D1474458

ELECTRIFIED

ELECTRIFIED

THE ART of the CONTEMPORARY ELECTRIC GUITAR

ROBERT SHAW

Sterling Signature
NEW YORK

Sterling Signature
NEW YORK

An Imprint of Sterling Publishing
387 Park Avenue South
New York, NY 10016

STERLING SIGNATURE and the distinctive Sterling Signature logo are registered trademarks of Sterling Publishing Co., Inc.

ISBN 978-1-4027-4774-8

Library of Congress Cataloging-in-Publication Data
Shaw, Robert, 1951-
Electrified : the art of the contemporary electric guitar / Robert Shaw.
p. cm.
Includes index.
ISBN 978-1-4027-4774-8
1. Electric guitar--History. 2. Electric guitar makers. I. Title.
ML1015.G9S509 2011
787.87'190922--dc22
2011015566

Distributed in Canada by Sterling Publishing
c/o Canadian Manda Group, 165 Dufferin Street
Toronto, Ontario, Canada M6K 3H6
Distributed in the United Kingdom by GMC Distribution Services
Castle Place, 166 High Street, Lewes, East Sussex, England BN7 1XU
Distributed in Australia by Capricorn Link (Australia) Pty. Ltd.
P.O. Box 704, Windsor, NSW 2756, Australia

Book design by Scott Meola and Rachel Maloney
Please see photo credits on page 263 for image copyright information

For information about custom editions, special sales, and premium and corporate purchases, please contact Sterling Special Sales at 800-805-5489 or specialsales@sterlingpublishing.com.

Manufactured in China

2 4 6 8 10 9 7 5 3 1

www.sterlingpublishing.com

To Nancy, Emma, and Georgia

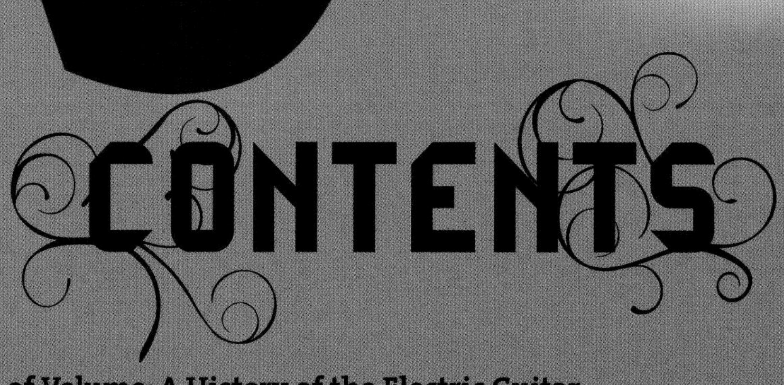

CONTENTS

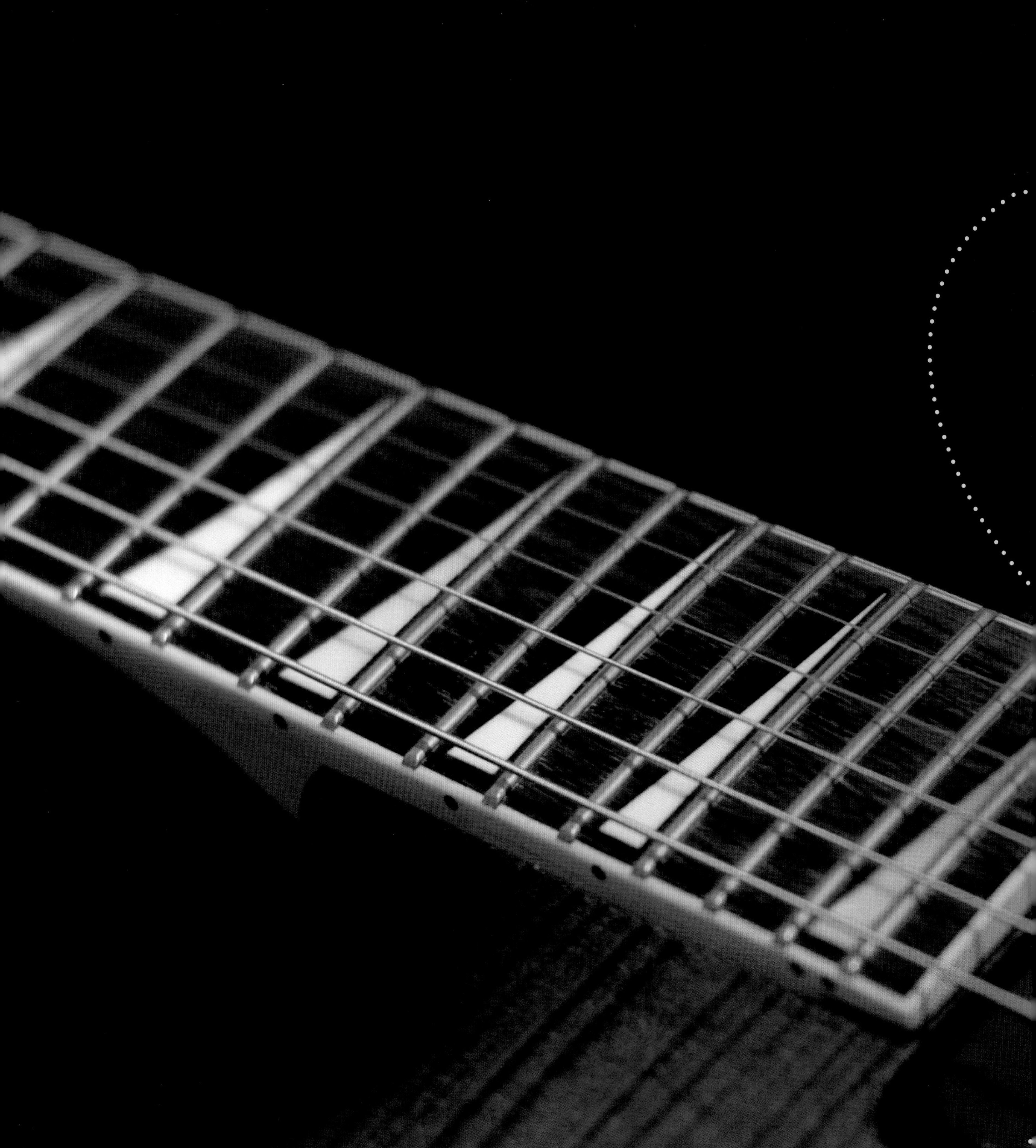

IN SEARCH OF VOLUME

A HISTORY OF THE ELECTRIC GUITAR

REPLICA OF LES PAUL'S LOG. CUSTOM, ART, AND HISTORIC DIVISION, GIBSON GUITAR CORPORATION. NASHVILLE, TENNESSEE, 2003.

This one-off replica of the solid-body electric guitar that renowned musician and inventor Les Paul assembled in 1941, using a length of four-by-four lumber as the body, was built in 2003 to honor Paul's performance in Nashville at an All-Star Guitar Night produced by Gibson. After getting negative reactions to his odd-looking instrument in clubs, Paul realized he needed to dress it up a bit for public consumption. To do so, he cut an Epiphone archtop in half and attached the sides to his four-by-four. Although the attached wings were purely cosmetic and did not affect the instrument's sound in any way, they allowed the Log to pass for a normal guitar. Paul's original Log is in the collection of the Country Music Hall of Fame in Nashville.

ELECTRICITY=VOLUME

The simple equation above sums up the early history of the electric guitar, which made its first public appearance in the 1930s. Volume became a major issue for Jazz Age guitarists working in noisy clubs or trying to compete with horns and rhythm sections in ensembles, and the search for volume preoccupied players and builders throughout the middle decades of the twentieth century. The electric guitar, which was first used by jazz and Western swing guitarists working in big bands, evolved as the ultimate answer to the working guitarist's problem of volume; it made it possible for the guitar to emerge as a solo instrument and allowed guitarists to compete with and eventually dominate every other instrument. "It was tremendous," the legendary guitarist and inventor Les Paul told the *Washington Post*. "I designed some amps that were pit bulls, and when I put my speaker beside a sax player, he reacted like he had a heart attack. We could walk all over the rhythm section. We had a knob, and all we had to do was turn it."

Electric instruments were made possible by the advances in radio and amplification of the 1920s. Guitars were electrified by fitting them with electronic pickups that converted the vibrations of metal strings into electric current, which could be transmitted to an amplifier and projected into a room through speakers. But it took nearly twenty years for instrument makers to overcome the problems electricity brought to guitar design and manufacture and to invent a new kind of guitar that could handle the volume that electricity made possible. Adding pickups to a hollow-body guitar increased its volume tremendously, but with that volume came a new problem—feedback, the result of sound produced by the amplifier looping back and keeping the strings vibrating. Although controlled feedback would become a staple element of rock playing in the hands of 1960s masters like Jimi Hendrix, Jeff Beck, and Pete Townshend, it was an undesirable nuisance and often an insurmountable problem for early electric guitarists.

Les Paul, who had toyed with electrified guitars since he was a teenager, realized that the way to circumvent the problems with feedback that are inherent in a hollow instrument—which, after all, is built around a resonating chamber—was simply to mount the strings on something solid that would not vibrate. To prove his thesis, he said, "I went to the railroad yard with some friends, and we stole a 2½-foot length of steel rail. I stretched a string the length of the rail and held it down with a spike at each end. Then I put a telephone mouthpiece underneath the string."

Paul kept experimenting with the solid-body concept throughout the 1930s. In 1937, he hired the Larson brothers, master luthiers from Chicago, to build him an instrument with a half-inch maple top, no sound holes, and two pickups, and he also worked with a number of other builders and inventors, including Epi Stathopoulo, the president of the Epiphone guitar company, on various designs. In 1941, he mounted strings and pickups on a length of four-by-four lumber with a spare Gibson guitar neck attached and actually played his "Log" in clubs, much to the confusion of his audiences. He also took the Log to Gibson and tried to persuade them to manufacture an electric solid-body, but recalled, "They laughed at me for ten years. They called me 'the guy with the broomstick with the pickups on it.' "

THE BIGSBY CONTRIBUTION

Southern California, where Paul spent a lot of time in the 1940s, was a hotbed of musical activity and invention, replete with jazz, pop, and country musicians and guitar makers. Many country-and-western guitarists in the area were already playing electric lap steels, which had been offered by a number of builders and manufacturers since the 1930s. In 1946, the country guitarist and singer Merle Travis, who wanted a Spanish-style electric that would sustain like a lap steel, drew a design for a solid-body electric and asked his friend Paul Bigsby, the foreman in a local motorcycle machine shop, to build it for him. Travis's most important design innovation was putting all six strings on the same side of the headstock, a configuration that would become standard in the years to come. Bigsby told Travis, "I can build anything," and went to work. Travis began playing the resulting guitar in 1947, but only a handful of others like it were ever made—all as custom orders that Bigsby built one by one, from the ground up. The bulk of Bigsby's orders were for his innovative electric steel guitars—which were much in demand from country players like Joaquin Murphy and Speedy West, for whom he built his first two—and for the Bigsby tailpiece vibrato system, which allowed players to raise or lower the pitch of a string or strings at will. (It is this vibrato system for which Bigsby is remembered today.) Because he could not keep up with orders for guitars, his business centered more and more on the vibratos in the 1950s and early '60s. Suffering from health problems, he ultimately sold the Bigsby name and his entire inventory to Gibson in 1966 and died two years later.

"IT WAS TREMENDOUS . . . WE COULD WALK ALL OVER THE RHYTHM SECTION. WE HAD A KNOB, AND ALL WE HAD TO DO WAS TURN IT."

BIGSBY BY-50. GRETSCH MUSICAL INSTRUMENTS. SCOTTSDALE, ARIZONA, 2003. COURTESY OF GEORGE BORST.

This recent limited-edition guitar is modeled after a groundbreaking solid-body electric that country musician Merle Travis commissioned Paul Bigsby to build for him in 1947. Bigsby, whom some consider the real father of the electric solid-body, made only a few guitars before moving on to pioneer the modern pedal steel guitar. Bigsby's distinctively shaped headstock clearly influenced Leo Fender's famous Stratocaster. The Bigsby original that this guitar is based on is in the collection of the Country Music Hall of Fame in Nashville.

DEBUT OF THE TELECASTER

It was another Southern California inventor with ties to country musicians who succeeded where others had failed. His name was Clarence Leonidas Fender, and he introduced the first commercially viable solid-body electric guitar in 1950. Initially called the Broadcaster but soon renamed Telecaster for copyright reasons (the Gretsch company, which built Broadkaster drums, objected), Leo Fender's revolutionary design was simple to the point of minimalism—a guitar stripped of everything nonessential. The body was a solid slab of blond ash with a single cutaway on the right side. Whereas previous guitar builders had attached fret boards of ebony or other hardwoods to the necks of their instruments, Fender streamlined his by making the head, neck, and fret board a single unit, which he attached to the body with four screws. This first "bolt-on" neck was made of solid maple and had frets

'51 NOCASTER NOS. FENDER CUSTOM SHOP, FENDER MUSICAL INSTRUMENTS CORPORATION. SCOTTSDALE, ARIZONA, 2006. COLLECTION OF THE SOUTHPAW SANCTUM.

Gibson and Fender began making exacting copies of classic early models in the late 1980s, when the market for vintage electric guitars from the 1950s and early '60s boomed and prices for choice original instruments soared.

Leo Fender originally called his revolutionary two-pickup solid-body guitar the Broadcaster, but he was forced to find a new name for it after finding out that Gretsch owned the trade name Broadkaster. To avoid legal problems between name changes, an estimated fifty guitars were sent out of the factory with the Broadcaster name stripped off the decal on their headstocks, and these rarities have come to be called Nocasters by collectors. Having learned their lesson, Fender later registered the trademark name NoCaster, and this painstaking recreation, with an ash body, U-shaped maple neck, single-ply black pick guard, and original-spec pickups, is accurate right down to the finest detail, including the paint "halo" beneath the pick guard. It also was given what Fender calls its New Old Stock (NOS) treatment—"built as if bought new in its respective model year and just found today." This one is, however, left-handed, making it something that no one could have bought in 1951 or could have found in any closet since.

mounted directly into its front side. A skunk stripe of dark walnut on the back of the neck, which filled the routed channel where a supporting metal truss rod was inserted, was the only contrastingly colored wood on the entire guitar. Fender followed the lead of Bigsby and Travis, whose work he knew well, by putting all the tuning machines on one side of the head, and he anchored the strings with six chrome ferrules set into the lower back of the body. All the guitar's hardware, which included a bridge pickup set at an angle so it would bring out the sound of the treble strings, was mounted on the top of the body, which was finished with a contrasting black plastic pick guard. The bridge was adjustable, allowing the player to modify the height of pairs of strings to improve playability and intonation.

Unlike anything that had come before it, Fender's guitar was expressly intended for mass production. It was a brilliantly realized industrial design in every respect. What's more, the guitar not only looked different from anything that had come before, it also sounded different. The pickup at the base of the neck was full and mellow, ideal for rhythm playing, while the angled bridge pickup produced a biting, trebly tone that, in the hands of master pickers like James Burton and Jerry Reed, came to define country "chicken pickin' " and that bluesmen like Albert Collins and Roy Buchanan used for their stinging, emotionally wrenching lead work. Amazingly, Fender managed to get almost everything right from the beginning, setting the standard for a two-pickup solid-body electric out of the starting gate. With just a few modifications, the Telecaster remains in production today, sixty years after its debut, and it has been copied by hundreds of other builders over the years.

FENDER VS. GIBSON

Prodded into action by Fender's success, Gibson decided that it was time to get back in touch with "the guy with the broomstick," and summoned Les Paul to help them design a solid-body electric that would compete with the Telecaster. In keeping with Gibson's well-established reputation and marketing strategy, company president Ted McCarty wanted to offer a refined product aimed at more affluent and sophisticated customers than those who were buying Fender's guitars. Paul, who had become a star in the years since Gibson rejected his Log, lent his name to the instrument as its endorser and consulted on a few details, but most of the design was already in place before he was brought in. The first Les Paul guitar, which Gibson introduced in 1952, had the rounded lines of a Gibson acoustic archtop and also sported a traditional glued-on fret board. To increase its elegance, it had a carved maple cap over its solid mahogany body, and, at Paul's suggestion, the entire body was painted metallic gold because, as he told guitar historian Tom Wheeler, no one else had a gold guitar and gold has "always been associated with quality and richness."

The original Les Paul model, which has become known as the Goldtop, was heavier and more expensive than the Fender Telecaster, with a distinctive sound of its own. Like the Tele, it carried two pickups, but the Les Paul's single-coil P-90s produced a fat, robust tone that was unlike anything the Tele offered. The decorative carved maple top also turned out to have a profound effect on the guitar's sound; the combination of the hardwood top on the softer mahogany body gave the Les Paul warmth and tremendous sustain.

Not to be outdone, Leo Fender decided he needed to one-up Gibson with a more sophisticated sister to his Telecaster. The new Stratocaster model, which he had been working on since 1951 and introduced in 1954, carried three pickups on a curvaceous body that was cut away from the neck on both sides to give players easier access to the upper frets. The distinctively shaped headstock, which, like the Tele, featured all six tuning knobs on one side, bore an uncanny resemblance to the Bigsby/Travis guitar. In addition to being the first double-cutaway electric, the Strat was also the first solid-body to have the input jack on the face of

TOP RIGHT **LES PAUL TRIBUTE.** CUSTOM, ART, AND HISTORIC DIVISION, GIBSON GUITAR CORPORATION. NASHVILLE, TENNESSEE, 2009.

Gibson introduced its Les Paul guitar in 1952, as a response to Leo Fender's highly successful Telecaster. This custom-shop limited edition was made as a tribute to Paul, who died in 2009 at the age of ninety-four, and follows his original design specifications more closely than Gibson did in 1952. Like the original Les Paul Goldtop, this guitar has a mahogany body and neck, a carved maple top, and a rosewood fingerboard. The bridge, however, is an exact replica of Paul's original 1952 patent, and the guitar carries a pair of P-90 pickups, which were his preferred choice.

Apparently, Paul and Gibson had a difference of opinion on the string-wrap direction for the guitar. Gibson wanted the strings to wrap underneath the bridge and Paul wanted to be able to palm-mute the strings, so he needed them to wrap over the top of the bar. When Gibson didn't see it his way, Paul designed and patented the bridge that this guitar now carries.

RIGHT **1956 STRATOCASTER RELIC LTD** (TAOS TURQUOISE). FENDER CUSTOM SHOP, FENDER MUSICAL INSTRUMENTS CORPORATION. SCOTTSDALE, ARIZONA, 2006.

The 1956 Strat is one of the most coveted and collectible of all Fenders, and, since the stunning "Taos Turquoise" finish was only available as a custom order in 1956, originals in this color are few and far between. This reproduction, made in a limited run of one hundred instruments, is part of Fender's Relic series and features all the original detailing and original tooling, including the October '56 "Boat Neck" shape and a reverse-wound, reverse-polarity middle pickup. Fender also re-created tooling holes and marks made during the original production process, and applied its Relic treatment to imitate "years of natural wear and tear; with nicks, scratches, worn finish, rusty hardware, and aged plastic parts."

the body rather than on the side, set at an angle to protect the connection if the guitar was dropped. The three pickups and a three-way toggle switch, which allowed the pickups to be played singly or in combination, gave the guitar enormous sonic versatility. Guitarists soon discovered that they could not only use the three designated positions of the toggle switch but could also stop the switch between positions for even more sound variation. In addition, the Strat carried a master volume control and two tone controls—one for treble and one for bass—and a unique new vibrato system that combined the instrument's bridge, tailpiece, and vibrato control into a single unit. The vibrato control, which Fender confusingly dubbed a tremolo arm, allowed greater pitch variation than the Bigsby, especially in up-bends, and created fewer intonation problems as well.

The Strat's versatility proved to be the key to its success. It was first championed by the seminal rockers Buddy Holly and Ritchie Valens, who helped popularize guitar-driven rock and roll, and surf rocker Dick Dale, who was given a Stratocaster by Leo Fender in 1955. The Strat has been identified with a wider array of prominent guitarists—including Eldon Shamblin, Buddy Guy, Jimi Hendrix, Bonnie Raitt, Stevie Ray Vaughan, and Richard Thompson—than any other guitar in history. It is also the most copied electric-guitar design of all time; its silhouette is so instantly recognizable that it has come to symbolize the electric guitar itself, and hundreds of individual builders and guitar manufacturers in America, Europe, and around the Pacific Rim have imitated, modified, or even blatantly copied Fender's design and manufacturing techniques over the years. And, like the Tele, the Strat has been in continuous production by the Fender company since its introduction, with no end in sight.

GRETSCH ENTERS WITH FLASH AND TWANG

Not long after Les Paul and Gibson combined forces, another master guitarist and manufacturer, the country stylist Chet Atkins and the aforementioned Gretsch Musical Instruments, teamed up to enter the growing electric-guitar market. Gretsch's instruments were known for their flashy looks—their popular drum sets were painted with metallic glitter—and their electric guitars followed the same mold. Atkins, who had made a name for himself backing everyone in Nashville from the Carter Family to Eddy Arnold, was a sophisticated musician who effortlessly combined his love of jazz and country in a distinctive solo style. Gretsch hired him as a consultant, and he worked closely with Gretsch designer Jimmy Webster. Their combined ideas were first made manifest in the Gretsch G6120 Chet Atkins Hollow Body, introduced in 1955.

Cosmetically, the G6120 was a cowboy's dream of a guitar, a thin-bodied acoustic-electric archtop aimed directly at the country music market that Atkins knew so well. It carried the image of a longhorn steer's head on the headstock, large rectangular ivory fingerboard inlays etched with the longhorn motif and pictures of cacti, and a huge *G* branded into the lower bout of its richly colored, reddish-amber body, which also carried a Bigsby vibrato. But in addition to its manly good looks, this first Chet Atkins guitar also offered some thoughtful new design

G6120EC EDDIE COCHRAN TRIBUTE HOLLOW-BODY. GRETSCH CUSTOM SHOP, GRETSCH MUSICAL INSTRUMENTS. SCOTTSDALE, ARIZONA, 2010.

The orange G6120 was the first Gretsch model released under the Chet Atkins name, and Eddie Cochran, whose hits included "Summertime Blues," "Somethin' Else," "Twenty Flight Rock," and "Nervous Breakdown," helped to make it the quintessential rockabilly guitar. Cochran bought one in 1955, when he was sixteen, and played the guitar for the rest of his all-too-brief life, which ended in a tragic auto accident while he was touring England in 1960. This exacting replica of Eddie's guitar, which was found unharmed in the trunk of the car in which he died and is now in the collection of the Rock and Roll Hall of Fame in Cleveland, is one of fifty made by the Gretsch Custom Shop in tribute to Cochran and his seminal place in rock-and-roll history.

"THE STRAT HAS BEEN IDENTIFIED WITH A WIDER ARRAY OF PROMINENT GUITARISTS THAN ANY OTHER GUITAR IN HISTORY. IT IS ALSO THE MOST COPIED ELECTRIC-GUITAR DESIGN OF ALL TIME."

MICHAEL BLOOMFIELD AGED 1959 LES PAUL STANDARD. CUSTOM, ART, AND HISTORIC DIVISION, GIBSON GUITAR CORPORATION. NASHVILLE, TENNESSEE, 2009.

Gibson's "sunburst"-colored Les Paul was originally manufactured from 1958 to 1960, and only about fifteen hundred of them were made during those years. Remaining originals are the most coveted and valuable of all electric guitars and can sell for well into six figures, as guitar expert Tony Bacon documents in his 2008 book Million Dollar Les Paul: In Search of the Most Valuable Guitar in the World. *Collectors admire the beautiful carved flame-maple tops, while players like Jimmy Page and Billy F. Gibbons have built legends based on the Les Paul's tone and undying sustain. Gibbons dubbed his favorite Les Paul Pearly Gates in honor of its celestial sonic capabilities, and Gibson has produced exacting reproductions of both it and Page's '59 "Burst" as well as LPs owned by Jeff Beck, Slash, Don Felder, Mike Bloomfield, and a number of other prominent guitarists.*

This custom-shop limited edition is a replica of Bloomfield's 1959 Les Paul, the guitar he played with the Paul Butterfield Blues Band on Bob Dylan's immortal Highway 61 Revisited *album, and on his* Super Session *collaboration with Al Kooper. The first one hundred guitars in Gibson's limited-edition run were given the full replica treatment, down to the finish on the Burst top, which was achieved by carefully examining hundreds of photos of the original guitar.*

ideas, including a metal bridge and nut, and, most important, a distinctive twangy sound that was completely different from a Les Paul or either of Fender's models. The G6120's signature twang was popularized in the 1950s by the guitar-driven sounds of best-selling instrumentalist Duane Eddy and rocker Eddie Cochran; Pete Townshend, a huge Eddie Cochran fan, used it as his main studio guitar throughout the 1970s; and rockabilly revivalist Brian Setzer has played a 6120 since his days with the Stray Cats.

MORE GIBSON INNOVATIONS

Meanwhile, back at Gibson, company president Ted McCarty and his team were moving in several different directions, tinkering with the Les Paul to improve its sound and looks and working on a new semi-acoustic electric archtop while at the same time contemplating some of the most radical design concepts for solid-body electrics ever to hit the drawing board. To begin with, in 1955, Gibson applied for a patent on a new "humbucking" pickup that had been invented by engineer Seth Lover, and the company began employing the new pickup on its standard guitars in 1957. The humbucker represented a big leap forward from earlier electronic pickups: it set two single coils in an out-of-phase series so that they canceled out each other's signal noise—the constant hum that had interfered with the sound produced by Gibson's P-90s and Fender's single coils.

Then, in 1958—a year that marked a turning point for Gibson and electric guitars in general, although it would take some time before the impact of the new models the company introduced that year was clear—Gibson introduced a revamped Les Paul, the Les Paul Standard. In addition to humbucking pickups, the Standard's maple top was left unpainted, showing off the beautiful grain to full advantage for the first time. Each of the humbuckers had its own volume and tone knobs, and the toggle switch allowed them to be used separately or in tandem. Although these changes did not improve contemporary perceptions of the Les Paul—Gibson actually stopped production between 1960 and 1968—the Standard was destined to be rediscovered by '60s blues-rockers, and original Les Paul Standards are today the most valuable and sought-after guitars on the planet. In the mid-1960s, blues-oriented musicians like Mike Bloomfield, Eric Clapton, Jeff Beck, and Jimmy Page discovered that the Standard has unique virtues, especially when played at the bone-shaking new volume levels made possible by hooking stacks of Marshall amplifiers together. The Standard's thick, fat tone and seemingly endless sustain made it ideal for their new approach, and, by 1968, it was back in production, where it has remained ever since.

Another 1958 Gibson introduction, the ES-335, was a successful attempt to combine the best aspects of hollow- and solid-body electric guitars in a single instrument. In *Gibson Guitars: 100 Years of an American Icon*, Walter Carter quotes Ted McCarty, who developed the idea for the new model: "Some players didn't like the acoustic-electrics because they had the same

"ORIGINAL LES PAUL STANDARDS ARE TODAY THE MOST VALUABLE AND SOUGHT-AFTER GUITARS ON THE PLANET."

problems all acoustics do. They weren't loud enough, or if you did turn them up they were hard to control. And other players thought the sound of the Les Paul was too bright. So we need[ed] something for the player who wanted the body reverberation of an acoustic and more highs . . . but not as much treble as a solid-body. The 335 was an in-between deal." The ES-335 was thinner than any previous hollow-body electric, and its deep double cutaways reminded contemporary eyes of Mickey Mouse's ears. It had f-holes, as did other hollow-bodies, but, like a solid-body, it had a stop tailpiece mounted on its face. The guitar's real innovation lay inside, however, where a four-inch block of solid maple ran through the body, effectively turning its wings into separate sound chambers. The maple block cut down on feedback at the same time as it provided more of the sustain and biting treble of a solid-body instrument.

Unlike the rest of Gibson's 1958 crop of electric models, the ES-335 was an immediate hit with jazz, blues, and rock guitarists alike. Its earliest advocates included Otis Rush, whose deep Chicago blues was a huge influence on Eric Clapton, and Detroit bluesman John Lee Hooker. Over the years, the ES-335 and its later and somewhat fancier sister instruments, the ES-345 and ES-355, have become closely identified with B. B. King, who has played the ES-355 exclusively for decades. For musicians like King, the new guitar felt light, comfortable, and responsive, the cutaways made it easy to play high up on the neck, and it produced a wider rage of sound than any other guitar on the market. It was an ideal working musician's guitar, and it became one of Gibson's all-time best sellers. Like Fender's Tele and Strat, the ES-335 line has remained in continuous production from its inception.

Gibson's final 1958 introductions broke the mold for the solid-body electric guitar form forever. As Les Paul and his Log had proved, an electric solid-body did not have to resemble a

50TH ANNIVERSARY ES-335. CUSTOM, ART, AND HISTORIC DIVISION, GIBSON GUITAR CORPORATION. NASHVILLE, TENNESSEE, 2009.

The double-cutaway Gibson ES-335, introduced in 1959, is the quintessential semihollow-body electric guitar. The 335 is most closely identified with B. B. King, who has played a variation of the design throughout his long career.

conventional guitar at all. Any shape would work, including one that was made up of straight lines. Ted McCarty decided that it was time to shake up the market and alter Gibson's somewhat stodgy image. He also wanted to settle a score and have a little fun. In a 1993 interview, McCarty recalled that Leo Fender "was going around saying that Gibson had not had a new idea in a hundred years, and I guess my attitude was, 'Well, we'll show 'em.' " So, with the help of a local artist, he drew a number of angular, straight-edged shapes for his team to work with, and they built three wild-looking prototypes that were trotted out at trade shows.

In addition to being oddly shaped, all the guitars were made from korina, an exotic, light-colored, tight-grained African hardwood that made them look even more strange. Fender general manager Forrest White told Tom Wheeler, "When I looked over and saw those things, I looked at [McCarty] and he looked at me and he had this big grin on his face. He was making fun of what Leo had done. He thought I would be mad, but I had to laugh. I thought Leo's stuff looked crazy, [but] I thought [to myself], 'This guy must be nuts.' " Two of the prototypes, the lightning bolt–shaped Explorer and the appropriately named Flying V, were manufactured for market. However, their novel appearances worked against them, and both guitars were commercial flops; fewer than two hundred of the new models were shipped before production was stopped in 1959. But while McCarty had misjudged the market for his edgy guitars, the Flying V, like the Les Paul Standard, found new life in the mid-1960s, when it was played by Dave Davies of the Kinks and bluesmen Lonnie Mack and Albert King. Both the Flying V and the Explorer are now recognized as classics: McCarty's daring drawings, done on a lark, ultimately freed generations of electric guitar designers to push the envelope of form.

THE 1960s REVOLUTION

As the 1960s began, the models that would form the pantheon of electric guitars—Fender's Telecaster and Stratocaster; Gibson's Les Paul, ES-335, and Flying V; and Gretsch's Chet Atkins line—were all in place, waiting for the unimaginable storms to come. The first of those storms came out of England, arriving on American shores little more than two months after the assassination of John Fitzgerald Kennedy. It came in the form of four long-haired kids from Liverpool called the Beatles, who appeared on *The Ed Sullivan Show* on February 3, 1964, before the largest audience in television history. Modeling themselves on Buddy Holly and the Crickets and on American R & B and blues groups of the '50s and early '60s, the band was made up of electric bass and electric rhythm and lead guitars backed by drums, a configuration followed by most other British Invasion bands and the hundreds of British and American groups that sprang from their influence.

What most American fans didn't realize was that the Beatles, the Rolling Stones, the Kinks, the Animals, the Searchers, the Who, Them, and other bands from the British Isles had cut their teeth on American pop, R & B, and blues, which they were channeling and feeding back to kids across the pond who had either never heard it or—in the case of artists such as Chuck Berry, Bo Diddley, Buddy Holly, Little Richard, Carl Perkins, Gene Vincent, Eddie Cochran, and other '50s rockers—were too young to have experienced it firsthand. John Lennon, who sang "Roll Over Beethoven" and "Rock and Roll Music" on early albums, would later declare, "If you tried to give rock and roll another name, you might call it 'Chuck Berry.' " Other young English guitarists dug deeply into American blues repertoire, which few white Americans were aware of. The Rolling Stones took their name from the title of a Muddy Waters song, and Keith Richards, Eric Clapton, Jeff Beck, and Jimmy Page played the grooves off records by Waters and other American blues masters, including Howlin' Wolf, Sonny Boy Williamson, Otis Rush, John Lee Hooker, Buddy Guy, and B. B., Albert, and Freddie King, all of them largely unknown to white audiences in their native land. The British bands knew they had debts they could never hope to repay, and they were happy to give credit where credit was due. When the Beatles first came to America in 1964 and told everyone they wanted to see Muddy Waters, at least one reporter asked, "Where's that?" A surprised Paul McCartney chided, "Don't you know who your famous people are here?"

JIMI HENDRIX PSYCHEDELIC FLYING V. CUSTOM, ART, AND HISTORIC DIVISION, GIBSON GUITAR CORPORATION. NASHVILLE, TENNESSEE, 2006.

The angular Gibson Flying V and its sister instrument, the lightning bolt–shaped Explorer, were the first electric guitars to break away from the gently curved forms of traditional acoustic instruments. But they proved to be too far ahead of their time, and were commercial flops when they were introduced in 1958. The Flying V, however, was championed by '60s guitarists such as Lonnie Mack, Albert King, and Dave Davies of the Kinks, and Gibson brought it back into production in 1967. It is now recognized as a design classic, and thousands of V-shaped guitars have been built by Gibson and copied by other companies and luthiers since then.

This limited-edition guitar is a meticulous recreation of a Flying V that Jimi Hendrix used on tour in Europe in 1967 and 1968. It was one of three Flying Vs that he owned. It carries exacting reproductions of the swirling, psychedelic designs that Hendrix painted on his guitar, which were originally done in what appears to be nail polish. Hendrix's designs were painstakingly rendered by artist Bruce Kunkel in close conjunction with the Custom Shop.

Kids from the American suburbs got turned on to electric blues, and sales of electric guitars—which had burgeoned after the Beatles and other British Invasion bands landed—went into orbit. Suddenly, everyone wanted an electric guitar, and the guitar companies were more than happy to oblige by ramping up production. By the end of 1964, the year the Beatles conquered America, Fender was building fifteen hundred guitars a week; the company earned more than ten million dollars that year. Gibson, which had greatly expanded its plants, sold more than 100,000 guitars in 1965 and doubled its sales between 1964 and 1966. But there was a problem that quickly caught up to the big companies: the guitars that Clapton, Beck, Bloomfield, and others were popularizing were not newly minted, but were instead older models, most of them made in the 1950s. The instrument choices of these and other rock and blues virtuosos made it clear that the big companies just couldn't make them like they used to.

Leo Fender sold his company to CBS in 1965 for thirteen million dollars, and quality plummeted while serious musicians retreated to the "pre-CBS" models. Inexpensive Japanese knockoffs of Strats and Les Pauls flooded the market, and sales of American-made guitars fell off precipitously; Gibson's sales were down by half by the time the company changed hands in 1969. Even as '60s guitar gods continued to break new ground and inspire kids to pick up an "axe," the guitar industry was in trouble.

GUARDIANS OF QUALITY

The 1970s brought surprisingly little change from the major guitar manufacturers. After the tumultuous social and musical upheavals of the previous decade, the music and musical-instrument industries retrenched. By the end of 1971, the Beatles had broken up, Jimi Hendrix and Duane Allman were dead, and the Stones were tax exiles in France. Major manufacturers chased cheap Japanese imports to the bottom of the market, and the most desirable electrics remained vintage Fenders and Gibsons that had been made in the 1950s and early '60s.

A few intrepid individuals and small companies did attempt to fill the quality and innovation voids left by the ossified guitar corporations. Across the pond in swinging England, an independent London-based luthier named Antanus Casimere Zemaitis was building distinctive acoustic and electric guitars that became favorites of top British players. Tony Zemaitis became a full-time builder in 1965 and first achieved recognition for his acoustic twelve-strings, which were played by the likes of Eric Clapton and George Harrison. Around 1970, Zemaitis hit on the idea of putting a metal plate on the top of a solid-body electric guitar to shield the electronics and reduce hum. The metal-front guitars, which were decorated with detailed engravings by Zemaitis's friend Danny O'Brien, also looked great on stage; Ron Wood, then with Faces, caused a sensation when he appeared on the British TV show *Top of the Pops* with one of Zemaitis's first engraved metal-front electrics. Marc Bolan, Peter Frampton, and Greg Lake (of Emerson, Lake & Palmer) quickly joined Wood as metal-front advocates, and Zemaitis soon went a step further with the flashy stage-guitar concept, creating instruments with "pearl fronts," which were covered with mosaics of shimmering abalone. Although he worked alone throughout his

DRAGON METAL-FRONT LIMITED EDITION (MF500-FD). ZEMAITIS INTERNATIONAL. TOKYO, JAPAN, 2006. COURTESY OF GEORGE BORST.

The late English luthier Tony Zemaitis designed some of the most original and striking-looking electric guitars of the late twentieth century, including models with fronts of engraved metal and abalone-and-pearl mosaic patterns. Japan has had a long love affair with Zemaitis guitars, so it is not surprising that soon after his retirement in 2000, Tony Zemaitis began talks with a Japanese group interested in carrying on his legacy of quality craftsmanship. Zemaitis died in 2002, but his widow and son continued the discussions and ultimately reached an agreement to make the rebirth of Zemaitis guitars a reality. The new company has access to Tony Zemaitis's original drawings, specifications, and guitars—thanks to his family—and also has the benefit of the involvement of Danny O'Brien, who designed all the metal engravings on Zemaitis's original guitars. The metal front was originally intended to shield the guitar and reduce hum, but, then as now, O'Brien's gorgeous artwork lifted the model well beyond the realm of the practical.

On new Zemaitises like this one, O'Brien's designs are hand-engraved by a team of engravers. This limited-edition single-cut has a 25-inch scale length, a Honduran mahogany body and neck, an ebony fret board, and carries a pair of DiMarzio Custom DP103 PAF pickups.

career, creating only six to ten guitars a year before retiring in 2000, his concepts were widely copied and counterfeited.

Alembic, the world's first boutique guitar company, was founded in 1969 in San Francisco by electronics wizard, design engineer, and multitrack recording pioneer Ron Wickersham and his artist wife, Susan Frates. Susan and Ron thought Alembic was a perfect name for their company: the word "alembic" denotes a type of still used by medieval alchemists to distill liquids, and has, by extension, come to mean anything that refines or transmutes.

Alembic initially worked with the Grateful Dead, who, as Susan puts it, "had a larger-than-average interest in improving the quality of their sound." The original intention of the collaboration was to improve the quality of the final product—the record—but this soon led to new designs for guitar pickups and electronics, which in turn led to designing and building guitars from the ground up for groups such as the Dead, Jefferson Airplane, and Crosby, Stills, and Nash. Both the pickups and guitars were developed with the input and skills of musician-turned-repairman Rick Turner, who has continued to pioneer in both acoustic and electric guitar design since parting ways with Alembic in 1978.

The first Alembic guitar, a bass built by Turner for Jefferson Airplane's Jack Casady, was completed in 1972 and cost more than four thousand dollars, an absolutely unheard-of

sum at the time. The following year, the Wickershams negotiated an agreement with a distributor and began manufacturing a their first production instruments, and Alembic remains in business in 2010, with twenty-six people on its payroll. As Susan recalls, "Many people thought that no one would be interested in an instrument so dedicated to excellence . . . I guess they were wrong, weren't they? It was the advent of an entirely new genre in instrument-building."

THE ERA OF CUSTOMIZATION

Another answer to the declining quality of manufactured guitars was do-it-yourself customization. Over the years, many working guitarists, from Les Paul to Eric Clapton, altered their instruments, mixing and matching parts and tinkering with elements that gave them trouble or just didn't do what they wanted or needed them to do. For example, Clapton's favorite Fender Stratocaster, which he nicknamed Blackie for its finish color, was actually a composite of parts from three vintage 1956 and '57 Strats he bought in a Nashville guitar shop in 1970. (The guitar was ultimately sold at Christie's in 2004, where it brought $959,500 to benefit Clapton's Crossroads Centre for drug and alcohol rehabilitation.) In the mid-'70s, a Southern California guitar repairman named Wayne Charvel, who had been doing custom paint jobs and other work for Fender, started a business making and selling parts, including bodies, necks, and pickups, from which guitarists could build their own instruments. Word got around, and Charvel soon found himself not only making parts but building one-off guitars for the likes of John Entwistle of the Who and Billy F. Gibbons and Dusty Hill of ZZ Top. One of Charvel's other early customers was a local kid named Edward Van Halen, who often came into the shop and sat on the floor playing while Charvel worked on his guitars. Van Halen was developing a host of new playing techniques that would take the guitar world by storm when his eponymous band first hit the airwaves in 1978, including tapping notes on the fret board with his right hand in combination with notes fretted by his left hand and "dive-bombing" his low E string with the tremolo bar, taking it down as low in pitch as it would go. He needed a guitar that would help him do his bidding: he wanted to combine the Fender Strat's deep cutaways and tremolo bar with the big, fat sound that could only come from an overdriven Les Paul.

Van Halen bought an inexpensive Strat-type body and a thin, twenty-two-fret neck from Charvel and gouged out a hole near the bridge for a single Gibson humbucker pickup—the PAF (or Patent Applied For) model that the original Les Paul Standards carried. Because the Fender tremolo was never intended to do more than wiggle the strings a little, Van Halen's dive-bombing, as Jimi Hendrix's similar deep bending had done before his time, often left his guitar pretty badly out of tune. Van Halen initially dealt with the problem by tinkering with a standard Fender vibrato unit, widening the grooves and adding a little oil, but soon switched to a new locking vibrato system invented by machinist Floyd Rose, which solved the intonation problems and became the standard by which all others were measured over the course of the 1980s. Van Halen finished his "Frankenstein" by spray-painting it black,

SERIES ONE WITH CLASSIC DRAGON INLAY. ALEMBIC, INC. SANTA ROSA, CALIFORNIA, 2002. COLLECTION OF VINCENT D. MILLS.

Although Alembic is best known for its innovative bass guitar designs, it has also produced many outstanding six- and twelve-string guitars over the years. This custom-made cocobolo-bodied guitar is based on a 1973 template for Alembic's Series One model, which has a flatter bottom and slightly more curled horns than the company's current version. The guitar also has a five-piece maple-and-purpleheart neck and a dragon inlay that spans the ebony fingerboard. The dragon, which is based on one of artist Susan Frates's mid-'70s designs, is made up of 187 separate pieces of shell, ivory, wood, gemstone, and metal. The creature's body is fashioned from mother-of-pearl; the scales from abalone. The ridge down the dragon's back is sterling silver. The belly is brass and the legs are copper. The teeth and claws are made from antique ivory reclaimed from old piano keys, and the tongue is pink ivory, a rare African wood. The beast's breath is made from brass filings set in optically clear epoxy, and its eyes are pink sapphires.

EDDIE VAN HALEN FRANKENSTEIN REPLICA. E.L.V.H., INC. SCOTTSDALE, ARIZONA, 2007.

In 2007, Eddie Van Halen joined forces with Fender to create the EVH brand of guitars, pickups, amps, and other musical products. This replica of Van Halen's scruffy homemade Frankenstein Super Strat was issued in a limited-edition run of three hundred. The Fender Custom Shop put these guitars through an exhaustive aging process to replicate the original "down to every last scratch, ding, and cigarette burn." Fender craftsmen even scoured the land for 1971 quarters—just like the one Eddie stuck under the original tremolo bridge on the Strat body he bought from Wayne Charvel. The replica also features a Floyd Rose Original tremolo bridge, a single Seymour Duncan Custom Shop EVH humbucking pickup, and a single master volume knob (labeled Tone*, like the one Van Halen used) mounted on a partial black pick guard identical to the original. Also replicating the original is a nonfunctional three-way switch and unwired single-coil pickup that occupy two of the three pickup cavities. Van Halen's original guitar, concocted from parts he bought from Charvel, set him back a couple of hundred dollars, whereas the replicas list for twenty-five thousand dollars each. The price of fame?*

then putting strips of masking tape over the dried paint and adding coats of white and then Schwinn-bicycle red before stripping the tape off. The motley-looking, homemade guitar became his trademark.

Heavy-metal shredders were not the only players interested in customization or in the notion of combining the best of Fender and Gibson in a single guitar. Another was a kid from Maryland named Paul Reed Smith, who built his first guitar in response to a challenge from his college music professor. "I got an A," Smith recalled, "and decided to pursue my dream of making guitars for a living." After college, Smith worked as a guitar repairman and musician. In his spare time, he began working on an instrument of his own, trying to solve the myriad problems he saw in the guitars he was repairing. "I was trying to set it up so a repairman would have none of those problems," he told historian Tom Wheeler. "I was looking for an instrument that would be a really good tool for musicians."

Smith worked diligently, experimenting with a host of design elements and field-testing his work on gigs with his band. "I guess I made about one guitar a month for ten years," he recalled, "and I changed the design guitar by guitar until I came up with something that Fender and Gibson players would both like. We went through three headstocks, three body shapes, eight pickup designs, three renditions of tuning pegs, and four tremolo designs to get the right mix."

Smith started his own company, and its first guitar, introduced in 1985, was the PRS Custom, which set a new standard in an industry desperately in need of one. Like a Les Paul, the Custom had a carved maple top on a mahogany body and three tuners on each side of the headstock, but it also had double cutaways like Gibson's SG or Fender's Stratocaster and a tremolo bar similar to a Strat's. The Custom's 25-inch scale length—the length of the strings from the nut to the bridge—set it squarely between the Les Paul's 24¾ and the Strat's 25½. (Because strings vibrate only between the nut and the bridge, scale length affects a host of factors, including the spacing of the frets, the tone of the instrument, and its overall feel—i.e., whether the strings feel relatively loose or tight. The longer the scale length, the tighter the feel and the more difficult it is to "bend" notes up, a key element of blues and rock playing.) The original Custom also had twenty-four frets, more than either the Les Paul or the Strat. Smith's attention to detail was manifest throughout his thoughtful and pragmatic design. Among his innovations were a

DRAGON I PROTOTYPE. PRS GUITARS. STEVENSVILLE, MARYLAND, 1993. COURTESY OF GEORGE BORST.

As a budding luthier, Paul Reed Smith had two dreams. First, he wanted to build a guitar that possessed the best qualities of the '50s Stratocasters and Les Pauls he loved to play but that also employed new technologies to address some of their problems and limitations. Second, he wanted to build a guitar with the image of a dragon on it. This is a prototype for the first of several Dragon models that PRS has built over the years. It embodies the realization of both dreams in a single guitar.

friction-relieving headstock angle, a patented tremolo system that was far more effective than Fender's, and locking machine heads that held the guitar firmly in tune by eliminating the string slippage that plagued other guitars. Perhaps most influential of all was the Custom's finish: the beautiful figure of the maple Smith used was enhanced by multistep staining that gave a three-dimensional feel to the top, unlike anything that had been seen before.

VINTAGE GOES VIRAL

Another offshoot of the decline in quality from big manufacturers was the rise of the market for vintage guitars. Professional musicians were the first guitar collectors: Steve Miller, Stephen Stills, and John Entwistle were among those who built great collections of old guitars. But as more baby boomers grew up—guys who had dreamed of being rock stars as teenagers but ended working for prestigious law firms, Wall Street investment banks, or other lucrative businesses—began investing in guitars. Dealers like Nashville's George Gruhn, L.A.'s Norman, and Staten Island's Mandolin Brothers began catering to the new collectors, more than a few of whom were Japanese, and prices rose exponentially.

Large guitar companies, which were looking for ways to revitalize their sinking reputations and business, watched all this activity with great interest. Push had come to shove: CBS sold the money-losing Fender company to a group of employees and investors headed by William Schultz in 1984, and Gibson, which was on the verge of bankruptcy, was purchased by a trio of Harvard MBAs who were looking for a turnaround investment in January of 1986. Under new management that understood the need to get back to the basics of quality guitar making, Fender and Gibson began to reinvent themselves and rebuild the confidence in their products that had been so badly eroded over the years.

To that end, Fender established its own custom shop in 1987. The shop was originally manned by just two master builders, John Page and Michael Stevens. Page had worked for Fender in a variety of roles since the late 1970s, and Stevens, who hails from Texas, had built guitars and pickups for a number of prominent players in his home state, most notably bluesman Stevie Ray Vaughan. According to Page, who was the foreman of the new venture, Fender CEO Schultz's original idea for the custom shop was "to have a couple of guys 'out in the back forty' making a few really cool guitars a year, [which] would help raise the quality perception of [the] Fender product." Professional musicians were delighted to finally have someone at Fender who could build or customize whatever they wanted. The shop also began producing limited-edition artist signature models, starting with an Eric Clapton Strat. Orders for limited production runs also came in from Japan, and Page and Stevens soon found themselves with more work than two builders could possibly handle.

As part of their effort to capitalize on the interest in their vintage models, both Fender and Gibson also started making exacting custom-shop reproductions of specific well-known instruments, including Stevie Ray Vaughan's battered 1963 Strat and Jimmy Page's 1959 Les Paul. These proved so successful that both companies went on to offer a host of replicas of vintage classics, some of which artificially reproduce the wear and tear of years of hard use—tarnished metal, paint scratches, yellowed plastic pick guards, cigarette burns, etc.—with scary accuracy. To cite just a single example, one can now buy an exact copy of the hopelessly ravaged and much altered 1954 Fender Esquire that Jeff Beck played with the Yardbirds—a guitar that is so close to the original that Beck thought it was his when he first saw it. There are now far more of these replicas in the marketplace than there are authentic original examples of guitars that were made in what is now considered the classic era of production.

VISIONS OF THE FUTURE

While Gibson and Fender were busy trying to recapture the glory of their past accomplishments, a few independent builders were looking far into the future and reimagining what an electric guitar could and should be. One of these visionaries was a New York custom guitar craftsman named Ken Parker, who told *20th Century Guitar* magazine that he saw the guitars available to modern musicians as "clumsy, limiting, and gimmicky. They [can't] respond to the changing and increasingly sophisticated needs of the guitar player." Parker, who, like Paul Reed Smith, built his first guitar while he was in college, can build or modify anything with strings on it: he had made archtops, electric guitars and basses, fiddles, cellos, harps, and even a Japanese koto. During his years in New York, Parker made a reputation for himself by designing and crafting replacement parts for a wide range of instruments, and by building custom guitars for Pete Townshend, Andy Summers of the Police, and other musicians who know exactly what they want from their instruments.

Working with electronics wizard Larry Fishman, Parker spent nine years reexamining every aspect of electric guitar design. Throughout that process, the pair followed the dictum

FLY DELUXE. PARKER GUITARS. WILMINGTON, MASSACHUSETTS, 1996. COURTESY OF GEORGE BORST.

At the time it was made, Ken Parker's Fly represented the first complete redesign of the electric guitar since Leo Fender's introduction of the Broadcaster in 1950. This example was boldly autographed by Ken, who, in recent years, has turned his attention to a similarly thorough reconsideration of the acoustic archtop.

The Fly's name was a reference to boxing's flyweight category: the guitar weighed in at a mere four and one-half pounds, about three pounds less than a Stratocaster and half the weight of a Les Paul. This huge reduction was made possible by Parker's study of Renaissance lutes, which he knew were often made of soft wood that luthiers had strengthened with veneers of ebony and other hard woods. Parker built the guitar's body from poplar and the neck from basswood, and covered both with an extremely strong space-age "exoskeleton" of carbon and glass fiber bonded with epoxy resin that could handle string tensions that would normally tear a soft-wood guitar to shreds.

The fingerboard was made of the same less-than-half-millimeter-thick composite material as the exoskeleton; this further stabilized the neck and allowed Parker's wear-resistant stainless-steel frets to be glued directly onto the fingerboard rather than hammered into grooves, as they are on a conventional guitar. The Fly also differed from previous electric solid-bodies in another game-changing way: whereas most earlier guitars had relatively little resonance because of their stiff hard-wood bodies, and could barely be heard without amplification, the Fly's lively, tone-rich body allowed it to be played acoustically. Electronics wizard Larry Fishman fitted the guitar with a combination of standard magnetic pickups and bridge-mounted piezo pickups (generally used on acoustic instruments) that could conjure both a typical range of electric guitar sounds and a realistic amplified acoustic sound. This was revolutionary in and of itself, but the new Fishman technology also allowed players to blend electric and acoustic sounds at the same time, resulting in hybrids that had never been heard before. The Fly was therefore capable of being two, or even three, guitars in one, and of freeing working musicians from hauling multiple instruments from gig to gig.

of the great Chicago architect Louis Sullivan—"form ever follows function"—and allowed what Sullivan had called the "rule that shall permit of no exception" to take them wherever it led. Unbound by previous design models, the instrument that he and Fishman ultimately introduced in 1994, the Parker Fly, was so unlike anything before it that Parker has said, "The only things on a Fly that will attach to a standard guitar are the strings and the strap button."

The new guitar incorporated eleven new design, technology, and manufacturing-process patents, but, unfortunately, despite all its technological advances, the Fly did not sell nearly as well as Parker and Fishman had hoped. The problem was its decidedly nontraditional look, which pushed contemporary standards of acceptability just as the Flying V and Explorer had done more than thirty-five years earlier. Joni Mitchell, who played a Fly live and in the studio, thought it looked like a piece of driftwood that Parker had found on a beach, but most other professional musicians refused to be seen with it. Keith Richards, for example, only played one behind closed studio doors. He told Parker he thought it was a great guitar but wondered why he had made it look "like a bleeding assault rifle." Once again, convention and tradition trumped innovation. "This is rock and roll!" Parker told *The New Yorker* in 2007. "You would think that guitar players would be open and brave and experimental. And they are not. As a group, they are not. That guy with the purple Mohawk? He won't play anything made after 1960. Wait a minute, dude! *You* were made after 1960."

Like virtually everything else in our consumer-oriented society, the world of guitars today is splintered, diverse, and replete with a vast and at times bewildering array of choices, both large and small. The guitar, which has been dominated by American designs for a hundred and fifty years, remains the most popular instrument in the world. Millions are made and sold every year, along with modifications and accessories that no one could have dreamed of a generation ago. Electric guitarists can choose from a wider array of instruments than ever before. There are robot guitars that tune themselves, guitars with skeleton-like metal bodies, guitars that fold in half for travel, guitars made of prehistoric wood, guitars designed for women and young girls, and guitars that glow in the dark, like B-movie flying saucers. Collectors pay tens or even hundreds of thousands of dollars for rare 1950s Fenders and Gibsons and guitars played by famous rock stars, many of which are going into museums or being put away as investments, too valuable to play. Sotheby's, Christie's, and other auction houses sell guitars, and vintage guitars show up fairly often on PBS's popular *Antiques Roadshow*, where their owners are invariably astonished by their value.

But despite all these past and present distractions, we also are living in the greatest age of guitar building in history, with more highly skilled luthiers at work than ever before. Hundreds of custom-shop master builders and independent luthiers around the world now specialize in handcrafting fine instruments for discriminating clients. Paul Reed Smith, whose company celebrated its twenty-fifth anniversary in 2010, articulates the ethos of today's builders with these words: "Guitar building is an ongoing process of discovery. We are devoted to the guitar's rich heritage while committed to new technologies that will enrich our products with uncompromised tone, playability, and beauty. Our success depends on our ability to listen, implement positive change, and continually refine our craft." Most of today's best builders work closely with their clients to design guitars specifically tailored to their personal needs and desires. Others go their own way, listen to their own muse, as they push the traditional boundaries of form and sound toward their vision of the ever-elusive guitar of tomorrow. Whatever their approach, the best of today's electric guitar builders are driven toward a goal of perfection that they can visualize but know they cannot reach. But after all the unpredictable changes of the past century, who really knows what the future holds for the electric guitar? Maybe, some day, some kid with a crazy dream will build a guitar that can, like Spinal Tap's amps, "go to eleven." Stay tuned.

"[WE] ARE LIVING IN THE GREATEST AGE OF GUITAR BUILDING IN HISTORY, WITH MORE HIGHLY SKILLED LUTHIERS AT WORK THAN EVER BEFORE. . . . THE BEST OF TODAY'S ELECTRIC GUITAR BUILDERS ARE DRIVEN TOWARD A GOAL OF PERFECTION THAT THEY CAN VISUALIZE BUT KNOW THEY CANNOT REACH."

MARNIE STERN WITH HER PINK PAISLEY SF3-CLF BY SCOTT FRENCH.

Today's guitarists and builders work closely together, inspiring each other to new heights. Marnie Stern, seen here with a custom-built guitar by luthier Scott French, is a cutting-edge progressive rocker whose heady, virtuosic finger-tapping puts her in a league by herself. In a January 3, 2011 profile, The New Yorker *called her playing "rapturous" and declared that her eponymous 2010 album "feels like a single emotional eruption, even when melodic lines pile up in dizzying aggregate, like film spooling onto the floor." (See p. 179 for more information about the guitar and luthier.)*

PARTS OF AN ELECTRIC GUITAR

CARVED-TOP

On a carved-top electric guitar, the instrument's top—i.e., the front; the side that faces the audience—is gently curved, whereas that of a solid-body guitar (see opposite page) is completely level. No one instrument contains all the features discussed in this book, but the labels here identify most of the basic elements of an electric guitar and should help identify some of the terms in the captions that follow.

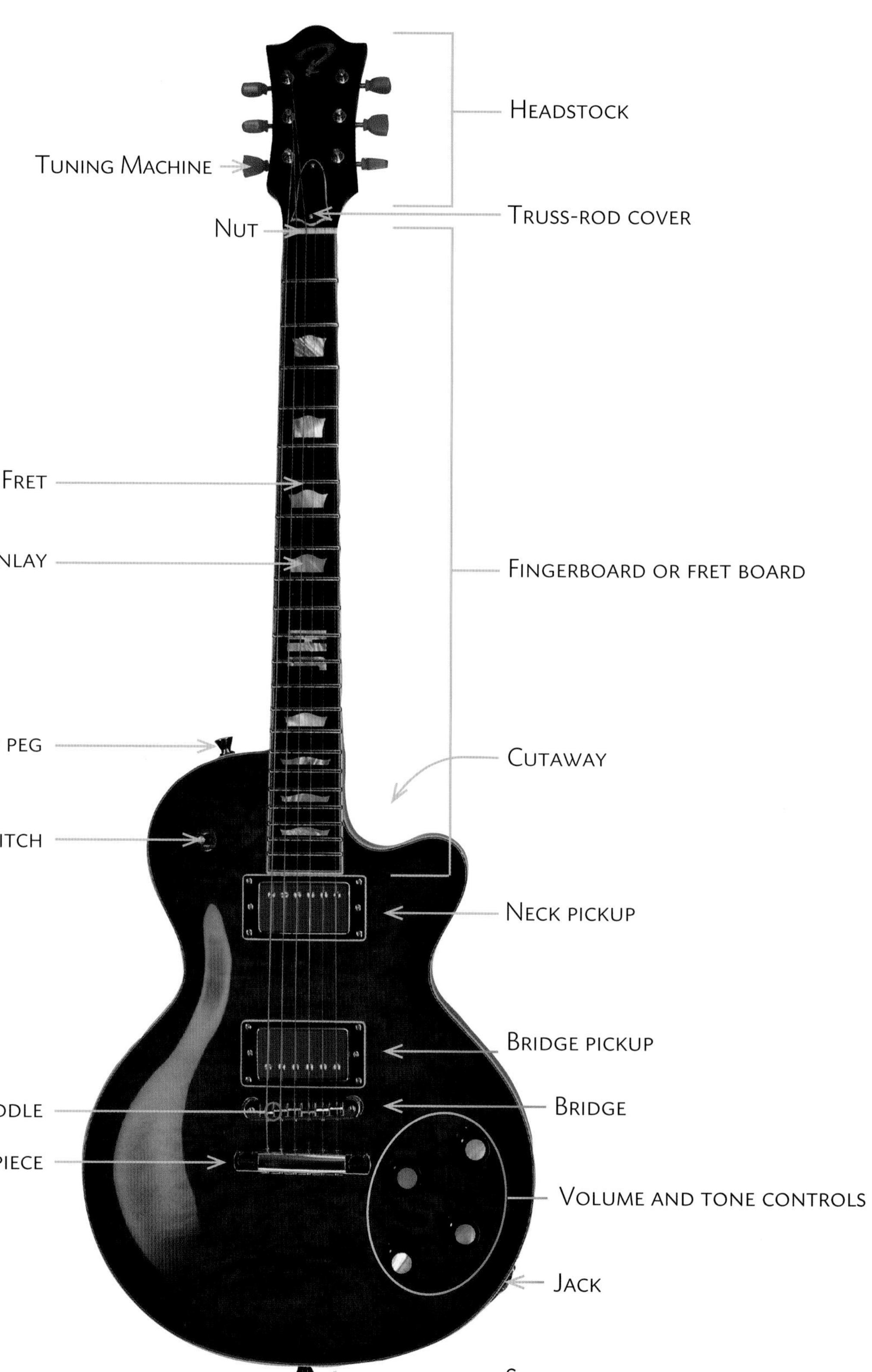

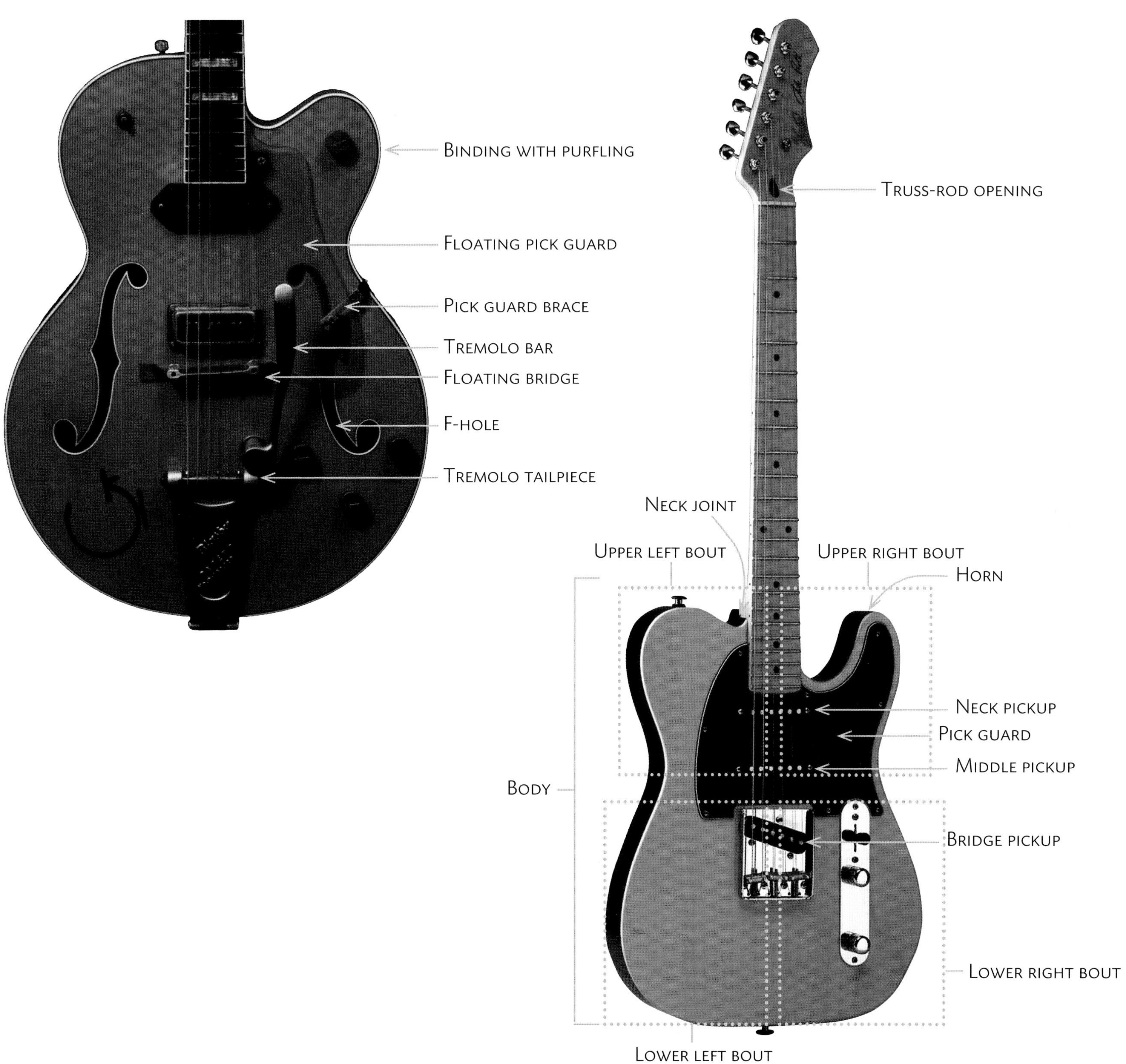
HOLLOW-BODY
Binding with purfling
Floating pick guard
Pick guard brace
Tremolo bar
Floating bridge
F-hole
Tremolo tailpiece
SOLID-BODY
Truss-rod opening
Neck joint
Upper left bout
Upper right bout
Horn
Neck pickup
Pick guard
Middle pickup
Body
Bridge pickup
Lower right bout
Lower left bout

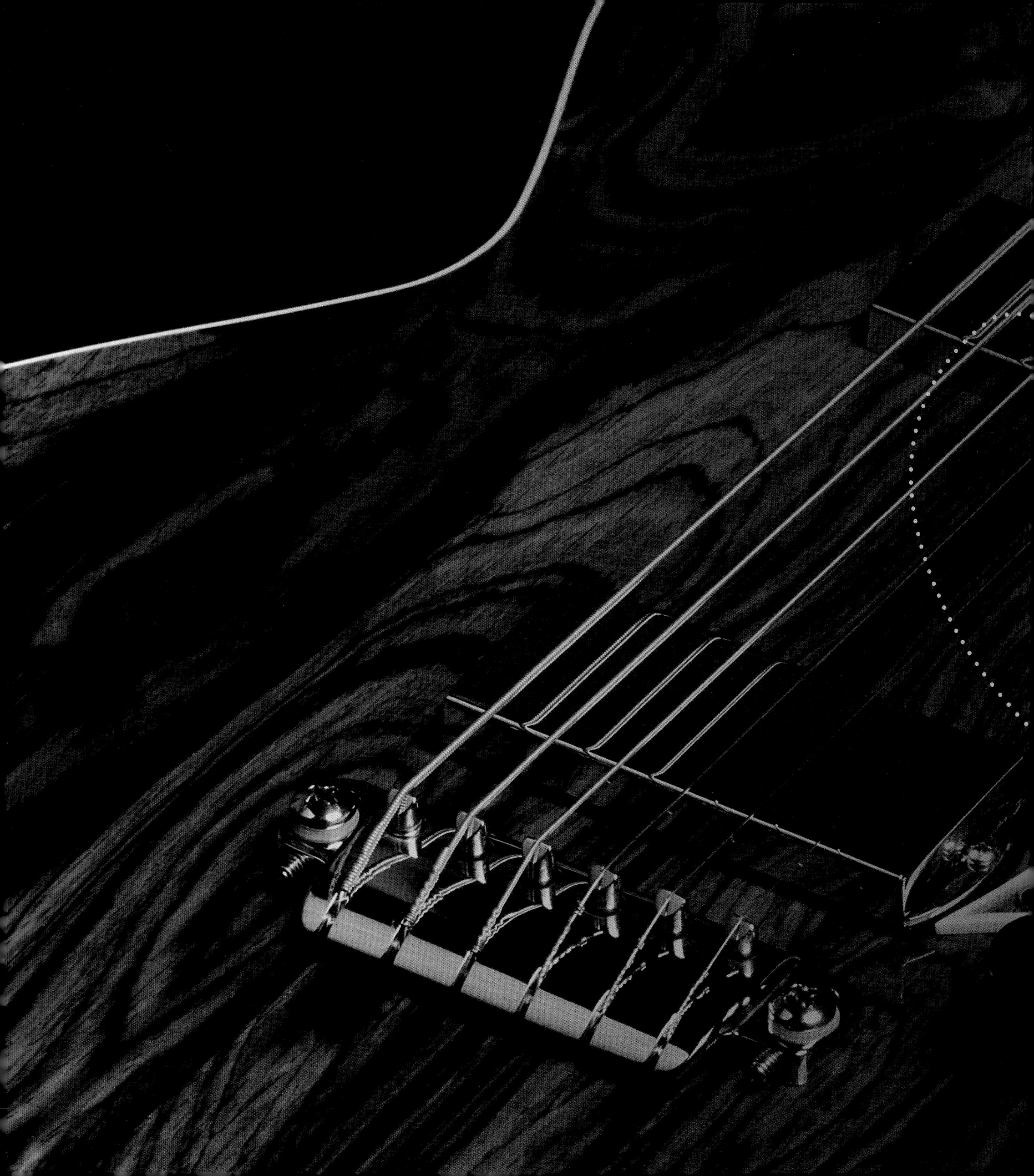

MODERN MASTERS

PORTRAITS OF ARTISTS AND THEIR WORK

MATT ARTINGER

Matt Artinger has been fascinated with all things guitar from nearly as far back as he can remember. "As a kid, I saw the inception of MTV and was immediately hooked," he recalls. "Although it's a bit embarrassing to admit now, I was in awe of all of the crazy-looking guitar shapes and clothing styles of the early '80s and remember cutting out cardboard air guitars and headbanging in front of the likes of Van Halen and Poison. Who would imagine what it would lead to! I'm five-hundred-plus guitars into this fantasy that some call a career, and I'm still excited about every guitar that I complete . . . every one has its own personality, and I remember them all!"

Happily, Matt also had a stepfather who had spent his college years amassing an enormous live-tape collection, "everything from the Grateful Dead to Springsteen to Alice Cooper to Traffic and beyond . . . it was all playing in our household during that time. Although the '80s hair-metal fad was wild and fun for my musical upbringing, it was the older bands like the Dead, Zeppelin, the Allmans, etc., who shaped my musical tastes."

After spending most of his grammar-school days sketching guitars (and cars) on every paper surface he could find, Matt finally got his first electric guitar when he was twelve. He immediately wanted to take it apart to see what made it tick, but soon realized he didn't know how to put it back together again. His obsession led to buying inexpensive damaged guitars on which he could safely practice disassembly and reassembly. He built his first real guitar—a Martin Dreadnought he made from a kit—when he was sixteen. He then apprenticed under a local master cabinetmaker named John Angelino, acquiring the skills that would allow him to create his own guitars. After finishing high school, he dove into guitar making headfirst, repairing friends' instruments and pursuing his own ideas about guitar design, which eventually evolved into the instruments he is building today.

MATT ARTINGER OF MATT ARTINGER CUSTOM GUITARS, LTD., EMMAUS, PENNSYLVANIA.

Matt Artinger, whose intense dedication to his work and clients has led friends to jokingly call him a guitar monk, began tinkering with guitars when he was twelve, and founded Artinger Custom Guitars shortly after graduating from high school. Matt's designs, which often reflect considerable input from his clients, are continually evolving, and no two of his cutting-edge hollow-, semihollow-, and solid-body guitars and basses are exactly alike.

NUB CHOPPER, 2006.

This guitar was painted by the artist known as Nub, who is best known for his work at the Orange County Choppers motorcycle shop in Newburgh, New York. Matt met Nub while they were both doing design work for Martin Guitars in 2006. The Chopper is built entirely from mahogany. It features a 25-inch scale, a brushed aluminum neck and headplate binding, brushed aluminum logo and inlay, blue fiber-optic side and top fret markers, skull knobs, and stainless .22-caliber shells outlining the body and capping the switch top. After a jet-black base coat, Nub laid down the pearlescent plum flames, which he edged with light blue pinstripes.

Matt says this is one of his favorite guitars, and one of the few that he'd have a hard time parting with. But, as he told Modern Guitars *magazine, "I think a guitar maker is like a car dealer. You're always driving new cars, but you never own any of them. That's just the way it has to be in order to pay the bills. I still don't officially own any of my own guitars."*

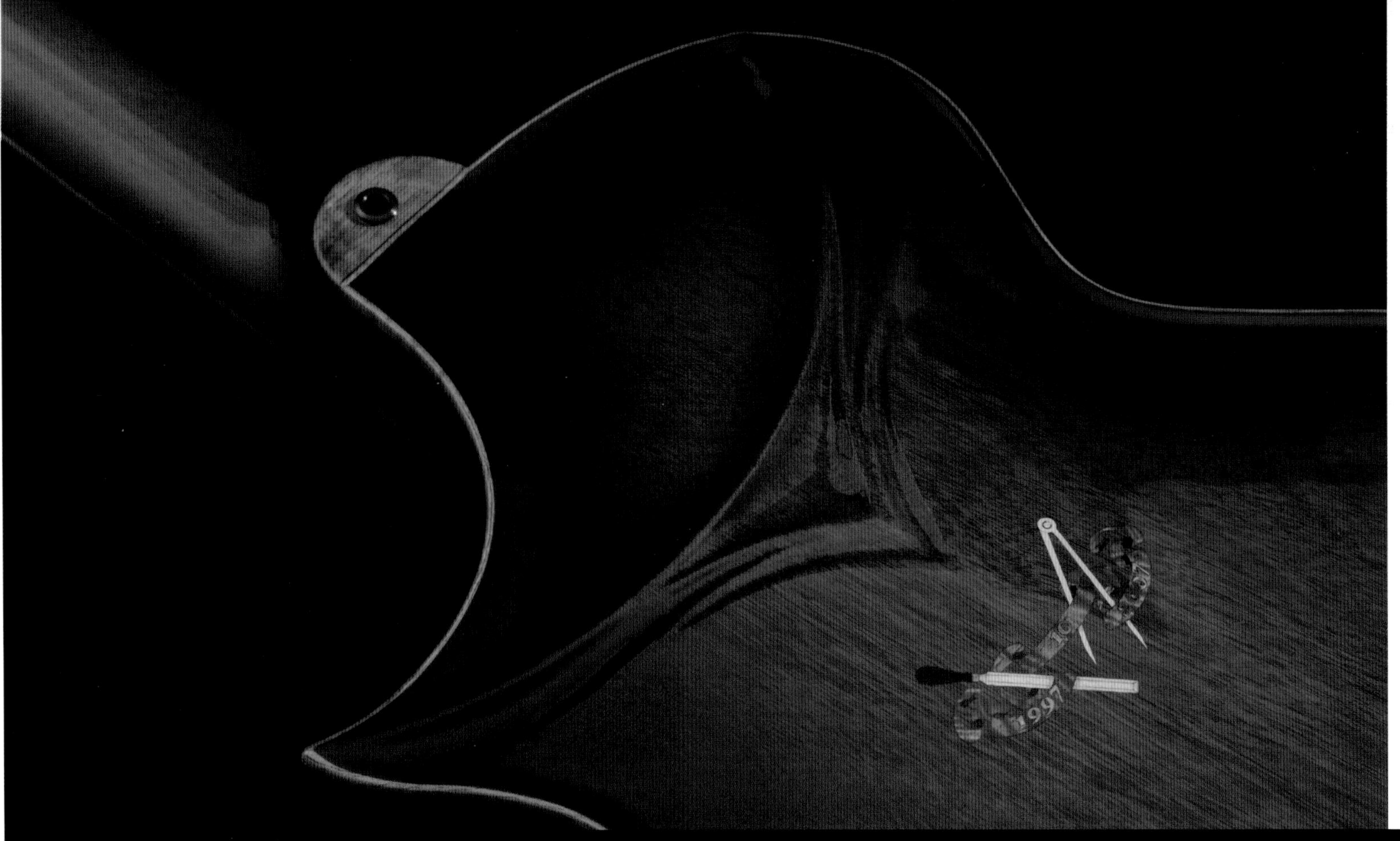

10TH ANNIVERSARY SINGLE-CUTAWAY HOLLOW, 2007.

Matt made this one-of-a-kind guitar to mark a major milestone—the anniversary of his first decade in business. It features a 25-inch scale, a quilt-maple top, a mahogany back, a carbon fiber–reinforced mahogany neck, and a full flame-koa binding. Both the top and back have chevron patterns carved in deep relief, and the back is further embellished with a tenth-anniversary banner of koa, brass, and aluminum. The banner wraps around two of the major hand tools of Matt's craft, a rasp and a two-legged drawing compass. A smaller version of the banner and tools appears at the twelfth fret.

The sound ports at the edge of the top were inspired by archtop innovator Ken Parker, who has incorporated similar ports into his recent work on acoustic archtops. The guitar also has a Brazilian rosewood headplate and matching pick guard, a pair of ebony-and-koa-covered Seymour Duncan 59 pickups, a custom one-off bridge and tail, and a one-off brass headplate logo featuring an inlay of one of Matt's favorite little palm planes. According to Matt, who has lived with the guitar since it was finished, "It's one of those special guitars that will reveal new secrets about itself, even after you think you've seen every individual detail on it."

Matt has been in business for himself since 1997, when, as a nineteen-year-old, he founded Artinger Custom Guitars. His business grew by word of mouth, first in the area near his hometown and then out of state. With demand steadily growing, he teamed up with Rick Dorfman in 1999 to form Artinger Custom Guitars, Ltd. Matt explains that although Rick spends only a small portion of his time in the shop helping with the construction of the instruments themselves, he's the administrative backbone of the company, handling everything from the Web site to marketing. "It's been a fantastic partnership, and we're both proud to be keeping the company at a grassroots level, getting to know each customer individually, and tailoring every instrument to that individual's needs and desires."

Matt currently produces between thirty-five and forty-five instruments per year in his shop in Emmaus, Pennsylvania, about twenty-five miles southwest of Nazareth—the home of the legendary C. F. Martin guitar company. He befriended folks at Martin early on, and has done occasional custom inlay work for them over the years. He also collaborated with the company to develop the Martin OMC Artinger 1 model, which was introduced in 2007. Matt says the project was an absolute dream come true, even though it took two years to come to fruition. "When I was five, holding a cardboard air guitar in front of MTV, I certainly would never have imagined my name on a Martin!" he says, shaking his head in disbelief.

He says that one of the big challenges he sees in being a very small operation is resisting the temptation to grow "beyond your particular guitar's market share. I've been in business for myself for fourteen years now," he explains, "and I've seen the rise and fall of quite a few builders who have grown too quickly and turned from independent

ROMEO Y JULIETA
OLIVA
COHIBA
100 AÑOS
ASHTON
VSG
C.A.O.
PUNCH
MADE
FLOR DE JUAN LOPEZ
HAND MADE

CIGTAR, 2008.

Matt Artinger's artist friend Douglas Vokes inspired this unique theme-based guitar, and Matt says he had "a blast" creating it. The Cigtar is an all-mahogany 25-inch-scale chambered solid-body with a tortoiseshell binding and headplate. The body is decorated with more than one hundred cigar labels that Matt collected from clients over a period of several months, and the handmade lipstick-tube single-coil pickup was created from two Romeo y Julieta cigar tubes. The rear control plate was made from a cedar Partagás box top. Matt explains that he sealed the guitar's top with a vinyl sealer to provide a moisture barrier and fill any small holes in the surface. "Then, on a coffee-fueled Saturday night, I just went at it with a glue stick, an X-Acto knife, and the labels. I can't even explain how the layout came together—I had labels spread all over my main workbench and was in a complete art/Zen blackout. When I came up for breath several hours after I started, there it was—done! I finished by cutting off any overhanging labels and X-Actoing in the binding line around the top face. I love projects like that—the ones where I know that no matter how hard I try, I'll never be able to duplicate them!"

artisans into small manufacturers. Then they go under, only to revive themselves again as independent artisans . . . the temptation is great, but sometimes we need to consider the intimacy of our craft and our individual relationships with our clients before taking any growth risks that may tarnish those relationships and our reputations." Continuing on the same theme, he told *Modern Guitars* magazine, "I'm not an administrator by nature. I'm a craftsman and I truly have a passion for what I do . . . I don't see how I could successfully [be an administrator] and have the same guitar and the same quality, that same intimacy that I know. I mean, when you carve an individual piece of wood and you're spending hours and hours over the top of it, you really get to know that piece of wood and that guitar inside and out. I don't want to lose that connection."

Asked about the future, Matt replies that he likes the trajectory his business is taking right now. "I'm still independent, and creatively charged with my own designs, but I would really like to collaborate more with larger companies in the future, and I think there will be some opportunities for that!"

BILLY F. GIBBONS AND JOHN BOLIN WITH **THE NEW BO FUR GUITAR AND BASS**, 2010.

The fur-covered guitar and bass seen here (the bass is standing at the lower right) were created to update and honor ZZ Top's original pair of fur-covered guitars, which were made by Gibson in 1983 and featured in the band's hit music video for the song "Legs." Since covering guitars with sheep fur was Bo Diddley's idea to begin with, John and Billy decided that the bodies of the New Bo Fur guitars should be rectangular, like Diddley's most famous guitar design.

JOHN BOLIN

John Bolin was born into woodworking and fine craftsmanship; his father was a contractor and master carpenter who built custom houses, and John worked alongside him from an early age. "Pop taught me how to work," John explains, and the work ethic and quest for quality his father instilled in him has served him well over the years.

By his early teens, John was deeply into cars, guitars, and motorcycles. He could only afford pawnshop guitars, which he took apart and tinkered with just as he did with the cars and bikes that surrounded him. He says he played (and still plays) the guitar well enough, mostly for himself, but even back then he was more interested in what made the instruments tick than in being a rock star.

By chance or fortune, John ultimately came across an ad for a guitar school in a neighbor's music magazine and ended up serving an apprenticeship with a pair of acoustic-guitar makers—"a Martin guy and a Gibson guy"— in Spring Hill, Tennessee. "I had a head start," he recalls with obvious pride. "I was probably one of the few who walked into that shop and said, 'I know how to use all those tools, so let's build some guitars!' " After finishing his apprenticeship, he came back to Boise, his hometown, and opened Bolin Guitars in 1978. Like his mentors, he made only acoustic guitars at first, because he thought they were more challenging to build, and in 1980, he had the good luck to be asked to make a flattop for flat-picking legend Doc Watson.

But one day the following year, fate intervened again when someone walked into the shop and asked if John could make an electric. It only made sense to diversify, especially at a small shop in Boise, so John thought, Why not? "The customer wanted a black reverse Firebird," he recalls, "so that became my first electric build. Little did I know what lay ahead."

John's big break came in 1985, when a friend told him that ZZ Top was coming to town and suggested he build a guitar for Billy F. Gibbons. "I had *Tres Hombres* when it came out," John recalls, referring to the band's 1973 breakthrough album, "but I hadn't seen them live and wasn't familiar with their eccentric guitar 'thang.' " The gig was only two weeks away, so John did some intense homework and somehow managed to build a matching guitar and bass that he describes as hot rod–influenced designs finished in candy-apple red metal-flake paint.

The night of the show, John slipped backstage and introduced himself to Billy, who told him, "Get your best and meet me in the green room in ten." After Billy ran both the guitar and bass through their paces, John handed him his card, and, he says, "Twenty-four hours later, we struck our first deal."

As can be the case when dealing with Gibbons, one thing quickly led to another, and, as John explains, "For the next three or four years, I attended the 'Billy F. Gibbons School of Rock and Roll.' That, I can assure you, was no cakewalk. Billy makes strong demands about what he wants and needs." It proved to be a match made in creative heaven: stimulated by Billy's genre-bending ideas and precise requirements, John stretched himself and earned his teacher's trust and respect. Since that first deal, the two have collaborated on more than two hundred unique guitars and basses, including a number of ZZ Top's best known and wildest-looking

JOHN BOLIN OF BOLIN GUITARS, LLC, BOISE, IDAHO.

John Bolin celebrated his thirtieth anniversary in the guitar business in 2008. Over the years, John and a small team that now includes his son, Jake, have built some of the most innovative and visually distinctive guitars in rock-and-roll history. Their satisfied customers include Billy F. Gibbons and Dusty Hill of ZZ Top, Steve Miller, Jimmy Page, Lou Reed, Albert King, Bo Diddley, Joe Perry, and Keith Richards and Ron Wood of the Rolling Stones. John says his forte is "thinking outside the box—way outside the box." But however outrageous Bolin guitars may look, John is adamant that "it's about the music," and, as his client list testifies, the quality of his instruments is second to none. He is seen here holding his thirtieth anniversary limited-edition model, an understated archtop that demonstrates another side of his multifaceted work.

instruments. Gibbons also turned some of his friends on to John's work, including Steve Miller, a fellow Idahoan with whom John has since collaborated on more than one hundred and fifty guitars, and Keith Richards and Ronnie Wood of the Rolling Stones, to whom Gibbons gave guitars he commissioned John to build as surprise gifts.

Billy delivered Richards's guitar, a metallic silver-and-pink Tele he dubbed the Blues Basher, when the Stones played Houston during their 2002–3 Licks world tour. He handed it to Richards's guitar technician, Pierre de Beauport, before the show and told him that he and his mom would be in the audience that night. Pierre in turn presented the guitar to Richards, who asked, "Has Billy played it?" Assured that he had, Richards told Pierre to put it in the rack for the night's show, and, though he had never played it before, he picked it up for "Satisfaction" that night, a ritual that continued throughout the tour. Richards has been a Bolin customer ever since.

Steve Miller provided John with another life-changing connection in the early '90s, when he commissioned the incomparable archtop luthier James D'Aquisto, then at the peak of his innovative powers, to build a number of guitars for him. "Steve wanted some of them to be electrics, but Jimmy wasn't into doing the wiring," John explains. "So he gave his blessing to let me finish them. When I got the guitars, they only had holes in them for the pickups, nothing else. I had all kinds of questions, and Steve's response was, 'I'll give you Jimmy's number. Why don't you talk to him?' "

The two master luthiers, who were aware of each other's work but had never connected before, soon became phone pals. "We were like two mad scientists working on the same experiment," John recalls. "Jimmy took me to a whole new level. He was very generous, but if you went too far, he would get quiet. So I was careful not to cross that line. But one day I just came out and asked him, 'So, what *is* the big secret?' And he told me, 'John, you just have to build the archtop lighter and lighter, to the point where it actually fails. That's the only way you'll ever know what the limits are.' It blew me away that he was willing to push things that far. He also told me I had to listen to what the wood was trying to tell me, which I thought sounded kind of mystical at first, but he said, 'No, you just keep tapping and carving, it knows what it wants, and it will guide you.' And he was right."

Bolin Guitars is a family affair: John and his wife, Cristi, live above the shop, and their children, Celeste and Jake, have grown up immersed in the world of guitars and guitar heroes. All of them have taken turns in the shop when help was needed, but Jake, who remembers sharing an after-school snack with Steve Miller the day he first walked into the shop and says Billy Gibbons bought him his first skateboard, has followed in his father's footsteps. He started as an apprentice in the shop after graduating from high school in 2001 and became head of production two years later. His proud father says that Jake is a great luthier who can build anything, but is not sure what the future holds. "Jake is really smart," John says. "He could be anything he wants to be. He could be a businessman or the president of a company or even a lawyer, for that matter."

Whatever Jake ultimately decides, John neither plans nor desires to stop. "I'm like an old pirate," he says with a hearty laugh. "I'll stop building guitars when I'm dead." His work still challenges and fascinates him, because his clients and his own restless imagination keep pushing him into unknown territory. "It isn't just one thing that goes into making a guitar," John told *Boise Weekly*. "It's all my influences, and hundreds of hours spent with guitars and guitarists, with these geniuses and their collections, finding out what they need. And the devil's in the details."

JUPITER THUNDERBIRD BILLY-BO "PRO" PSYCHE, 2010. COLLECTION OF BILLY F. GIBBONS.

The Billy-Bo is named after two of rock and roll's great characters and showmen, ZZ Top guitarist Billy F. Gibbons, whose idea it was, and the immortal Bo Diddley, for whom Gretsch built the wildest and most radical-looking guitars of the 1950s. The Billy-Bo is based on the Jupiter Thunderbird, a futuristic, automobile-influenced guitar that Diddley designed in 1959 and which he and the Duchess, a.k.a. Norma-Jean Wofford, both played on stage together in the early '60s.

Diddley later presented his original Jupiter Thunderbird to Gibbons, who explains that during a recording session, "when the engineering crew and I snaked through the guitar vault searching for that 'certain-something' guitar, there it was! We didn't want to risk subjecting such a rare instrument to the rigors of the road, so this new, reproduction model was re-created [by Gretsch] with some BFG mojo thrown in for good measure." Gibbons's update reversed Diddley's original body design and added a number of modern sonic bells and whistles, resulting in an instrument that has, as only Billy F. Gibbons could put it, "enough 'vibe' to make space aliens dance the alligator."

Enter John Bolin, who, under the auspices of Gretsch, had built several custom Jupiter Thunderbirds for Gibbons to use on stage. He and Gibbons were talking about the design one night and decided to add some new twists to it. They cut, pasted, and photocopied designs until they came up with a shorter, thinner, and lighter body—this guitar actually fits in a Telecaster case—added some curves, and turned the surface into a psychedelic extravaganza. As fellow gearheads, they hit on the idea of covering the back of the guitar with House of Kolor "Shimrin Kameleon" car paint, so called because it changes color when seen from different angles, and Billy found a psychedelic motif on an old playing card that he and John manipulated to create the painted design on the front. The net result was the Jupiter Thunderbird Billy-Bo "Pro" Psyche.

HIGH DESERT
HARLEY-DAVIDSON
TWIN CAM
USA

TWIN CAM HARLEY-DAVIDSON GUITAR, 2009. COLLECTION OF BOB AND DAVE THOMAS, HIGH DESERT HARLEY-DAVIDSON.

This wild new Bolin creation is one of a pair of guitars John designed and built as a trade for a custom Harley-Davidson motorcycle from High Desert Harley-Davidson in Meridian, Idaho.

John's original pitch was to trade a custom guitar for a bike, but, as he warns, "Be careful what you wish for!" Co-owner Dave Thomas convinced John that what he really wanted was a custom bike, which would cost him two custom guitars. After the deal was struck, John stayed up all night drafting two designs, one built around a fuel tank and the other around a Harley Twin Cam engine. The latter design was everyone's favorite, so then John had to figure out how to build it.

"I wanted lots of metal parts to make it convincing," he explains, "but the prototypes were way too heavy, and I had to figure out how to put an air cleaner on a guitar and make it playable!" Ultimately, each cylinder was made up of fourteen pieces of aluminum and rosewood, and John found a shop in Las Vegas that could do a diamond-cut tool pass on the metal, so it would look just like the sparkling cylinders and heads on a real Harley. The final touch was the Harley-Davidson eagle logo on the fingerboard, which is a dead ringer for the decal on a bike (Dave got special dispensation from Harley to allow the design to be copied), but was actually all hand-inlaid by John. "That," he says, "was a real pain in the neck!"

STEVE MILLER WITH THE TWIN CAM HARLEY-DAVIDSON GUITAR, 2009.

Over the course of a career that dates back to the 1960s, Steve Miller has built one of the world's most extraordinary collections of antique and contemporary guitars. Miller has worked closely with John for many years and commissioned more than one hundred and fifty Bolin guitars, but the Harley-Davidson guitar came as a complete surprise to him.

John took it and "a carload of other guitars" to an all-night gathering at Miller's home studio. "We didn't get started until about midnight," John recalls, "and Steve and a bunch of friends had a stack of Marshalls going and had a great time trying out all the guitars I brought. About four-thirty in the morning, we were winding down, drinking coffee and smoking cigars, when I said, 'Hey, I have one more guitar for you to try.' I had put the HD in a bag and when Steve pulled it out, he flipped. He plugged it in, and, after a minute or two, he turned to me and said, 'This plays really good, really good.' I knew I had hit the nail on the head. Then, to show everyone the guitar's hidden feature, I said, 'Push the button on it.' Even though he was puzzled, Steve pushed it and all of a sudden you had the sound of a Harley revving up and going into idle, all through a stack of Marshalls cranked up to ten! We must have talked and laughed about that until seven AM!" John adds that Steve has promised to end his next show in Boise by playing the Twin Cam Harley Guitar.

BRAZILIAN '52, 2009.

This DeTemple '52's distinguishing feature is its beautifully grained Brazilian rosewood top. Rosewood was far too rich for Leo Fender's blood, but the company he founded did make a few rosewood-topped instruments after it was sold to CBS in 1965—guitars to which this gorgeous DeTemple pays proper homage. In particular, there was a rosewood Tele model that Fender launched in 1969: one was presented to George Harrison, who played it on "Let It Be" and in the famous rooftop documentary film of the same name. Rhythm guitarist Steve Cropper also played a rosewood Tele in the early '70s, but that model was discontinued in 1972. Fender also made a one-off rosewood Strat in 1969, which was given to Jimi Hendrix.

This Spirit Series '52 started out to be a standard two-pickup model, but as soon as Mike saw how beautiful the book-matched, two-piece Brazilian rosewood top looked, he decided to use a bridge pickup only, as on a Fender Esquire. He also decided he couldn't put a pick guard on the guitar, which, like a neck pickup, would cover up the natural beauty of the grain and mar its color and overall presentation. Instead, Mike made the guitar one-sixteenth of an inch thicker than normal (the thickness of a single-ply pick guard) and then routed the top down, leaving a raised pick guard shape intact. The grain thus continues off the "pick guard" and is the same on the top of the body as it is on the pick guard shape.

The body is one-piece featherweight swamp ash bound with cream-colored ivoroid, and the neck is one-piece, quartersawn Brazilian rosewood with a flame-maple skunk stripe. The neck is finished with true gun oil, and the body with a thin coating of see-through nitrocellulose lacquer in seafoam green. The position markers on the fingerboard are made from fossilized walrus-tusk tapioca (the material inside the tusk itself), and the Gotoh tuners are a special open-back design. Mike adds, "I installed my titanium saddles and ferrules and my SweetSpot Alnico II bridge pickup on the guitar. The truss rod design and installation is proprietary, but I will say that the truss rod is tuned to pitch, and the neck is made with my special pre-tensioned technique."

MICHAEL DETEMPLE

Michael DeTemple makes what he calls "vintage-design solid-body electrics"—guitars so good that *Premier Guitar* magazine said Mike's Spirit Series '56 model "may well be the best built, most thoroughly actualized guitar of its kind out there." Master luthier Rick Turner has called the DeTemple '56 "the one out of five thousand—the top half of one percent of all these types of guitars . . . the dream Strat-style guitars that everybody's chasing after."

Mike was born and raised in L.A. He started playing guitar, banjo, and mandolin at twelve, and grew up not only playing but maintaining a large assortment of stringed instruments for the legendary guitarist and music business entrepreneur Ernie Ball, who traded Mike old guitars in exchange for work in his store in Tarzana, California, one of the first all-guitar shops in the country. Mike's earliest musical influences came while hanging out at the legendary Ash Grove music club in L.A., where he spent time with the likes of Taj Mahal, Doc Watson, Lightnin' Hopkins, and Clarence White (who was then playing with the Kentucky Colonels).

Mike won his first Topanga Banjo·Fiddle Contest when he was fourteen, and, after competing against the likes of David Lindley and winning four times in five years, he was invited by the Academy Award–winning composer Earl Robinson to perform Robinson's *Concerto for Five-String Banjo* with the Los Angeles Philharmonic. One of the conductors with whom Mike performed was Elmer Bernstein, whose connections in the movie industry enabled Mike to obtain work playing on film scores, including the Academy Award–winning *Bonnie and Clyde*. He worked as a road and session musician throughout the '70s, playing with Dave Mason, Eric Clapton, Van Morrison, Bob Dylan, Neil Young, Pete Townshend, Ron Wood, Booker T., Paul Butterfield, and others—many of whom he met through his close association with bassist Rick Danko of The Band. Mike toured with The Band in the late '70s and also served as house guitarist during the filming of Martin Scorsese's classic 1978 rockumentary *The Last Waltz*.

Because he wanted to have more time with his wife and young children, Mike eventually phased out of touring and dedicated his professional life to instrument restoration, repair, and building. He became a trusted resource for many top artists and studio musicians, including Bob Dylan, Joe Walsh, John Fogerty, Lee Ritenour, and Michael Thompson. By the mid-'90s, his own collection of vintage electric guitars was rapidly increasing in value and therefore becoming impractical to

MICHAEL DETEMPLE (LEFT) AND HIS ASSISTANT, JOHN CAREY, OF DETEMPLE GUITARS, SHERMAN OAKS, CALIFORNIA.

Mike DeTemple is a former professional guitar, banjo, and mandolin player who is recognized as one of the reigning masters of the art of building Tele- and Strat-style guitars. Mike's son-in-law, John Carey, is his right-hand man, and has assisted in the building of DeTemple guitars alongside Mike for the past seven years. Johnny and his wife (Mike's daughter, Annie) play and sing with Old Man Markley, a rising and rousing nine-piece bluegrass band that—in a twist on tradition—also includes a drummer.

Mike's solid-body Spirit Series '52, '56, and Modern Jazz guitars are handcrafted to order with an absolutely minimal use of machinery, and bring classic Fender concepts to an unparalleled level of contemporary refinement. "The Spirit Series guitars are a labor of love," explains Mike. "I baby each and every one of them into existence. I craft each guitar with the attitude that it's mine, and they're usually really difficult to let go of."

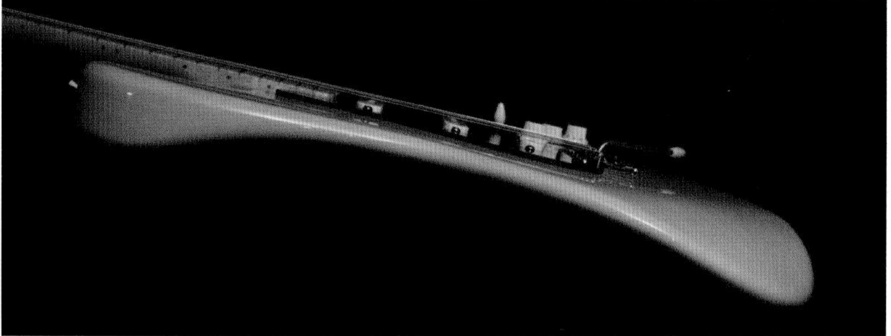

'56, 2008.

Although 1950s Strats have a graceful body form, Mike gives his '56s a longer, deeper, more ergonomic body contour that makes them more comfortable to play and also increases tone and resonance.

PERSONAL '56, 2008. COLLECTION OF MICHAEL DETEMPLE.

Mike built this guitar for himself. Weighing in at six and one-half pounds, it has a body crafted from a single piece of featherweight swamp ash; a quartersawn, one piece, flame-maple neck with a bocote skunk stripe and gun-oil finish; a stunning faux-tortoiseshell celluloid pick guard; DeTemple SweetSpot pickups; a fossilized mastodon-ivory nut and fossilized walrus-tusk string trees; a titanium tremolo block and saddles; and a push/pull knob on the second tone control, which allows Mike to select from among seven different pickup configurations.

play during gigs. So, after years of restoring and repairing some of the great old Fender instruments, he decided to build his own, using what he describes as "the ones that really had the magic" as templates for new re-creations. He studied every conceivable nuance of what set these particular instruments apart from the others, and incorporated his discoveries into his own guitars, including the DeTemple '56—a variant of the mid-'50s Stratocaster—and the DeTemple '52, a variant of the early '50s Telecaster. Friends such as pedal steel master Red Rhodes of Velvet Hammer pickups fame helped uncover the enigma of early Fender electronics, and Mike's acute sense of "touch memory," developed over his many years as a working musician, helped him establish the ideal neck shape as well as a long, accumulated list of proprietary "secret recipes" for fingerboard and tone treatments. He says he is frequently told, especially by seasoned players, that his guitars have an immediate "old friend" feel, and adds, with a gratified smile, "That's exactly what I set out to accomplish." Mike says the idea of the Spirit Series is that these models capture the essence, or spirit, of the 1950s originals they were modeled after. "They are essentially a composite of the cream of that period," he explains. "And I personally feel that there are no better guitars than Fender's 1950s-era models."

Mike continues to keep a hand in the music business, most recently playing his prized Lloyd Loar–era Gibson F-4 mandolin on John

SPIRIT SERIES TWINS, 2009. COLLECTION OF KIRK HAMMETT.

Mike has made a number of handsome twin sets of his '52 and '56 models over the years. This pair, finished in a custom black nitrocellulose lacquer, was commissioned by Kirk Hammett, the lead guitarist for Metallica, who were inducted into the Rock and Roll Hall of Fame in 2009.

Both guitars have matched featherweight swamp-ash bodies; book-matched maple necks; hundred-year-old book-matched Brazilian rosewood fingerboards; fossilized mastodon-ivory nuts, switch tips, and string trees; titanium neck plates; custom Italian celluloid tortoiseshell pick guards; special open-back tuners; and DeTemple SweetSpot pickups. The '52 (at bottom) has DeTemple compensated titanium saddles and titanium ferrules, while the '56 has a DeTemple titanium tremolo assembly.

Fogerty's *Deja Vu All Over Again* album. As a builder, he is fastidious about every part of his guitars, and constantly tweaks different aspects of them to improve their tone. For example, he began building his own pickups, which he calls SweetSpots, because he couldn't get the results he wanted from those made by others. Mike has been making tremolo blocks, saddles, and back plates from titanium since 2004, and says the titanium trem assembly made an overwhelming difference when he first tried it out on his favorite Strat. "Not only did it reduce the weight of the guitar, but it was so musical," he recalls. "I never heard any upgrade on a Strat that seemed so dramatic and dynamic." His necks are carved from one-piece quartersawn flame maple, and he also carves the nuts (and sometimes the switch tips) for his instruments from fossilized mastodon ivory. No detail is too small to escape his attention, and that, he believes, makes all the difference.

'52 SWITCH TIP, 2009.

Mike often hand-carves special switch tips from fossilized mammoth ivory or walrus tusk. This one, which graces a DeTemple '52, portrays a Polynesian tiki god.

FIBENARE

"We have a long story," says Attila Benedek of Fibenare Guitars, in his customarily colorful narrative style. "Once upon a time, in a country far, far away, where the Iron Curtain was real and the Communist regime was in charge, we, the three Benedek brothers, were born in a city known for its appreciation of classical music."

The Benedeks of Kecskemét, Hungary—also the birthplace of composer Zoltán Kodály, a strong advocate of elementary music education—came from a family of musicians, and all studied classical music as youngsters under the Kodály Method, which was developed in the mid-twentieth century by the composer and his followers. It is now used in more than fifty countries around the world, including the United States.

Although they maintained their interest in classical music as they grew older, the Benedek brothers—Csaba, Árpád, and Attila—became increasingly interested in rock, blues, and jazz. Therefore, as Attila—who speaks the best English in the family—puts it, "electric guitars became the most important for us. The question was, how you could get one? In Eastern Europe? In the countryside, where we had only one music shop? The shop had only one Gibson guitar at that time—which was far too expensive—and there were three of us. There was not any Internet connection or Skype, Facebook, or MySpace to look for instruments. Our father gave us the solution: we should build a bass and two electric guitars of our own. Oh my God, but how?"

Somehow, the brothers managed to build some workable instruments. "We started to build the first guitars by heart," Attila recalls. "We talked to woodworkers, carpenters, and turners to become experts about different materials. We learned a lot from musicians and guitarists. Our friends who were guitar players already

LEFT TO RIGHT: CSABA BENEDEK, GENE BLACK (ONE OF FIBENARE'S CUSTOMERS AND A GUITARIST FOR JOE COCKER), ÁRPÁD BENEDEK, GÁBOR GOLDSCHMIDT, AND ATTILA BENEDEK OF FIBENARE GUITARS, BUDAPEST, HUNGARY.

Fibenare is a small Hungarian guitar company founded in 1998 by the Benedek brothers, who advertise their guitars as being "from behind the curtain"—i.e., the Iron Curtain. The company is named in honor of their parents, who played a key role in its formation: "Fibenare" is a mashup of the Hungarian words for "sons of Benedek and Clare." With the help of luthier Gábor Goldschmidt, who joined the team in 2004, the brothers take the art of hand-building about as far as it can go, crafting every part of their instruments except the tuners in their own shop—they even machine their own bridges, tailpieces, and pickups—and offering their costumers a host of options in everything from electronics to neck profiles.

MATTE HENDERSON SIGNATURE BASIC JAZZ, 2009. COLLECTION OF MATTE HENDERSON.

Session guitarist Matte Henderson's weapon of choice is a seven-string electric, a configuration that adds a low A string to the standard EADGBE layout. Seeking the advantage of an extended range, jazz guitarist George Van Eps had a seven-string built for him in the late 1930s, and a number of other prominent jazz guitarists, including Bucky and John Pizzarelli, Howard Alden, and Lenny Breau have played seven-strings over the years.

The guitar that the Benedek brothers designed with Matte's input has a solid white-limba back with a carved flame-maple top and a white-limba set-in neck. Limba, also known as korina, is an African hardwood that was first introduced into the guitar world when Gibson used it to build its Flying V and Explorer models in 1958. The fully scalloped ironwood fret board is bound but has no inlays. The guitar has a Fibenare brass-and-aluminum tremolo bridge, and is equipped with a Fibenare HSH "Matte" pickup set. As with Fibenare's standard fixed bridge, the tremolo bridge allows the player to set the strings' action and intonation individually, or to set global action with the two stainless-steel pivot screws. The saddles can be fixed to the bridge's base plate, which makes tuning very stable.

10TH ANNIVERSARY EROTIC, 2010.

This is one of ten special-edition Erotics made to celebrate Fibenare's tenth anniversary. The suggestively named Erotic, which is the company's most popular and distinctive model, is named for its decidedly sexy lines and unusually shaped horns. The anniversary edition has a radius-carved Hungarian-ash back, a hand-carved Hungarian 5A-grade poplar-burl top with maple binding, a laminated set-in neck of padauk and 5A-grade flame maple, and a padauk fret board. The fret board is double-bound with maple, mahogany, and ebony, and has mother-of-pearl dot inlays and an anniversary X inlay at the twelfth fret. The guitar carries a gold Fibenare wraparound bridge, a pair of Fibenare's own ALV-63 hand-wound wooden-coil humbuckers, and is finished in a special anniversary "cherryburst" color.

had some nice Western guitars and some asked us to repair them, so step-by-step we found our style. Later, when the Internet came into our daily life, it became easier to get the information we needed. We were heavily influenced by the Gibson, Fender, and PRS guitars of the past, and by the Nik Huber, John Suhr, Juha Ruokangas, Ervin Somogyi, and George Lowden guitars available nowadays."

The Benedeks attracted a lot of attention when they began playing their handmade guitars in public. "We love many music from all styles," says Attila. "Fortunately, we have different tastes among the brothers so we can cover almost everything—from the Beatles, Rolling Stones, Eric Clapton, Santana, Police, Sting, and Pink Floyd to Guns N' Roses, Metallica, and AC/DC, just to name a few. Our favorite guitarists include Eric Clapton, Sting, Dominic Miller, David Gilmour, Monte Montgomery, Eric Johnson, Jeff Beck, Jeff 'Skunk' Baxter, Sándor Szabó, Lance Keltner, Joe Satriani, Roine Stolt, and Gabor Szabó."

Because, by building their own guitars, they had solved a problem that frustrated many of their peers, they soon found themselves making guitars not just for their own use but for others as well. At first, their guitars were used by friends, but eventually professional musicians also bought them, and the brothers' work gained a very good word-of-mouth reputation in Hungary. As demand grew, the self-taught brothers conducted many experiments. Some of them were failures, but as time went on they met with more and more success. "The hobby activity became professional," Attila explains. "Parallel with this, the quality of the guitars continuously improved, and we worked out our production processes, technologies, and procurement resources, but manual fabrication remained our hallmark."

The trio established Fibenare Guitars in 1998 and began to promote their work at Hungarian trade shows. "By 2003," Attila says, "we were strong enough to exhibit at the largest expo in Europe, the

10TH ANNIVERSARY BASIC JAZZ, 2010.

This double-cutaway guitar is part of another special edition of ten made in celebration of Fibenare's tenth anniversary. It has a semihollow, one-piece mahogany back, a hand-carved 5A-grade maple-burl top, a mahogany set-in neck with an ironwood fret board, and the same double binding, inlays, bridge, pickups, and finish color as the 10th Anniversary Erotic.

Frankfurt Musikmesse. We've been there every spring since then. Then another step forward was our first North American exhibition, at the Winter NAMM [National Association of Music Merchants] show in 2007. Today, you can find Fibenare Guitars' stand at some of the national exhibitions in Europe, like the London Guitar Show in England, the Dallas Guitar Show in America, and the Montreal Guitar Show as well. If you ever visit us, we are happy to show you our instruments and have a nice talk or a cup of coffee."

Luthier Gábor Goldschmidt, who joined the company in 2004, works with the Benedek brothers to create Fibenare's guitars. The four men use the latest technologies, but still rely on traditional manual craftsmanship for both rough and fine work. The brothers advertise that they specialize in "constructing and manufacturing high-grade, quality handcrafted guitars to create an individual world of sound," and their distinctive designs and fastidious workmanship have built them an international clientele that continues to grow. They have built signature models for the session guitarist Matte Henderson, California fusion guitarist Ed DeGenaro, and the Canadian guitarist Mark Potvin. Attila adds, "We are happy to have a good reputation. From the beginning—getting the most appropriate wood—till the final step, the right strings, we take care of every little detail. Even the bridges, electronics, and pickups are designed and produced by Fibenare itself. Manufacturing anything is extremely hard work these days. We want to ensure that our designs meet the needs of guitarists in a way that says something new or extreme." Asked where they would like to be in five years, the brothers say they would like to reach an output of 150 first-class manufactured guitars per year. Asked what excites them, aside from music and guitars, the Benedeks respond, "Family in the first place, then girls, and seeing the world."

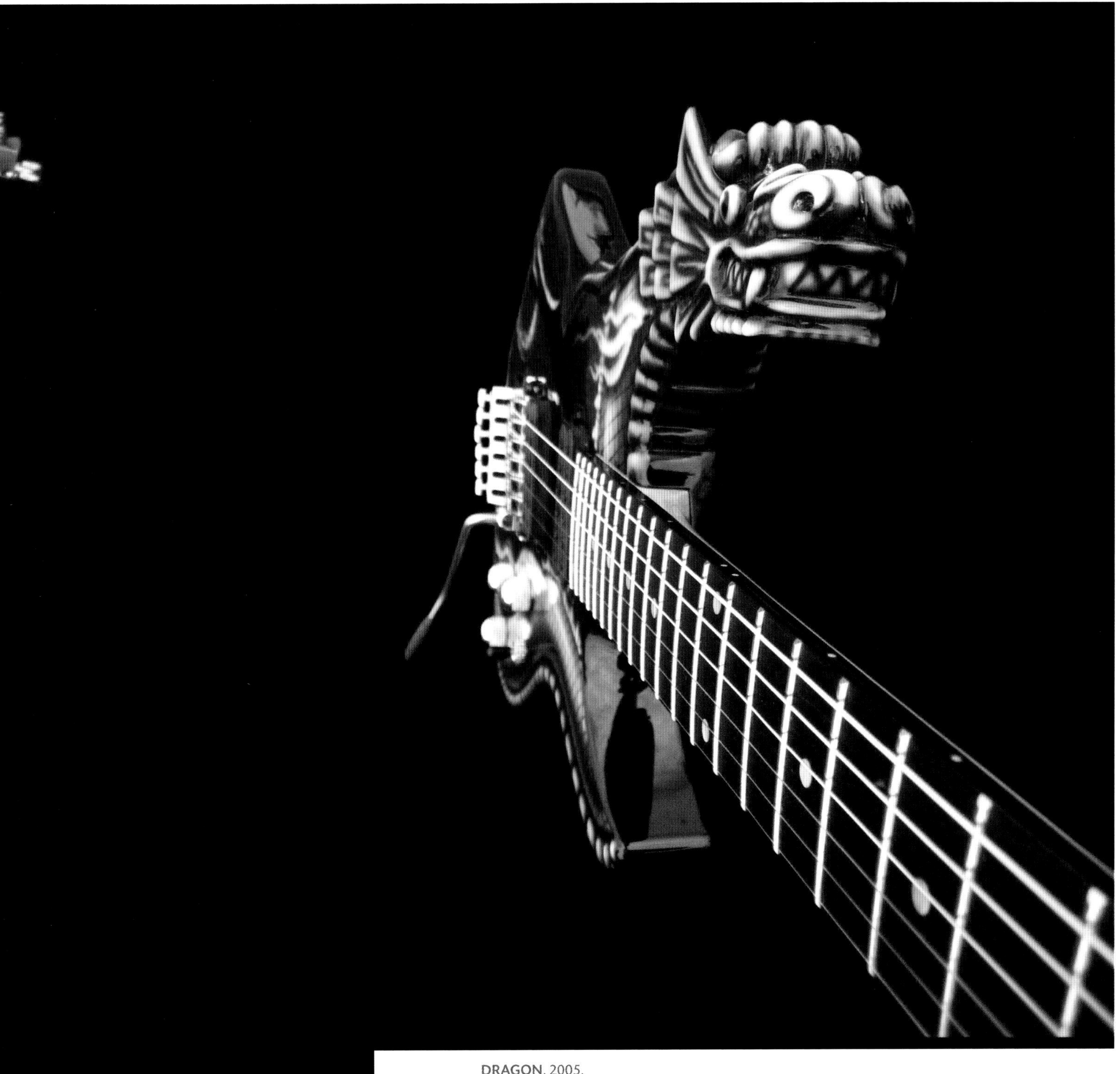

DRAGON, 2005.

This wild custom Fibenare guitar—one of their Art Model series—features a ferocious-looking dragon head carved into its upper horn. Among those who have played a Fibenare Dragon are the ambidextrous American heavy metal guitarist Michael Angelo Batio, who was voted the Number One Shredder of All Time by Guitar One *magazine in 2003, and János Solti of the long-lived Hungarian band Locomotiv GT, which has been in existence since 1971.*

ROGER GIFFIN

The English-born luthier Roger Giffin has played guitar ("badly," he says) since he was ten years old, and got interested in building after he was shown a guitar that a friend of his dad's had made from a kit. "I guess I would have been around fifteen at the time," he recalls. "So I got a similar kit and built an acoustic." His father, a former cabinetmaker, gave him woodworking tips and helped him build two more guitars, one electric and another acoustic: the latter, unfortunately, collapsed because it was not braced strongly enough. "This was real 'seat-of-the pants' stuff," Roger recalls. "There were no books or lutherie schools in Great Britain at that time, so everything I learned about guitar building was self-taught. I just had to figure it out for myself."

As a teenager, Roger remembers playing air guitar along with some very early Elvis records, and later became a fan of the British instrumental group the Shadows—"then the Beatles, the Stones, Johnny Kidd and the Pirates, and Beck, Page, and Clapton, no matter who they were playing with." He also says he loved Peter Green's guitar work—"so much feeling there"—and "Hendrix, of course! . . . [I] managed to see him play in England in '68 or '69. It was the loudest and most impressive gig I had heard."

All along, Roger continued to learn on his own and from anyone he could find who knew more than he did. At one point he asked the prominent luthier Tony Zemaitis—"almost the only guy in England at the time doing what I wanted to do"—if he could work for him to learn the trade, but Zemaitis said he wouldn't have the time to teach him. Dick Knight, who had been building jazz archtops since the '40s, proved more helpful, and Roger says he "learned a good few tips from him." In the late '60s, with enough experience under his belt to feel confident in his abilities, Roger opened a shop in London under a bridge by the river Thames. Word got around, and Giffin Guitars soon became a meeting place for people seeking

ROGER GIFFIN OF GIFFIN GUITARS, BEAVERTON, OREGON.

Roger Giffin is an English-born luthier who has been building outstanding guitars since the late 1960s. He came to the U.S. in 1988 to head Gibson's first custom shop, where he worked for five years, and he has continued to hand-build a wide variety of world-class instruments under his own name ever since. As Cliff Cultreri of the artisans' collective Destroy All Guitars puts it, "Roger is a true master builder, one of the finest alive and working today."

VALIANT CUSTOM, 2010.

This custom Valiant has a mahogany body and neck and a maple top. The fingerboard and headstock are Brazilian rosewood, and the snowflake-shaped fingerboard inlays are abalone. The pickups are Amalfitanos, which are deliberately out of phase magnetically—a feature that Roger says "gives the classic Peter Green sound when both pickups are on."

Roger adds, "It took a while to figure out what bridge to use with the Bigsby B5 [tremolo], but in the end it made sense to use a Wilkinson wraparound. This bridge is solid and stable, and it also allows the musician to bypass the tremolo when stringing the guitar. The instrument also has two volume controls, which produce some very interesting sounds with both pickups on and the volume backed off a little. The vivid canary yellow finish hits you square between the eyes—in a very good way!—and contrasts very nicely with the tortoiseshell binding."

STANDARD HOLLOW-BODY, 2009.

Roger Giffin says he first came up with the Giffin Standard guitar in the late '70s at the request of a customer who wanted a "Strat-meets-Les-Paul" type of instrument. "The body shape that I ended up using evolved from guitars I had been building since back in the early '70s," he explains. "It's not surprising to see that many other builders hit upon this type of design at about the same time. It was a very logical guitar that needed to be invented." Giffin makes the Standard in both hollow- and solid-body models. The hollow-body has a 24¾-inch scale length. Its body is Honduran mahogany with a hand-carved hard-maple top, a laminated Honduran mahogany neck, and Brazilian rosewood veneer on the fingerboard and headstock.

VALIANT SINGLE CUT, 2009.

Roger Giffin says that he designed this guitar after many years of being asked, "Can you build me a Les Paul?" and having to politely say no. Like a Les Paul, the Valiant has a figured maple top on a mahogany body. But, Roger explains, "I went with a slightly offset body shape to get away from the traditional look, and I used a thicker body for a little added depth to the sound and to give it a different tonal quality than my Standard model."

In the neck joint, Roger used an extra-long tenon that runs under the neck pickup position, which he says "really helps to generate great string vibration transfer into the body." The cutaway is extra deep to give the player good access to the upper frets, and he designed a straight-pull three-on-a-side headstock to avoid any hangups at that end of the neck. He also points out that the front strap button sits parallel to the neck instead of at ninety degrees to the body edge, and explains, "This small but maybe useful detail will prevent the strap from pulling off under 'battle conditions.' The guitar balances really well, both visually and physically, and I'm endeavoring to keep the weight limit for this guitar to no more than eight pounds."

great guitars and guitar repair services. Roger built hundreds of high-quality, reasonably priced guitars and worked on hundreds of others: regular customers included Eric Clapton, Pete Townshend and John Entwistle, Mark Knopfler, Andy Summers, David Gilmour, and many other British stars.

After Roger worked on a headless prototype for what became Ned Steinberger's M Series guitar, Gibson offered him an opportunity he couldn't resist—running the new Gibson Custom Shop with Gene Baker and fronting the company's West Coast repair shop in Los Angeles. He moved to the States in 1988 and plunged into custom work for Gibson, which left little time for his own craft. His client list during this time included names like Eddie Van Halen, Peter Frampton, Joe Walsh, Malcolm Young, and Jimmy Page, for whom Giffin built a replica of his famous 1958 Les Paul for use as a backup. After Gibson decided to shift its entire operation to Nashville in 1993, Roger ran a busy service business for three years before founding Giffin Guitars in 1997. He moved once more—to Beaverton, Oregon, outside of Portland—in 2004, where he continues his decidedly hands-on approach to guitar building, emphasizing extensive handwork and close interaction with clients.

Roger has worked on a huge number of classic guitars over the years, and says he has so many favorites that he couldn't possibly list them all. "I worked on a lot of D'Angelico guitars . . . love those! An all-gold 1955 Les Paul with P-90s—how cool is that? A Brazilian rosewood Martin D-45, a '57 Les Paul Junior—enough said! A '58 Mary Kaye Strat—wonderful. The list goes on . . ."

T2 CUSTOM (BLACK LIMBA), 2010.

With a body carved from African black limba, this guitar is Roger's take on a Tele. The neck is made of black limba combined with maple, and the dark South American rosewood fingerboard has abalone inlays and white binding. The "Model T" is equipped with a pair of vintage Amalfitano P-90 pickups—a soapbar at the neck, and a dog-ear at the bridge—which produce a big, round, smooth, rich sound. Roger comments, "This black limba T is an example of the many different visual results this wood can have. Some black limba is almost white with virtually no dark wood, while other limba can be the complete opposite. Some wood can be evenly colored, while other pieces can look pretty wild, with orange and black streaks. All good stuff, and never a dull moment!"

Roger's main objective as a luthier is to make guitars "that people *want* to play because they are graceful and uncomplicated. I've always tried to go for the simple approach—the minimum number of knobs and buttons wherever possible." He is also determined to prove that a traditional approach to the building process can produce guitars that stand up well against anything else in the marketplace. But, he adds, "there are so many good builders now, here in the States and back in England, that I'm often shocked by some of the amazing guitars they all turn out. Things have sure come a long way since the '60s."

Asked about the future, Roger says he hates to try and see what's ahead. "I think it sets you up for a fall! Twenty years ago, I sat down and thought to myself, Wow! I'm still here doing the work I love—how long can this continue? Now here I am, and I'm still asking myself the same question. I think I will just wait and see what happens."

SOLID-BODY TWELVE-STRING CUSTOM, 2010.

Roger has been a twelve-string freak since hearing Erik Darling play an acoustic twelve on the Rooftop Singers' version of "Walk Right In," a number one hit in 1963. (The song was written by Gus Cannon and Hosea Woods and originally recorded by Cannon's Jug Stompers in 1927.) Hearing Roger McGuinn's "jingle-jangle" twelve-string electric Rickenbacker on early Byrds records sealed the deal for the young luthier—he was a twelve-string devotee from then on.

Roger has made many electric twelve-strings over the years and is recognized as one of the masters of the instrument. This Giffin twelve has a solid swamp-ash body with a carved curly-maple top and a curly-maple neck. The fingerboard and head veneer are ebony, and, although the neck is unbound, the body and head are bound in black and white. The pickups are a matched set of Seymour Duncan Antiquity Strats, and all the hardware is gold. Roger adds, "One slight departure from my usual twelve-string specifications is that I have strung this one Rickenbacker-style, with the low string first— usually I do it the other way around. It gives the guitar a certain 'voice' that you don't get with the octave string first. I stained the wood in multiple layers of pale blue and turquoise to give it a washed-out denim look. This guitar plays easier than most six-strings!"

JOHAN GUSTAVSSON

Swedish luthier Johan Gustavsson has been a professional touring and session guitarist for more than twenty years, so he knows his way around an electric guitar.

Johan's older brother worked in a record store when they were young, so, as Johan explains, "he was always bringing home cool records. He totally spoiled me! I almost never had to buy any albums. I listened a lot to the Beatles . . . Later came Roxy Music, David Bowie, Lou Reed, Alice Cooper, Bob Marley, Status Quo, etc. One of my early guitar heroes was Phil Manzanera of Roxy Music, I think mainly because he had this cool-looking red Firebird. We listened a lot to Lou Reed, particularly *Rock n Roll Animal*. Steve Hunter and Dick Wagner played this great instrumental intro to 'Sweet Jane' that I just loved."

Johan's first guitar was an Italian Eko solid-body, which he and his brother spotted in the local Hagstrom store. (Hagstrom is Sweden's leading guitar manufacturer and has been building electric guitars since 1958.) "We thought it was awesome," he recalls. "It looked a bit like a reverse Firebird, covered in that plastic faux pearl that we guitarists lovingly call 'mother of toilet seat.' " The guitar was an immediate disappointment, however, because it proved almost impossible to play. "It had very heavy-gauge flat-wound strings and terribly high action," Johan explains. "The neck was a total baseball bat and two of the four [!] pickups didn't work. It was just terrible!"

So Johan started rebuilding the guitar. He took it to his school, where his teacher was kind enough to let him work on it during

BLUESMASTER CUSTOM '59, 2008. COLLECTION OF CHARLES DAUGHTRY.

Johan has built his reputation on his carved-top Bluesmaster models, which combine elements of classic Fenders and Gibsons—one player described the Bluesmaster as looking like the love child of a Tele and a Les Paul—with extraordinary levels of refinement and craftsmanship. The Custom '59 has a Honduran mahogany body with an AAA-grade carved flame-maple top, a glued-in mahogany neck, and a Brazilian rosewood fret board with crown inlays. Like a Les Paul, the Custom '59 has a 24¾-inch scale length, a custom-made wraparound bridge, and Sperzel machine heads. It comes equipped with either a pair of humbuckers or P-90s, and the top is available finished in either "Vintage Cherry Sunburst" or "Tiger Eye Burst." As is the case with vintage Les Pauls, the color and grain of every carved-top is different.

As a member of the Gear Page's "Burst Mafia" put it, "Johan has incorporated my favorite aspects of a Les Paul Burst, Les Paul Junior, and Telecaster . . . [He] has reinvented the wheel with class and taste . . . We may have an iconic instrument on our hands." Charlie Daughtry, another member of the Burst Mafia and the owner of this guitar, adds, "Words can't describe the joy I've experienced on the guitar since I got this thing. I'm so blown away I can't even begin to describe it . . . It's the tone I've always heard in my head on the best-built instrument I have ever played. It's that good."

JOHAN GUSTAVSSON OF JOHAN GUSTAVSSON GUITARS, LIMHAMN, SWEDEN.

Swedish guitar maker Johan Gustavsson's guitars channel the best elements of classic Gibsons and Fenders, filtering them through his own obsessive attention to every aspect of design and detail. He has built a worldwide reputation for his masterful work entirely by word of mouth: his only advertising has been through his unpretentious Web site and the raves of the many serious guitarists who have discovered and spread the word about his meticulously crafted instruments.

HAND MADE GUITARS

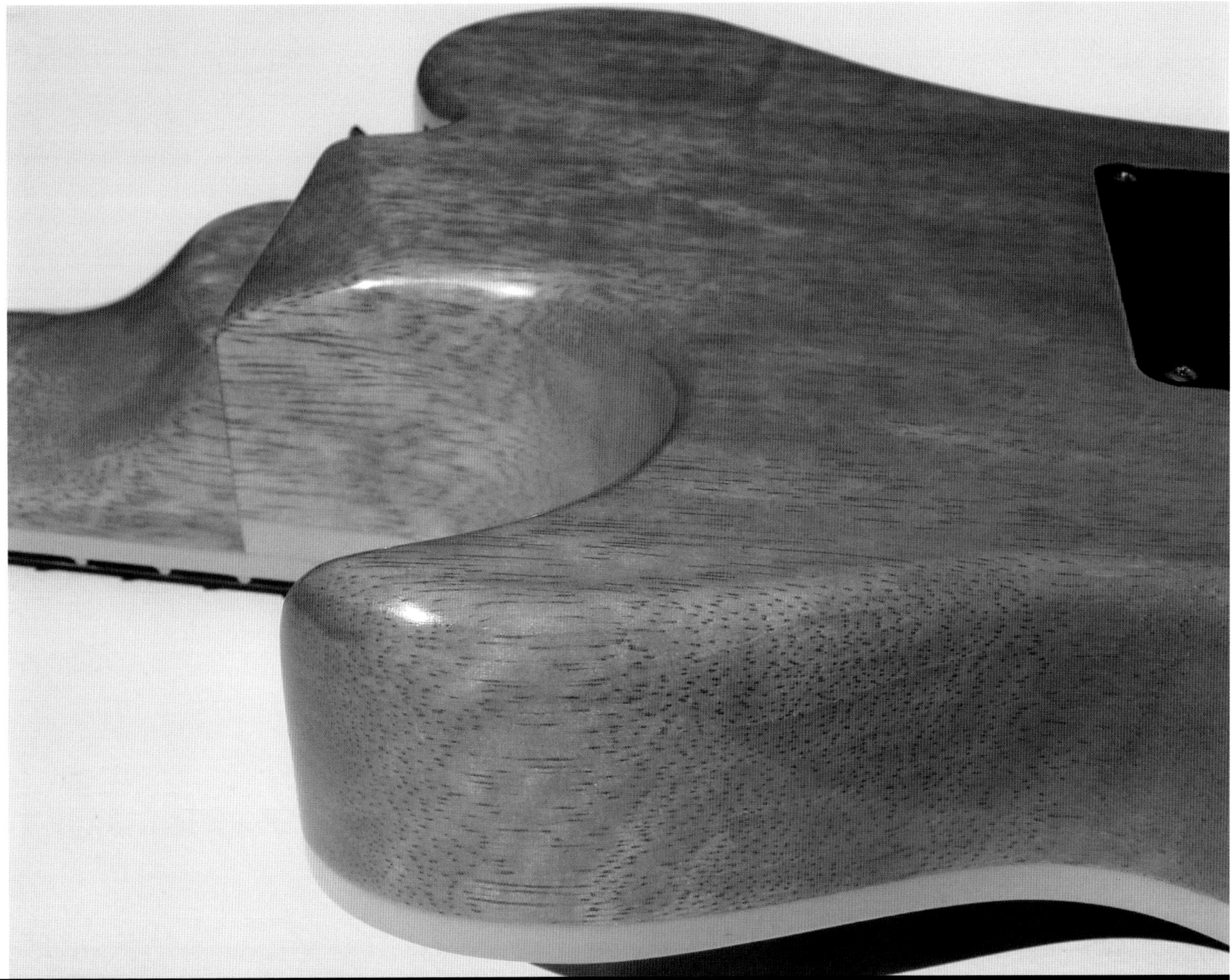

BRUISEMONSTER, 2006. COLLECTION OF MATTE HENDERSON.

The aptly named (albeit with tongue in cheek) Bruisemonster is a seven-string signature model custom-made for session guitarist Matte Henderson. Like other Bluesmasters, the Bruisemonster has a Honduran mahogany body with a carved AAA-grade flame-maple top, but the cutaway was redesigned for easy upper-fret access. The bound Brazilian rosewood fingerboard has crown-shaped pearloid inlays, and the straight-pull headstock and Gotoh "tulip" locking tuners provide stable tuning. The three pickups include Seymour Duncan custom-wound SH-4 JB and SH-1N '59 humbuckers and an Antiquity Strat single-coil. The bridge is a Gotoh six-string tremolo, while the additional low A string is attached to a separate hardtail bridge.

carpentry classes. He found an old Hagstrom neck and a fret board that he tried to attach to the Eko body, but that didn't work out so he started making a new (non–reverse Firebird) body. "The Eko pickups weren't too hot, either, so I found a better-sounding humbucker pickup in a store, better tuners, etc. When the 'rebuild' was ready, the only thing that remained from the Eko was the output jack—although later on I replaced that, too."

Another player who inspired Johan was his first real guitar teacher, Robert Larsson. "He knew everything you could ever wish to learn, and he had this old beaten-up 1960 Les Paul Standard. Even though I was a lousy guitar player back then, I immediately realized that this guitar was so much better than anything I had tried before. It was just magnificent! After that I found a 1964 Telecaster that I picked up for a thousand kronor [about one hundred U.S. dollars]. It was refinished, and the neck pickup had been changed to a P-90, but it was pretty cool."

Those two guitars gave Johan his first insight into the magic of classic-era American guitars, which have been his main inspiration as a builder ever since. As he explains, "I think the thing that set off the whole vintage guitar market was the fact that the quality of the seventies and eighties Fender and Gibson instruments was nothing like the fifties and sixties guitars, which were generally much better built and were often made of lightweight, high-quality wood. This made them more resonant and inspiring to play."

As a player, Johan says he was constantly trying to improve his guitars—adjusting, taking them apart, refretting, and changing pickups. Eventually the rumor started to spread that he could fix guitars, and he got a part-time job repairing guitars at the first vintage guitar store in Malmö, Sweden. "I think this was in 1978," he recalls. "We imported a lot of cool guitars from Guitar Trader in the U.S.—fifties Gibson Les Paul Goldtops, Juniors, Melody Makers, pre-CBS Fender Strats, Jazzmasters, Telecasters, etc. The fact that I did a lot of work on vintage guitars and had access to a lot of great instruments very much influenced my work as a guitar maker. I've always gravitated toward the more 'crafted' Gibson style of making guitars, with carved flame-maple tops and glued-in necks, as opposed to Fender's Model T 'assembly line' style."

Johan built his first complete guitar while he was apprenticing in a furniture workshop. "There was lots of wood and machinery right in front of me," he says, and "that first fully handmade instrument, which was heavily influenced by vintage Les Pauls, won first prize in a contest arranged by the magazine *HiFi & Musik*." After completing a three-year apprenticeship and mastering all the elements of fine woodworking, he founded JG Guitars.

A chance encounter with U.S. session guitarist Matte Henderson proved to be Johan's big break. "Matte is the man who brought JG Guitars to the U.S.," Johan explains. "I showed him a guitar on an Internet forum, and he immediately wanted to buy it. He also offered to show it to some important people in the business. Next thing I knew, I got a large order of guitars from Wildwood Guitars in Colorado! Matte has been very supportive of my work from the start of our interaction. He has also been a great source of ideas and a great friend.

"Matte is a very talented and demanding player, and he's got a unique playing style that has made him seek an instrument that best serves his particular musical needs and proclivities. I made him a seven-string guitar to his specs that we call the Bruisemonster. One very special feature is the bridge setup. The lowest string, tuned to A, is fixed, and the other six go through the vibrato unit. This keeps the tension down on the bridge, which enables him to use the bar for very expressive and wide-ranging bends and vibrato. It also anchors the low A securely in the body, hardtail-style, which seems to give more body to the string.

Johan only has one other luthier, Fredrik Rosén, working with him at JG Guitars. Fredrik, whom Johan describes as "a lovely guy and a wonderful guitarist," trained at London Guildhall University and has vast experience working on guitars. The two are currently working on two new JGG models, the Junior and the Special, which will be manufactured under license in the U.S. by the Premier Builders Guild, a small collective of master luthiers and amp builders that also includes Gene Baker, Roger Giffin, Saul Koll, and Jason Z. Schroeder. "Gene is supervising the production of all PBG-licensed instruments," Johan explains. "I have a lot of faith in him and his crew and I have no doubt that they will make a great guitar. I think it's a wonderful thing to see other people make my guitars," he adds with a smile. "It's a bit unreal."

FUTUREMASTER, 2010.

The Futuremaster is another one of Johan's collaborations with Matte Henderson. Matte has admired the sound and feel of Gibson's korina-bodied guitars for many years, but found that the angular designs of the Explorer and Flying V, while definitely cool-looking, made them poorly balanced and impractical as working instruments. So he asked Johan if he could take the best aspects of the two designs and create a less cumbersome instrument to gig with. The Futuremaster, which aims to redistribute the mass of the original korina designs, is the result.

The Futuremaster has the neck feel of a Flying V; the neck tenon extends halfway between the neck and bridge pickups to create as much coupling as possible. Matte and Johan searched high and low for the best materials with which to build the guitars, including old-growth Brazilian rosewood and a supply of korina they located in Germany, which was far superior to anything they could find in the United States.

FRANK HARTUNG OF FRANK HARTUNG GUITARS, LANGEWIESEN, GERMANY.

Frank Hartung is a perfectionist—a master carpenter and luthier whose obsessive, hands-on approach gives him the freedom to work with flexibility and incorporate special requests from his clients. Frank hand-carves the tops of his guitars with sensual, flowing lines to create his proprietary three-dimensional forms, and has also developed unique two-piece three-dimensional headstocks that complement the bodies and add visual appeal to his creations. "And," he says, "the possibilities for a personal touch are endless."

FRANK HARTUNG

Frank Hartung is a professional carpenter and self-confessed guitar addict—"Once you are infected, there is no cure for that," he says without a hint of concern or remorse in his voice—who has been building guitars full-time since 2001, when he first visited Ulrich Teuffel's shop. Teuffel, he observes, "is like no other guitar maker. He knows how to create modern interpretations of these instruments. Ulrich has had a great impact on my work, and he has lent me his support and advice."

Frank explains his start as a luthier this way: "I am a skilled carpenter; that is, a craftsman who acquired the skill from the bottom

DIAVOLO CC, 2008.

Frank calls his Diavolo CC "a guitar for real players," in part because it has four aces inlaid on its fingerboard and mother-of-pearl dice on the electronics cover on the back.

CC stands for Color Concept, and this example is finished in a gorgeous "Glacier Blue," one of nine colors Frank offers. The guitar has a lightweight basswood body with a maple top, a bolt-on maple neck with a Macassar ebony fingerboard, and a pair of high-output Häussel humbuckers. The neck is stained, and the headstock overlay is cut from the same wood as the fingerboard.

up. This provided me with the technical understanding of the material. Then I picked up the guitar and got interested more and more in woods, construction, and the ingredients and details of a guitar. So it was bound to happen that I made my very first guitar, the Enigma Blue, and it wasn't half bad—as other luthiers, including Ulrich [Teuffel] and Nik Huber, whose guitars are built on a very high level of craftsmanship, confirmed." With the encouragement of successful luthiers whom he respected to buoy him, Frank felt confident enough to follow his passion and start his own business. As he puts it, "Since then, I make guitars."

Frank says that part of his passion for building guitars comes from the fact that the instruments come into being through him—from the raw slab of wood to the first ringing note. "For me," he continues, "This makes it a very personal affair. It's not just a finished product, but rather like a baby that becomes dear to my heart."

Frank grew up listening to classic '70s rock and blues from the likes of Billy Idol and Gary Moore, and later became obsessed with a band from the Netherlands called the Gathering. "Their guitarist, René Rutten, was the one who actually brought me toward the guitar and eventually also to guitar making," Frank recalls. "His sound fascinated me and made me want to pick up the instrument. Actually, I only play my own instruments now, but there are also repair jobs—e.g., on old Strats, Les Pauls, etc.—that enable me to test-drive these guitars and learn about the work of other guitar makers."

The first "reasonable guitar" that Frank owned was a vintage Les Paul that he later sold to raise funds to buy a supply of wood and lutherie tools. Perhaps because of his familiarity with it, and because he really likes its shape and overall appearance, the Les Paul became a model for his own work. "But," he adds quickly, "simply cloning it was out of the question. Instead, my interpretation needed to incorporate distinct features of my own design and thus become unique."

Primary among the unique features of Frank's guitars are his distinctive three-dimensional headstocks and "flow-carved" bodies. The headstocks, which are topped with two cleverly shaped curved pieces of wood that interact visually, are kept compact to enhance overtones and leave enough room for unhindered access to the tuning machines. The design also leads the strings over the nut in an almost straight line. Frank developed his proprietary flow carving in 2002 as he searched for ways to make his guitars stand out. The upper bout of his tops is carved with decidedly feminine contours, including a waist that runs fluently onto the surface of the nearly circular lower bout and gives a layered look to the overall appearance. As Frank puts it, "It seems as if the two top planks melt into each other and shape a perfect object."

Frank says his main objective as a luthier is simple: to have happy customers who are pleased with his guitars. Getting there is not so simple, though. "A custom guitar is often very special," he explains, "and the completed instrument should fit the player perfectly in terms of vibe, sound, and looks. These are important criteria to meet, and a satisfied customer is the ultimate reward for all my hard work." He hopes to be able to expand his company and increase production to reach an output of between eighty and one hundred instruments per year. "It may sound like this is not an awful lot," he says, "but due to the high amount of handwork involved, it really is a lot. My company will not become a large factory with many employees. Quality and close customer contact are important to me, and I would like to keep it this way."

Asked what excites him other than guitars and music, Frank responds that his family has top priority. "I have two little kids. My son is six and my daughter is two, so they always keep me on the run, but I do enjoy the time I spend with them. Time allowing, I like to play snooker, ride my bicycle, do sports, and I am also interested in architecture and like to travel."

Summing up, Frank says, "I love what I do and I believe that you can tell from my instruments. These are guitars for individualists and lovers of exquisite guitars, but most certainly are also musicians' tools for everyday use on the stages of this world. I am convinced that my guitars express a uniqueness and that high-level craftsmanship and attention to the detail make the difference."

LP SPECIAL CUSTOM, 2009.

LP is, of course, short for Les Paul, the instrument on which this custom-designed guitar is based. Like its forebear, it has a 24¾-inch scale length and a mahogany body topped with maple, which in this case is curly. Custom features include a Brazilian rosewood neck, a Brazilian rosewood fingerboard bound in maple with crown-shaped mother-of-pearl inlays, a curly-maple pick guard, and elegant hand-painted scrolls on the body sides and pick guard.

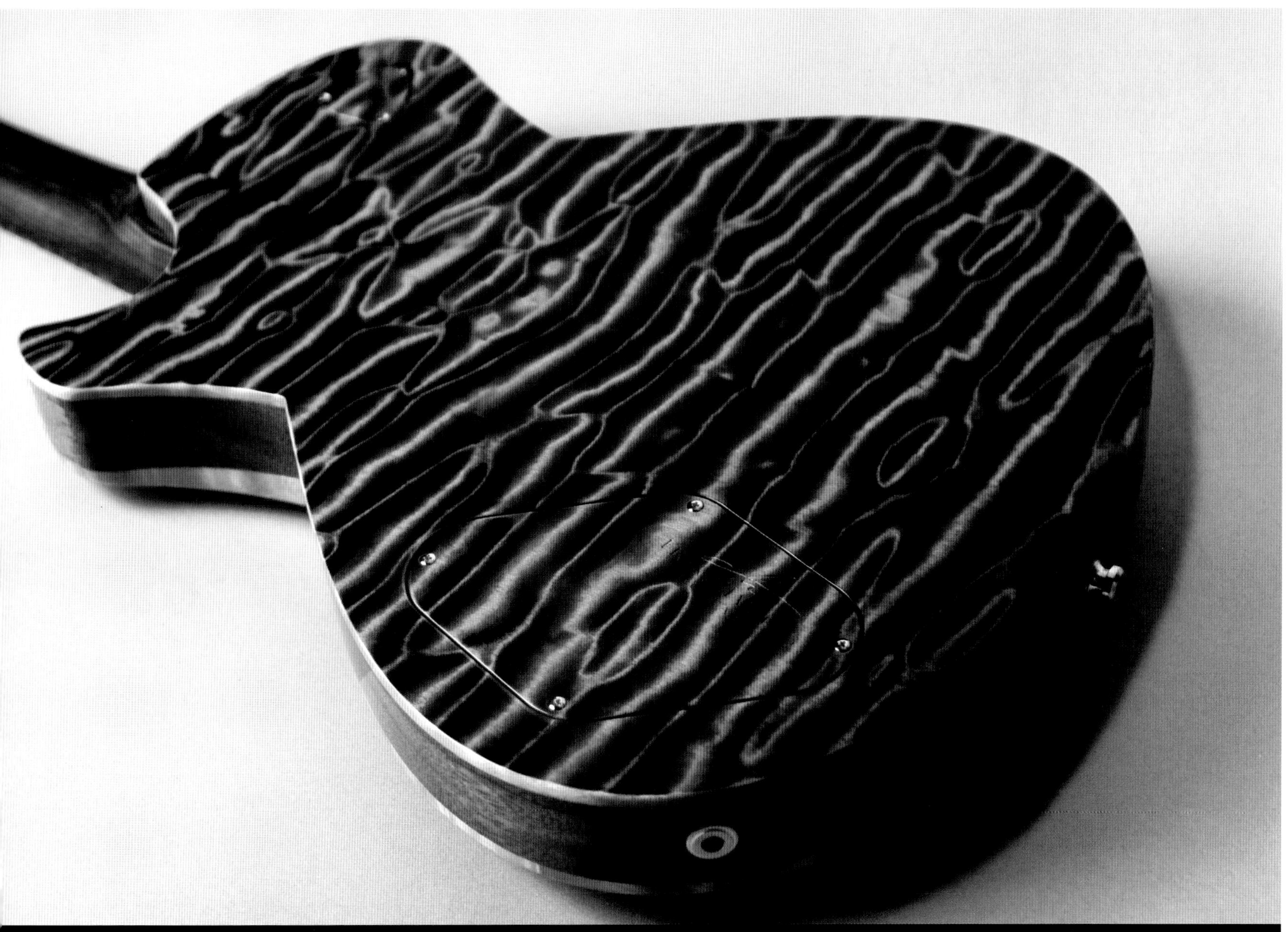

EMBRACE HOLLOWWOOD DELUXE, 2009.

Frank Hartung is a stickler for high-quality materials: this guitar's chambered Honduran mahogany body is backed and topped with quilted maple taken from a single spectacular piece of exhibition-grade wood. The neck was made from a single piece of scarce Brazilian rosewood, to which Hartung added a scalloped snakewood fret board. The guitar's intricate wiring offers the player a choice of twelve different sounds, and makes it suitable for an equally wide range of musical styles, including country, blues, and rock.

NIK HUBER
guitars

NIK HUBER

Nikolaus Huber IV carries on a family tradition that dates back to his great-grandfather, Nikolaus Huber I, who was born in 1896. "My family has a woodworking tradition going back four generations," he explains, "but not necessarily in guitar building. As a child I spent a lot of time in Dad's shop building ships, planes, and other wooden objects. Dad—or, way back, Grandpa, when I visited him during holidays—showed me how to use his tools and how to determine which wood could work for a given project. That was certainly the beginning of my passion for working with wood."

Nik fell in love with the Beatles and started playing piano at about age ten. But his affection for the Beatles was followed (but not substituted, Nik says) by a passion for AC/DC—a band whose lineup didn't include piano. That was when Nik decided he wanted to learn to play guitar. His father bought him one, but wasn't happy with it when they got it home. "In his opinion, it wasn't worth the money he'd laid down," Nik recalls. So Nik's dad built a better one himself, thereby setting an example and perhaps a future course for his son.

As he grew older, Nik decided he wanted to be an architect and, after finishing secondary school, he learned cabinetmaking as a base for that pursuit. He also found out about a guitar-making school in Formentera, Spain (where he later worked as a teacher), and, after attending that school for a few weeks, he got "a serious case of the guitar-making virus. I spent every minute working on guitars, building and repairing, and after a while I quit my part-time job as a cabinetmaker, kissed college good-bye, and opened a small guitar store with a small repair and building shop attached."

Nik Huber Guitars was founded in 1996. But before the guitar company was able to feed his family, Nik played in bands to pay the bills. "Today," he says, "I still play in two bands using pretty much every model I offer." As a player, he says he is not really into speed or shredding, and cites Jimi Hendrix, Stevie Ray Vaughan, Steve Lukather, and John Mayer among the guitarists he admires most. He says he loved grunge rock in the '90s (listing Pearl Jam, Soundgarden, Stone Temple Pilots, and Nirvana as favorites) and also started to get into Hendrix and Stevie Ray then. "Rock from all directions was and still is what I listen to most," he explains. "But this does not mean that I do not enjoy music from many other genres. The Beatles are always much appreciated. If you ask me for a favorite band at this time: Foo Fighters."

Nik's biggest influence as a designer and builder has been Paul Reed Smith, without whom, he says, there would be no Nik Huber Guitars. "He is an extremely important person in my life," Nik explains—"a friend, mentor, and teacher." Nik also expresses his admiration for the work of Joe Knaggs—the former director of R & D and the Private Stock department for PRS, who recently launched his own business—and says he is a big fan of '50s Les Paul Juniors. He owns a 1956 Junior, which is one of his favorite guitars. "Since I have been in the business," he adds, "I have met many great builders and become good friends with some of them, so this question of favorites is not easy to answer. I really like the guitars of Claudio Pagelli, Juha Ruokangas, and Jens Ritter, who are also close friends. And Paul's [Paul Reed Smith's] Private Stocks are amazing."

Huber Guitars has grown slowly but steadily since the company's first appearance at the Frankfurt Musikmesse in 1997, and now has a worldwide reputation as a serious manufacturer of high-quality electric guitars. In 1999, the expanding company moved to a commercial park in its hometown of Rodgau, Germany, about twelve miles south of Frankfurt, where a team of five highly skilled specialists currently handcrafts about 120 instruments per year. "Happily," Nik says, "we don't have problems getting enough work to keep me and my team busy. We have many orders and a lead time of at least six months. My biggest challenge is to become more efficient. I want to keep the quality as high as we can and not let customers wait too long. Ten years ago, I never thought that we would build fifteen instruments a month. Now, I can imagine us going up to about two hundred and fifty or three hundred per year

NIK HUBER OF NIK HUBER GUITARS, RODGAU, GERMANY.

Nik Huber sees his work clearly and simply. "Basically," he explains, "what we do is to turn beautiful pieces of wood into excellent guitars." Since founding Nik Huber Guitars in 1996, Nik and his small team of like-minded colleagues have established a worldwide reputation for the precision, quality, and playability of their carved-top and solid-body electric guitars. All Huber guitars combine Nik's elegantly understated design aesthetic with top-quality materials and meticulously crafted details.

if the market allows. But it is important for me to stay in the shop myself and 'make dust'—so we will probably not take steps to make Nik Huber Guitars produce thousands of guitars a year. Besides this, I am trying to spend more time with my wife and kids. I really worked a lot and probably too much to get my company going. Now that I am in a position to have a long order list and a good and reliable team, a 'normal' working day and having a weekend are certainly among the next goals.

"Generally speaking," he adds, "building fine instruments can be a very bumpy ride, a never-ending story of mishaps, dead-end streets, and tiny little pieces of metal that won't fit into their tiny little holes. Building guitars with your own hands, as good as possible and beyond, is nothing a high-school career counselor suggests, at least not a responsibly minded one. Guitar making is more a calling than a profession. It can be addictive. But it is not about 'more, more.' Our constant craving is 'better, better, better.' I try to do what I love to do—even for a living. I was lucky to have a very supportive dad and family, and for the chance to eat, live, and breathe the craft of fine woodworking."

REDWOOD, 2009.

The Huber Redwood, named for its gorgeous carved curly redwood top, is a semihollow-body instrument with a 25½-inch scale length. With its thin, heavily chambered mahogany body and soft-wood top, it is also an extremely lightweight instrument, tipping the scale at less than seven pounds. Its pair of Häussel humbuckers allows it to produce a wide range of tones, from bone-crushing Les Paul muscle to Tele twang, mellow jazz, and even a stinging, bluesy sound reminiscent of a vintage Strat in full cry.

ORCA 10TH ANNIVERSARY, 2008.

The Orca is distinguished by its bold fingerboard inlay of black-and-white killer whales. Nik explains the imagery by saying that being at the ocean with his wife and two young sons is a very important part of his life. "I love diving, and would like to learn surfing one day, though I think I am not [destined] to be very talented. Whales and dolphins are magical to me, and I am currently working on an idea to involve their protection in a guitar project."

BELOW KRAUTSTER, 2010.

The solid-body Krautster, which harks back to the classic simplicity of the Les Paul Junior, is Huber's latest model. The guitar has a mahogany body, a 25-inch scale length, and a glued-in curly-maple neck. This example is finished in "Onyx Black," and is equipped with a single custom Häussel bridge humbucker with an aged-nickel cover.

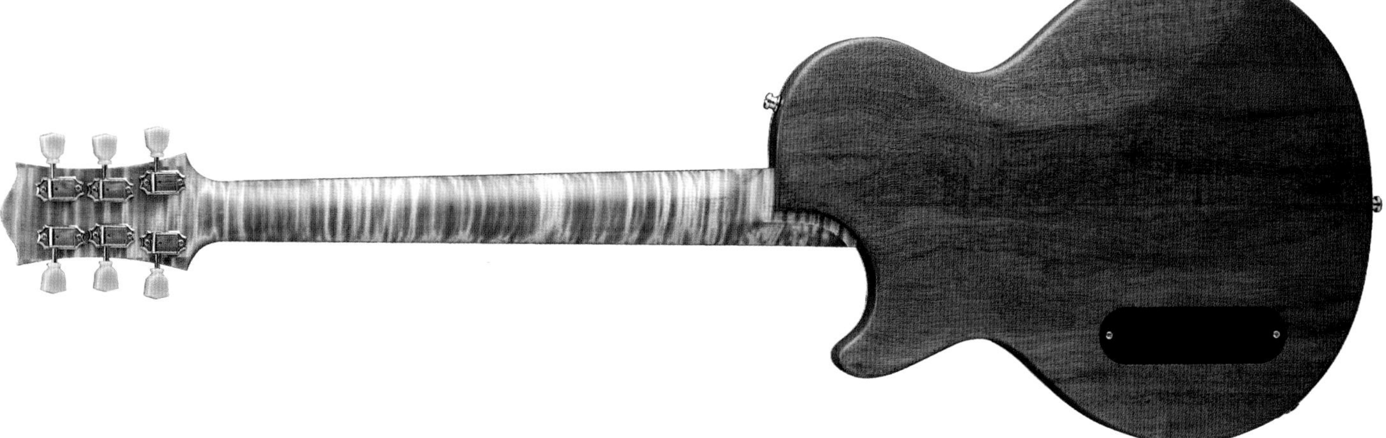

WILLIAM JEFFREY JONES

Jeffrey Jones can't really remember a time when he wasn't creating, drawing, designing, painting, building, sculpting, or making music. He has been an artist since he was a kid, and he says, "It amazes even me that as a seven-year-old, I was methodically doing exactly what I do now. I filled my Big Chief tablets with hundreds of designs of cars, airplanes, helicopters, houses... you name it." He played trumpet at the age of eleven and picked up the guitar when he was fourteen or fifteen. He was listening to and playing jazz in high school, everything from traditional to bebop to fusion, and he lists Andy Summers, Pat Metheny, Adrian Belew, Al Di Meola, and Robert Fripp of King Crimson among the guitarists who have influenced him the most over the years. "I also like some of the older jazz players like Tal Farlow, Joe Pass, Jim Hall, and, of course, Wes Montgomery," he adds. He also plays both fretted and fretless bass and has a special affinity for the fretless six-string guitar, which he has built a few of and still enjoys playing the most. "I find that when I play an instrument that's a bit different," he explains, "it shakes me out of my typical licks, patterns, melodies, and chord choices, pushing me in a new and exciting direction. I want to be a vehicle through which niche instruments, like a fretless tenor guitar or a five-string short-scale piccolo bass, can be created, inspiring new musical directions, compositions, and performances."

Jeffrey worked as a full-time commercial sculptor for more than twenty years, making a living sculpting prototypes for the toy industry as well as the giftware, display, and architectural ornamentation industries. For some years, he worked as an in-house sculptor for Todd McFarlane's toy company, and he sculpted toy prototypes for quite a number of films, comics, and video games, including *Buffy the Vampire Slayer*, *Battlestar Galactica*, the *Matrix* trilogy, the *Child's Play*/Chucky movies, *Pirates of the Caribbean*, *The Chronicles of Narnia*, and *Shrek*.

Recalling his transition to guitar making, he says, "As the toy industry began to allow less and less creativity on the part of the hired talent, my creative monsters had to be fed, so I was drawing, designing, and building guitars in my spare time. At some point,

JEFFREY JONES OF WILLIAM JEFFREY JONES GUITARS, NEOSHO, MISSOURI.

Jeffrey Jones is a professional carver and sculptor who created prototypes for toy manufacturers before he began carving guitars full-time in 2008. He hand-carves most of his instruments from local Missouri woods, such as walnut, maple, and sassafras, and finishes them only with Tru-Oil (originally made for gun stocks) to emphasize both the look and sound of the wood. Some of his guitars are smooth-bodied; others are deeply carved with figures and intricate designs. And, although Jeffrey emphasizes sculpture in his work, his guitars are also highly functional, precisely built musical instruments. Jeffrey used green masking tape to cover the spot where the carved fret-board end of this Dragonwing guitar was later glued on to the top. The tape kept that area clean and grease-free while he carved the body.

ARGOS, 2010.

"When I was first introduced to this particular piece of lumber," Jeffrey Jones explains, discussing the dramatic black walnut from which he carved the top of this guitar, "it spoke volumes to me. It was a much longer board then, and the sapwood swirled in a variety of patterns across much of it. I spent many hours just studying that board and how best to utilize it for the sake of conservation, stability, and visual impact, arranging templates of my designs on it in every imaginable way. The top for this guitar is the element I saved for last, the one I gave the most thought to."

The body is semihollow, constructed of a book-matched walnut back and a one-piece walnut top with a layer of black veneer between them. Both the top and the back were partially hollowed before being laminated together, leaving a block running down the center of the instrument. The inside cavities follow the outside contours very closely, with the top and back being just a bit over ¼-inch thick. The result is that the Argos is a very light and responsive guitar that weighs only seven pounds, three ounces.

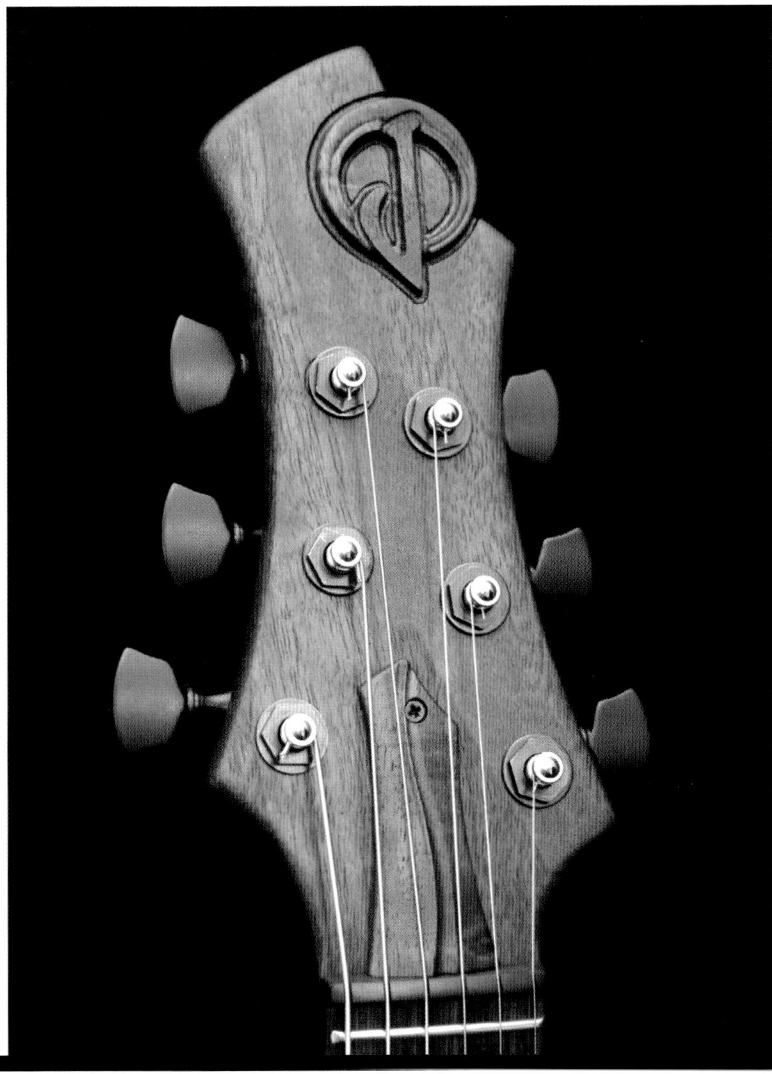

SYRENA, 2009.

Sirène is the French word for mermaid, and is closely related to the English word "siren." Sirène and "siren" both refer to the mythological sea creature—part woman, part beast—who lures mariners into danger with her mesmerizing songs. Because of the legend's musical overtones, it seemed to Jeffrey Jones that a mermaid would be a perfect motif for a guitar. Such a motif would allow him to combine certain elements of fantasy with the female form, explaining that he "wanted to develop a mermaid character that I could take a few creative liberties with—especially with the tail. I wanted an image I could coax into an involved and complex rhythmic form, in a fashion not dissimilar to the way I would approach her hair. I wanted to be able to feel the tail whipping through the water."

Jeffrey constructed the guitar's body from two layers of walnut that he salvaged from the Missouri River, then aged and air-dried. The front of the guitar is a single piece of walnut with "just the right amount of figure and a nice grain configuration that really enhances the form of the mermaid's tail, and vice versa." The back is book-matched, "also with a nice grain configuration that seems to follow the form of my body design."

Jeffrey adds, "I like to work with woods that exhibit or showcase the variation that nature provides. I take a lot of time to arrange the stock to suit both the shape of my instruments as well as whatever forms of embellishment I may choose to incorporate."

I just began to spend more time building instruments than sculpting prototypes and, financially speaking, the guitars began to take over as the primary provider of income, in addition to being the focus of my creative passion. I can't recall the day when I suddenly quit one type of job and went to a different kind of job the following week. It just fuzzily evolved that way."

Jeffrey freely admits that he is "all about the process and always will be," and that he always has several projects going on at once, in different stages. He currently completes about a dozen guitars a year, many of which are heavily carved. He says sculpture is "what I do, how I think," and that he has notebooks "jam-packed with concepts and drawings, so I'll never run out of projects that I'd like to create. I keep adding to those, virtually every day, so I hope that my work evolves and keeps evolving. I do aspire to build instruments no one has ever seen before. I've only scratched the surface of what I have planned for the future."

Of complex compositions like his Nocturne for iO guitar, Jeffrey says, "When I begin a piece like this, I'm immediately conscious that I'm in it for the long haul. Even the number of drawings I do—and changes I make to those drawings to develop one that is 'just so'—can take many hours, or even days. Once I arrive at a design that is acceptable to me, I begin work in a medium in which I've spent thousands and thousands of hours—clay. In clay, I can effectively develop a two-dimensional drawing into a three-dimensional form. The drawing contains minimal information, so the form comes to life nurtured by experience, observation, and imagination. When I have the form worked up sufficiently to use as a reference for my carving, then and only then can I comfortably start working in such a subtractive medium as wood. I could wing it or fly by the seat of my pants by just diving into the chunk of wood, but a few wrong turns can reduce a great piece of walnut into kindling. I'd much rather work from a detailed map that I've created from the ground up. The development of the form in clay gives me a familiarity with the subject that I wouldn't otherwise have . . . like a rehearsal of sorts."

Asked what excites him other than guitars, sculpture, and music, Jeffrey says, "I do like movies, literature, and animation, because I like to see what other artists, artisans, and writers are doing. When I watch a movie, though, I'm looking at the sets, at the props, at the costumes, and makeup—it drives some people crazy that I can't just watch a movie without deconstructing it. Hazard of the trade, I suppose. I also love the outdoors and nature. Here in the Ozarks, I live and work in it, and I have found a way to incorporate my love of nature into my work."

NOCTURNE FOR IO, 2009.

Jeffrey Jones hand-carved the top of this guitar with a scroll design he created specifically for this instrument. He says that each scroll and curve was painstakingly placed for a pleasing aesthetic relationship with the body shape, which is also an original design. The top, neck, knob, pickup cover, and tailpiece are bigleaf maple, and the back is aged and air-dried walnut that Jeffrey rescued from the Missouri River. Although the back is joined, both pieces were cut from the same board. The control cover, which is from a completely different board, was carefully matched to the grain of the back.

The "Nocturne" part of the guitar's name came about because ninety-nine percent of the carving was done late at night. The other part of the name refers to Io, the innermost moon of Jupiter and the mythological figure who was one of Zeus's lovers and a priestess of his wife, Hera. The jealous Hera turned Io into a beautiful heifer and sentenced her to roam the earth indefinitely. Io refers to herself as the horned virgin in Aeschylus's ancient Greek tragedy Prometheus Bound.

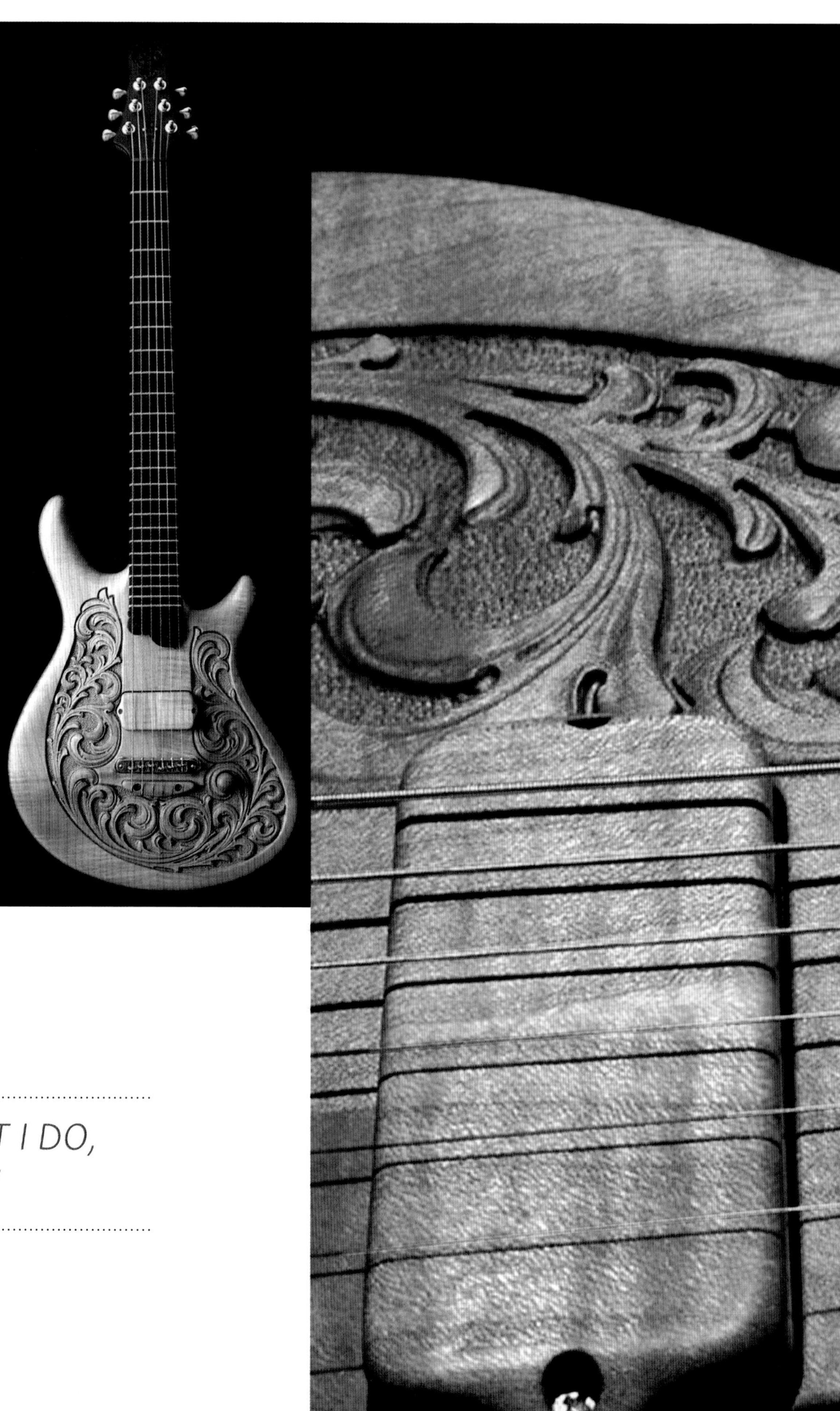

"SCULPTURE IS WHAT I DO, HOW I THINK."

STEVE KLEIN

Steve Klein is a legend among luthiers. He was one of the first independent builders to make a name for himself in the 1970s and '80s, and his innovative craftsmanship, creativity, and pioneering spirit have influenced nearly everyone who has followed him in the profession. Steve's acoustic, electric, and bass guitars have been played by artists as diverse as Roy Buchanan, Stanley Clarke, Bill Frisell, Michael Hedges, Henry Kaiser, Leo Kottke, Steve Miller, Joni Mitchell, Lou Reed, Carlos Santana, Martin Simpson, Stephen Stills, Sting, Andy Summers, David Torn, Joe Walsh, and Neil Young, and his work has been extolled by such master luthiers as Bob Benedetto, Harry Fleishman, Richard Hoover (the founder of the Santa Cruz Guitar Company), John Monteleone, Paul Reed Smith, and Ned Steinberger.

Steve began building guitars while he was still in high school, basically for his own use, and was lucky enough to live in the midst of the music explosion going on in San Francisco in the 1960s and '70s, when it was not unusual for Jefferson Airplane, the Dead, and the Butterfield Blues Band to appear together on a single bill. Through family connections, he also was lucky enough to meet Dr. Michael Kasha, a physical chemist who was working with classical guitar builder Richard Schneider on cutting-edge experiments with bracing and other design modifications that would make a guitar's sound-producing capabilities far greater and more efficient. While Kasha and Schneider were focused on nylon-string guitars, Steve applied many of Kasha's principles to the acoustic steel-string instruments he was designing, and ended up revolutionizing the way flattops could look, sound, and be built. Steve's innovations included guitars with decidedly nontraditional interior bracing patterns; guitars that include an interior "flying brace," which adds support to the top without actually touching it; guitars with asymmetrical bridges that are much wider on the bass side than the treble; guitars with maple or walnut backs and sides; guitars with the sound hole moved to one side of the upper bout instead of centered below the bridge; and guitars with massive lower bouts (Klein's L-45.7 measures 45.7 centimeters—17.99 inches—across its lower bout).

Then Steve's friend Carl Margolis, with whom he had learned to play the guitar as a kid, encouraged him to design an electric guitar that would be more comfortable to hold, whether a person is sitting or standing—in other words, an ergonomic guitar. Steve recalls that he reluctantly began experimenting, and between 1976 and 1981 ended up with a series of "large, strange, and very ugly electric guitars." But dozens of drawings and five completed instruments later, he realized that the "fundamental relationship between the center line of the neck and the waist, where the instrument rested on the leg, had to change." Those changes resulted in a guitar that studio wizard David Lindley nicknamed Lumpy, which made up in playability what it lacked in looks.

After designing a far more aesthetically pleasing electric with input from the versatile virtuoso Ronnie Montrose, Steve got to know the industrial designer and headless guitar pioneer Ned Steinberger and "had the realization that a headless neck would make Lumpy balance properly—and that Lumpy, with the aesthetic lines of the Montrose-Klein guitar, could work." Thus was born the Klein headless electric, which was as revolutionary as his acoustics had been. Steve also experimented with electric harp guitars, which he built for players like Steve Miller and Michael Hedges. Acoustic harp guitars, with a second neck supporting unfretted bass strings that extend the instrument's low end, were popular in the first two decades of the twentieth century, and adventurous players like Lindley were playing them again in the '70s. Steve brought the concept to the electric: he built a few guitars with five added bass strings and a few with added treble strings, extending the instrument's sonic capabilities in its upper range.

Now, after a number of years off the scene, Steve Klein is back, once again working with Carl Margolis on ergonomic electric guitars that are designed to be played while the musician is seated. Steve and Carl think these models are even more playable than his earlier creations. Because the new guitars are balanced at playing angle, the

STEVE KLEIN OF TIMBERDANCE ERGONOMIC GUITARS, ORINDA, CALIFORNIA.

Steve Klein has been one of the most innovative and influential luthiers in the world since the late 1970s, when his uniquely shaped and braced acoustic guitars first began turning heads. He pioneered ergonomic electric guitar design in the 1980s, built some of the first headless electrics, and crafted multistring electric harp guitars for the likes of Steve Miller and Michael Hedges. Now he is back with a batch of new electric and acoustic-electric guitars that are designed for perfect balance while the player is seated or standing, thereby freeing his or her hands.

musician does not have to hold the neck in place or wear a strap that suspends the weight from his neck. Instead, his hands are left free to simply play the guitar. In the earlier Klein electric model, Steve solved the basic balance problem—a guitar's neck is so heavy that it usually dips toward the floor—by removing the head. But he found that many players resisted headless guitars, and that removing the head severely limited the hardware that could be used, and thus affected sound options as well.

Steve's new Timberdance ergonomic guitars are designed to redistribute the instrument's weight so that the center of gravity lies over the player's leg, thereby eliminating the need for a headless tuning system. The curvature and hook of the underside of the Timberdance guitars resemble the original shape of the Klein electric, but Steve has redesigned the instruments for stability. Now, his guitars have greater mass at the head, a readily controllable neck-playing angle, and curvature behind the hook that allows the player to move the instrument around without changing the neck angle. The back of the upper bout is enlarged and shaped so that a right-handed player can use his left arm to control the guitar's angle relative to his body, since that arm is not needed to help grip the guitar and keep its neck up. And, although they are designed for seated playing, the new guitars retain their in-balance feeling when the musician is standing up.

With a full range of possibilities for the bridge hardware available, Carl has been focusing his attention on optimizing the sound. Since his background includes years as a gigging musician, his strategy has naturally been to use combinations of bridge and pickups that are well

32-STRING ELECTRIC HARP GUITAR, 2006. COLLECTION OF JEFF DOCTOROW.

The blueprint for this one-off guitar, which was originally intended for Steve Miller but left unfinished, is shown on page 54 of Art That Sings: The Life and Times of Luthier Steve Klein *by Paul Schmidt, along with a second harp guitar that Miller commissioned. Collector and master guitarist Jeff Doctorow saw the body years ago in Steve's shop, and says, "I told him if he ever built it I wanted it. So when he 'came out of retirement' a few years ago, that's the first thing he did." Unlike traditional acoustic harp guitars, which typically added six sub-bass strings, the harp strings on this instrument are all short treble strings that extend the guitar's range in the opposite direction.*

Acoustic harp guitars were a popular phenomenon in the first two decades of the twentieth century. In America, the concept was developed by a Norwegian-born luthier named Chris Knutsen, who experimented with a wide variety of forms. Knutsen's idea of supporting added sub-bass strings with a hollow arm, set parallel to the neck, was refined by the Larson brothers in Chicago, who marketed their harp guitars under the Dyer, Stahl, and Maurer brands. Gibson offered two harp guitar models, and C. F. Martin and several other companies and independent luthiers also tried their hand at the concept before the fad waned in the early '20s.

SWAMP ANGEL, 2010.

The solid-body Swamp Angel is named for its angelfish-shaped, swamp-ash body. Although the guitar was designed to balance perfectly in a player's lap for seated playing, its elongated tail also makes it easy to maneuver the guitar smoothly when the player is standing on stage.

balanced, with highly flexible passive controls that offer a variety of useful sounds and facilitate switching roles while playing—from solo to accompaniment and back again. The control-knob arrangement is Strat-like, with the knurled front volume control positioned so that the player doesn't have to move his hand away from the strings in order to access it for volume swells.

The two solid-body models, the Swamp Angel and Timberstrat, have swamp-ash bodies with a lightly tinted clear lacquer finish to show off the wood's dramatic grain, and the half-hollow, half-solid acoustic-electric Eklectric model has given Steve room to play with wood combinations—such as a spruce face with a walnut, maple, or rosewood back—and to experiment with the woods' effects on sound. The necks, like most other Klein instruments, are bolted on, and have a thick fingerboard. Steve's earlier acoustic guitars changed the perception that a glued-in neck was essential for superior sound; rather, bolted-on necks simply require high-quality craftsmanship in order to achieve good sound, and also offer ease of adjustment and maintenance as well as portability. The head design is new and features ergonomically slanted tuners with knurled buttons, both of which, like the control knobs, were designed in collaboration with Hipshot Products and produced by them. The detailing on all three guitars is simple yet elegant, a hallmark of a Klein instrument.

TIMBERSTRAT, 2010.

The Timberstrat, which has a Strat-like body and upper-bout horn, is equally as ergonomic as its sister, the Swamp Angel, and can be played balanced in the player's lap without a supporting strap. Like the Swamp Angel, it also has a solid swamp-ash body and a clear finish.

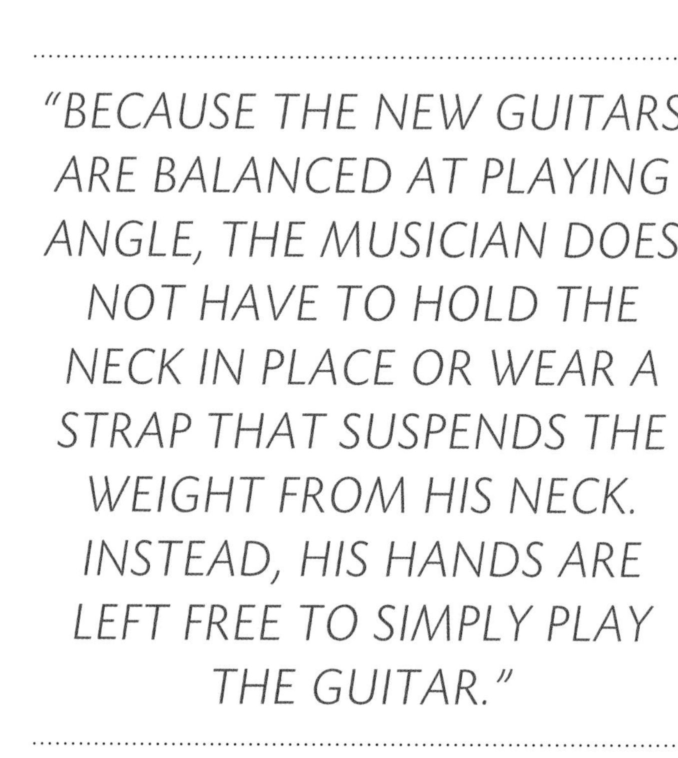

> *"BECAUSE THE NEW GUITARS ARE BALANCED AT PLAYING ANGLE, THE MUSICIAN DOES NOT HAVE TO HOLD THE NECK IN PLACE OR WEAR A STRAP THAT SUSPENDS THE WEIGHT FROM HIS NECK. INSTEAD, HIS HANDS ARE LEFT FREE TO SIMPLY PLAY THE GUITAR."*

EKLECTRIC, 2010.

As might be expected from Steve Klein, the Eklectric is not a traditional acoustic-electric guitar: rather, it is a fairly radical new concept—an instrument that attempts to blend the best of solid- and hollow-body characteristics. "I didn't want it to be a poor excuse for an acoustic," Steve explains. "Instead, the Eklectric is an 'acoustified' electric with its own voice."

The lower half of the guitar is mostly solid, which adds mass to the treble side and thereby increases sustain where it is relatively weak, whereas the hollow, thin-walled upper half contributes acoustic richness and complexity while reducing sustain on the bass strings, where sustain is already strong. The result is a more equalized sustain across the strings, and a guitar whose characteristics smoothly morph from flattop acoustic to solid-body electric as the player moves from the low E string to the high E string. Borrowing a detail from his acoustic guitars, Steve added a brace at the bridge, which allows the treble side to be tightened, thereby adjusting the differential and increasing sustain for the upper strings. The acoustically thin, nonlaminated face and back are arched to greater tension than in most guitars, making the body bright and alive. The instrument's voice is rich and surprisingly loud even when unamplified.

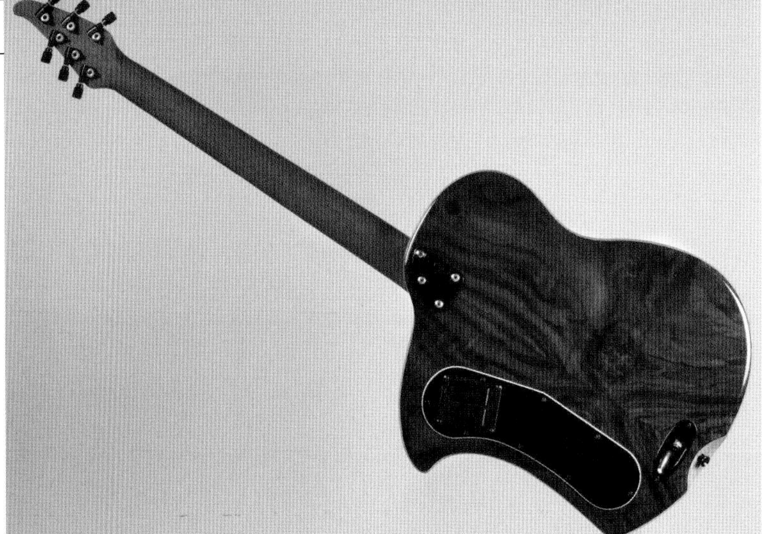

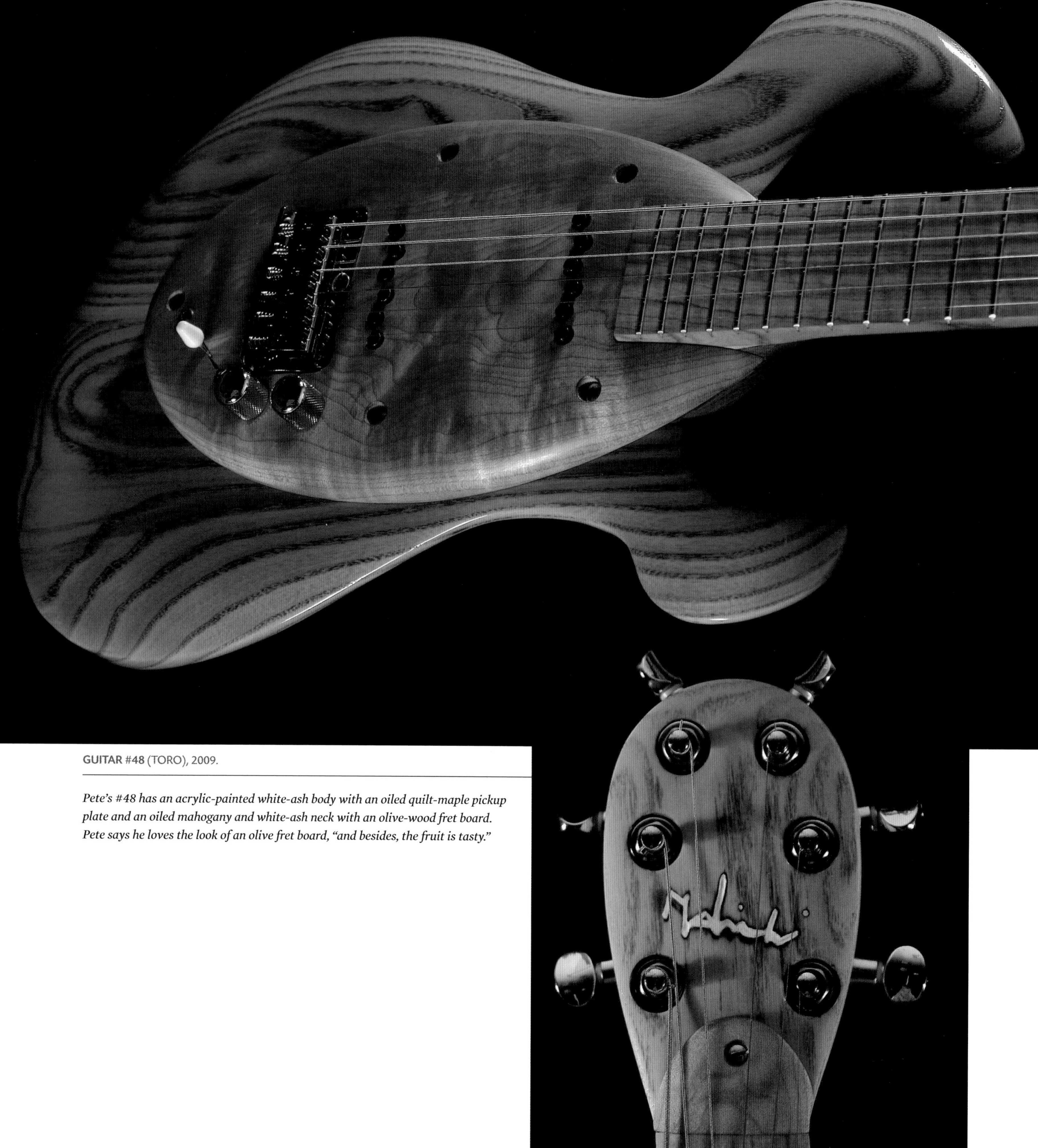

GUITAR #48 (TORO), 2009.

Pete's #48 has an acrylic-painted white-ash body with an oiled quilt-maple pickup plate and an oiled mahogany and white-ash neck with an olive-wood fret board. Pete says he loves the look of an olive fret board, "and besides, the fruit is tasty."

PETER MALINOSKI

Pete Malinoski is forthright about electric guitar design. "I think solid-body electric guitars are stuck in the past," he declares. "They have become stunted by their own success. It's my desire to give these wonderful instruments the respect they deserve by eliminating mass-production techniques and mass production–influenced design biases in favor of handcrafted individualism."

Pete came to guitar design and building by a circuitous route. "I always loved making things," he says. "It started with old cars—I got my first when I was fifteen years old. I've had twenty-four cars since. Never a new one, and the last two have lasted ten years, so it's safe to say I had a bad car habit at one time, sometimes owning two or three at a time. But before all that there were boats. I grew up on Chautauqua Lake in western New York State, which I loved, and one of my first jobs was as a boat mechanic. Because I was small, I was the one they stuffed under the dashboard and into the hold of old antique mahogany boats to rewire the instrument panels. Besides the mechanics, I learned how to refinish classic wooden boats and how to repair newer fiberglass ones.

"I went to college . . . I dropped out of college," he recounts, continuing his saga. "I built a cabin in the woods and lived there with no water or electricity through a frigid Snow Belt winter (two hundred inches—really!) and realized I'd better go back to college. I studied architecture for three years before tiring of it—I wasn't making anything, just drawing pictures and talking about things. I had friends in fine arts, and they were having a grand old time, so I made the jump to art. I became a sculptor, a gritty, dirt-in-the-teeth object maker who welded metal, cast metal, and assembled objects. I studied printmaking and learned the ancient art of stone lithography as well as modern silk-screening, and went deep into color theory."

But Pete's practical, pragmatic side wouldn't go away, and his art began to focus on common utilitarian objects. In the mid- and late 1980s, he built electric guitars and furniture and even built an automobile—a three-wheeled vehicle made from a Yamaha motorcycle and a Toyota. "It was registered and on the road at one time, a dangerous and crazy machine," he says with a laugh. He decided to seek a master's degree in functional design ("a loose term for furniture making"), and became a woodworker. After finishing that program, he became determined to get a second master's degree specifically in wood, in which he focused on the electric guitar as an art object and built one as his thesis project.

PETER MALINOSKI OF PETER MALINOSKIART GUITARS, HYATTSVILLE, MARYLAND.

In spite of the fact that he never expected to become an artist, Peter Malinoski has been making art objects for more than thirty years. He made his first guitar in 1986 because he was not satisfied with the "store-bought standard" he then owned, and there weren't many other options back then. "From that first instrument, I was hooked on the idea of making wildly different electric guitars," he explains. "The potential for their creation as beautiful functioning objects seemed endless. Guitars are the best art I can make, and I feel privileged to do so."

After earning his MFA, making lots of beautiful objects, spending nearly three years as a bike messenger in Boston ("I went insane for a while," he explains), and living on a boat on the Potomac while working for a major museum in Washington, D.C., Pete married, sold the boat, and paid off his school loans. ("A bittersweet trade-off," he laments. "I love boats.") Today, he and his wife, Nancy, and four lazy cats share a 1920s brick bungalow inside the D.C. Beltway, with a studio in the basement where Pete makes electric guitars "and/or repairs the old house."

Pete makes clear that it is not his intention to reinvent the electric guitar, noting that there are traditional ideas such as scale and

GUITAR #41 (SAGA), 2008.

This unpainted, natural-finish guitar has a 24¾-inch scale length, an oiled white-ash body with an oiled curly-maple pickup plate, and an oiled mahogany and white-ash neck with a bright red padauk fret board. Beneath the pickup plate is a proprietary humbucking pickup system with a bridge transducer. The controls include a single volume pot, a single blend pot, and a five-way selector.

dimension that are vital to the instrument's function. "Wire wrapped around a magnet to create sound-producing energy is a profoundly elegant idea that is central to the concept of the electric guitar," he points out. "But," he continues, "bolt-on necks, standardized body shapes, formless flat backs with hideous screw-in cover plates that survive as design afterthoughts are just dumb craft. There is no good reason for any of those things unless the object is just being stamped out in a factory like so many loaves of bread."

Pete has developed his own systems, shapes, and forms, which vary only slightly with each instrument he builds. "The last one always affects the next one, but no two are ever the same," he says. "My guitars are not simply collections of pieces and parts. I consider the guitar as a complete sculptural object in which form, shape, color, and material all share a design integrity—an object in which the back is as important as the front, and the sound is as important as the image." This sense of design integrity extends to Pete's pickups: although he buys standard components like strings, tuners, and bridges, he makes his own pickups and builds them into the guitar as part of the total design package.

"I am interested in pushing the boundaries of what an electric guitar should look like, but I want it to still look like a guitar," Pete explains. He points out that electric guitar designers like Leo Fender looked to the forms of acoustic guitars for their cues, but that unlike acoustic guitars, solid-body electrics are not dependent on their shape or construction to work correctly. "Electric guitars can be constructed from any random slab of wood and still function adequately," he says. "Technically, my guitars feel, play, and sound as good as any instrument can. Visually, I intend my guitars to have elegant and graceful lines with sometimes unexpected shape-and-form relationships. They have a look somewhat similar to or reminiscent of other guitars, but one that is uniquely my own."

That look manifests itself in the four basic styles Pete has designed—including the single-horned Rodeo, which has all six strings on one side of the headstock, and the deeply cut and spiky-horned Saga, which has a rounded headstock that resembles a six-toed cat's paw. His signature look also extends to his construction techniques. For example, the bodies of his guitars are in two parts. The back is attached to a glued-on neck, and the front, which houses the electronic components, is attached to the back half with screws or bolts. This sandwich-style body is a unique design of Pete's invention. "It allows for infinite component and wood combinations," he explains, "and the freedom of a sculpted body surface that is far different from the typical flat, paddle-like electric guitar body."

Summing up his work, Pete declares, "My guitars and basses aren't built the same, don't look the same, and don't sound the same as any other instrument. My intention is to create unique and beautiful instruments that are used to make unique and beautiful music."

GUITAR #49 (TORO), 2009.

This Toro model has an acrylic-painted white-ash body with an oiled, spalted curly-maple pickup plate, an oiled curly-maple and white-ash neck, and a bocote fingerboard. Spalting, which can create pink, gray, black, or multicolored streaking in wood, is caused by a wide variety of fungi during the natural rotting process. Light-colored woods like the maple seen here provide a dramatic contrasting background for spalting.

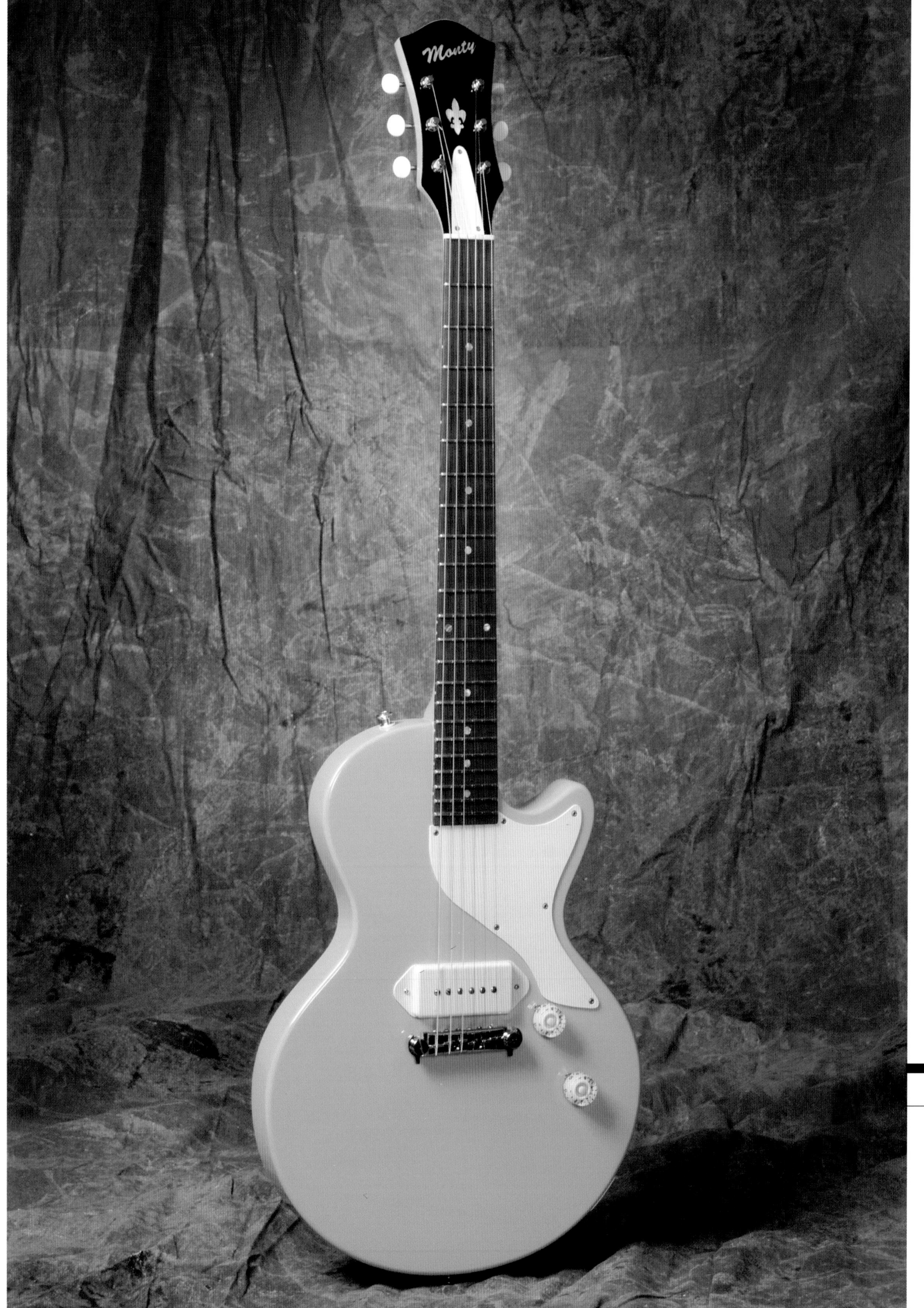
Monty

BRIAN MONTY

Canadian luthier Brian Monty has been playing the guitar for some forty-five years, and modestly says he still considers himself "a guitar player who makes guitars." But, he adds, after all those years of playing and holding guitars, "I do know what one should feel like in the hands of a player." He has been repairing and building guitars for more than thirty years, and although he has never advertised—aside from his Web site, a recent addition (he is more than a bit of a Luddite)—he has managed to build a worldwide reputation by word of mouth. His varied clientele includes Canadian singer-songwriter Bruce Cockburn, classical virtuoso Liona Boyd, Cheap Trick's Rick Neilsen, and members of the Dwight Yoakam, Conan O'Brien, and *Saturday Night Live* bands.

A working musician long before his was a builder, Brian had a Les Paul as a kid "because Mike Bloomfield had one," and his collection of guitars ultimately included "several Teles, an old fifty-seven Strat, a sixties ES 335, a Fender electric twelve-string that I tuned to open A for slide, and a collection of twenty-five-dollar Harmony archtops that I picked up on the road." He describes his musical influences as a bit of everything, from classical to jazz, with blues and R & B being the most influential. "I pretty well listen to whatever catches my ear these days, unless I'm going to do a gig," he explains. "When I have a gig to do, then I'll dust off the blues CDs and get to work." He adds that he owns a Hammond B3 organ that he is slowly learning to play, and laments with a chuckle, "I don't play much guitar these days. I mostly sand them."

Brian is completely self-taught as a luthier. "I decided one day—1975, I think—that I would like to repair guitars," he recalls. "I walked into a fellow's shop in Montreal, and I liked the look and the feel of the place, and I decided right then and there that that is what I wanted to do. I had always been a guitar player, so for me it was a natural step. In 1977, I set up a shop in the basement of Keen Kraft Music in Calgary, Alberta. I was armed with a couple of books that I referred to and went right at it. Two years later, I moved back east, set up my own thing, and have been at it ever since."

ROCKMASTER I, 2009.

Brian's back-to-basics Rockmaster I has a 24¾-inch scale length and a solid mahogany body and neck with a rosewood fingerboard. It comes with the choice of a single or a pair of P-90 pickups. The Rockmaster II, although similar, has a korina body and neck and a 25½-inch scale length.

BRIAN MONTY OF MONTY GUITARS, SAINTE ANNE DE PRESCOTT, ONTARIO.

Brian Monty is a decidedly old-school luthier who has been building world-class archtop acoustics and carved-top and solid-body electric guitars for more than thirty years. "What has always fascinated me," he says, "is how much the sound of a guitar is affected by the way the wood is shaped. To me, a guitar is a musical instrument that is meant to be played, not purchased and confined to a vault. With that in mind, I fashion a guitar that feels, sounds, and plays like you have had it for thirty years."

Brian built a strong reputation on the basis of his work repairing old Gibsons. Indeed, repair work was the backbone of his business for many years. "I have been in this business for thirty-five years and am just now getting really busy with orders for my guitars," he says. "I always made them and sold them, did repairs, etc., and made a living. I equate it with breaking into the movies: it can take a long time." He still offers a wide array of repair and rebuild services, including "retopping, renecking, and respraying Gibson guitars with old-fashioned nitro lacquer; complete conversions of Les Paul Specials,

ASH LP, 2009.

Brian is legendary for his precise repair work on vintage Les Pauls. His contemporary take on the Les Paul substitutes a hand-carved ash top for the traditional maple.

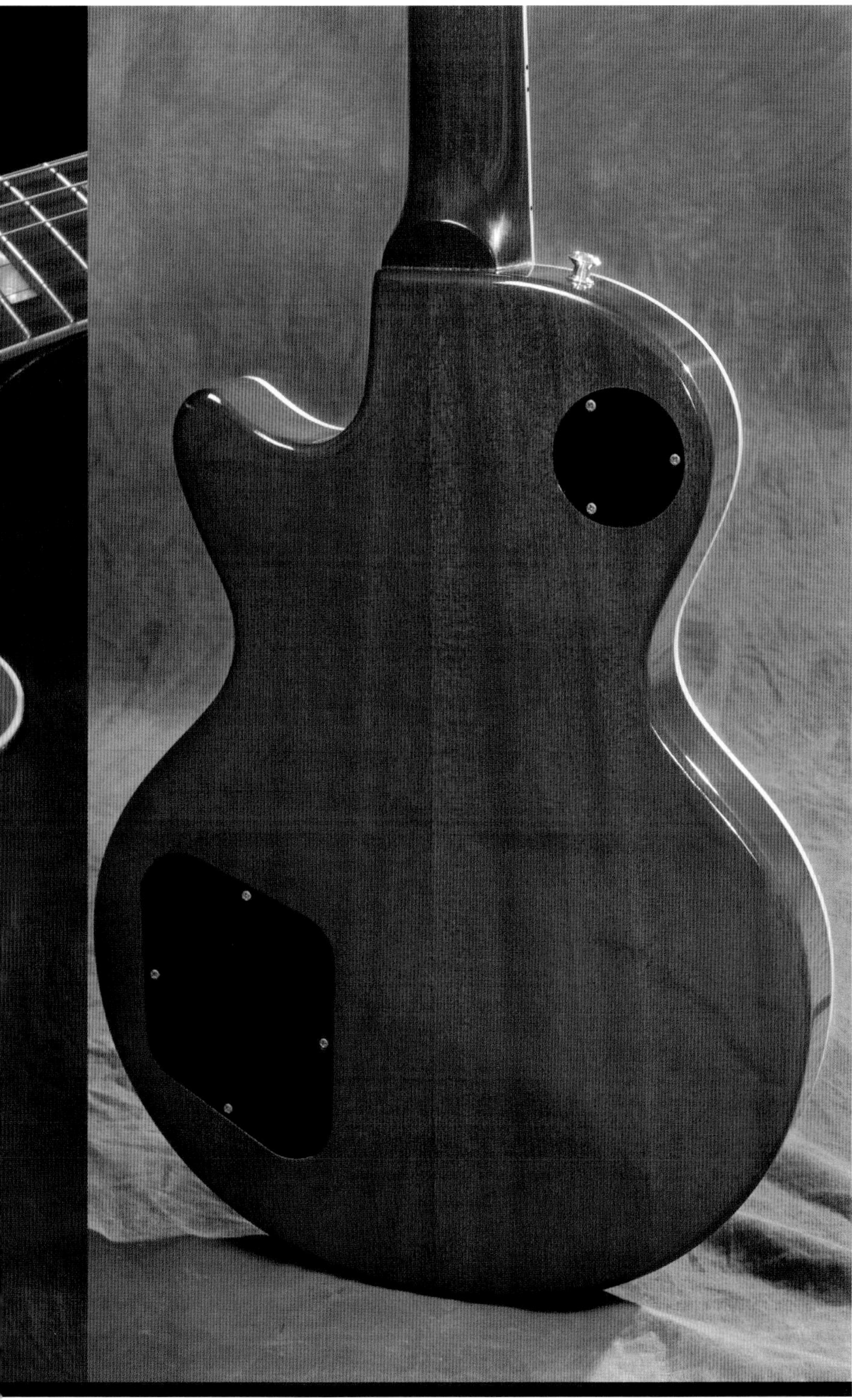

Juniors, and early fifties Les Pauls to the Les Paul '59 style; converting ES-335–style basses to dot-neck ES-335s; chambering guitars that are too heavy, and reconstructing necks that don't have that vintage feel." Monty told the Montreal *Gazette* that "a lot of famous people play parts of my instruments. What they like about the necks is that I make them the old-fashioned way—by hand. At one point, I was carving seventy-five necks a month. It nearly killed me."

Brian builds his own guitars one by one, working in a shop outside the nineteenth-century farmhouse he and his wife share, just over the line from Quebec in Ontario. Although he builds a wide range of instruments, from solid-bodied Rockmaster electrics to elegant acoustic archtops, he says the archtops are his favorite because "that's real craftsmanship." And, although he says he doesn't really have any favorite guitars by other makers, he admits when pressed that if he had to choose one it would be a D'Aquisto New Yorker. "I would have to say that Jimmy D'Aquisto was my biggest influence when I began making archtop guitars. I never met the man, although I spoke to him over the phone one day, asking him where he got his archtop cases. I had a book that had a section about him and his making of a New Yorker, and I studied the pictures and finally made my first one." Brian calls own version of the guitar the Montrealer.

Asked about other interests, Brian replies, "I like to cook and eat good food, and I like good conversation and good books. I would be a complete liar if I did not say that I enjoy playing music. If I were a wealthy man, I would have a seven- or eight-piece band on retainer and would only play good venues. Did I also mention that I am a great dreamer? To end with, I would just like to say that life is like picking fruit from the tree—all you have to do is go to the tree and pick the fruit. When I first struck out on my own, I had two kids in diapers and a five-year-old adopted boy, and I kept a saying in the back of my head that my grandmother once told me: 'It's a poor man's business that won't pay one man's salary.'" Happily, although the path he chose has not been an easy one, Brian has been able to make a living doing what he loves, and he continues to pick choice fruit from the tree.

Monty

FAR LEFT **BLUES QUEEN**, 2009.

The Blues Queen is modeled after the Gibson ES-335, a model that Brian knows literally inside and out, because he has worked on dozens, if not hundreds, of them over the years. The guitar has a 24¾-inch scale length; a hand-carved, solid, book-matched maple top and back; solid bent-maple sides; a mahogany center block; and a mahogany neck with a rosewood fret board.

LEFT **BLUESMASTER, 2009.**

Brian's single-cutaway Bluesmaster is informed by his decades of working on and playing vintage Les Pauls. He builds the model with the customer's choice of a solid or chambered mahogany body and a hand-carved curly-birch or curly-maple top. It has a rosewood fingerboard with block inlays on its mahogany neck and carries a pair of humbuckers. The body and neck are perfectly balanced, and happy owners invariably rave about the way the guitar feels. Like all of Brian's guitars, the Bluesmaster is built entirely by hand in his shop, from the ground up. He even machines his own truss rods and truss-rod nuts.

JOHN PAGE

John Page grew up in Whittier, California, a conservative Quaker community best known as Richard Nixon's hometown. His father was a preacher in an even more conservative religious sect, and John was compelled to do some preaching himself before surfing and rock and roll took over his life. He fell in love with Elvis, and says that when the Beatles and other English bands came along, that was it—he wanted to be them, to be a musician. He started working full-time as a janitor in the oil fields when he was fourteen, surfed with his friends every chance he got, and started designing and making jewelry. Then, because he couldn't afford to buy one, John crafted his first electric guitar with just a "camping knife, a cheapie scroll saw, and a file." That first guitar was so poorly made that John eventually threw it into a Dumpster, but, he told *Modern Guitars* magazine, "it made me try again, and again, and again."

After applying five times, John finally landed an entry-level job on the factory floor at Fender. Although he was initially dismayed by the disconnect between management and labor, he stuck it out and spent twenty-one years there, quickly moving from sanding necks on the floor to designing guitars in the research and development department. There, he was mentored by Freddie Tavares, who had worked alongside Leo Fender on the design of the Stratocaster. John then spent twelve years as the head of the Fender Custom Shop, which he cofounded with Michael Stevens in 1987. During those years, John worked with a team of other world-class luthiers, including Jay W. Black, John English, Fred Stuart, Steve Boulanger, and Vince Cunetto, and created guitars for Eric Clapton, David Gilmour, Pete Townshend, Elliot Easton, César Rosas of Los Lobos, and many others. Working with the artist Pamelina H. (Pamelina Hovnatanian), John pioneered the painted art guitar and designed limited-edition guitars for Harley-Davidson, Playboy (the Fender Playboy guitar features Pamelina's rendering of the Marilyn Monroe centerfold published in the first issue of the magazine), Jaguar, and other iconic companies.

Another influential custom-shop concept, the "relic" guitar, began when Keith Richards convinced Page and Black to artificially age a couple of guitars he had commissioned. Page hired Cunetto, who had developed special techniques that imitated the effects of age on wood, paint, and metal, to "devolve" the guitars so they looked like they had been played for many years, and the idea soon became a commercial success that has since been picked up by almost every other manufacturer. "It's like buying preworn jeans," Page told *Wired* magazine. "What's the appeal of a worn pair of jeans? They're more comfortable—not only do they look cooler, they feel better."

John says that at Fender, he "designed, built, and led with the passion of an artist. Having to combine business with art is a tough gig, and I bucked the system a lot. It wore me out. After almost a quarter of a century, I lost the passion for guitars." So he left the Fender Custom Shop in November of 1998 to become the founding executive director of the Fender Museum of Music and the Arts. He spent the next four-and-a-half years creating a 33,000-square-foot museum, education, performance, and recording facility for kids in Corona, California. "It was a gas!" he says. "It allowed me to pour all my energy into a 'feel good, do good' project . . . free music education for kids. But after the center was built and the programs developed, it was time for me to move on again."

In January of 2003, John and his family moved to land he had bought in the forests of southern Oregon to build a new life and a new home. "The first year I built my shop. The next several years I concentrated on my non-guitar-related art . . . functional art furniture. I'm not sure where my interest in art furniture came from, but I'm pretty sure it stemmed from the same core as my guitar-building desire; i.e., I didn't have the finances to buy the quality I wanted, so why not build it? And if I'm going to build it, why not make it really unique and cool? I was always challenged and intrigued by the process of identifying a necessary function and creating a utensil to achieve that function in a unique and beautiful way. Unfortunately, I never seemed to get around to building my own furniture. Everything I built usually was sold . . . pretty much just like the guitars. Funny how life works, eh?"

JOHN PAGE OF JOHN PAGE GUITARS, SUNNY VALLEY, OREGON.

John Page views himself as an artist who makes functional objects, and, in addition to guitars, he is currently designing and building unique wooden tables, lamps, cabinets, guitar stands, and boxes. John worked for Fender for twenty-one years, initially as a designer in R & D and ultimately as the foreman of the original Fender Custom Shop, which he and Michael Stevens cofounded. After a few years off the scene, he is back, making the guitars he has always wanted to build.

WOMAN IS THE MACHINE, 2010.

This one-off art guitar is based on a mixed-media piece John created in 2005, which won an award in the Southern Oregon Art Show. He explains that the guitar came about because he had a client who had commissioned him to build a guitar, but hadn't quite decided what he wanted. "So the client asked me if there was anything that I had wanted to do but hadn't yet," John says. "I told him about my idea of building the art piece inside a guitar . . . he loved the idea and said go for it . . . so I did.

"I have always been very influenced by art deco and the feminine form. When I created the initial work, and the subsequent guitar, in which the interior sculpture is encased in Plexiglas, I was shooting for a very industrial-deco vibe. Woman Is the Machine is my statement of how women make everything in the world possible. They are integral to every facet of life. The combining of the sensual lines of the feminine form with gears and buildings was my way of showing their oneness with industry . . . and their difference from it at the same time. Whether it is obvious or not, I use the feminine form in most of my creations. On a personal level, my wife, Dana, is my muse. She has supported me in every artistic venture I have ever undertaken . . . she has raised our children . . . she is my inspiration. She has made everything possible in my life. On a larger scale, when men took over religion, they basically killed off the goddesses that came before them. In my small way, I try to bring them back to the forefront anytime I can."

Soon, however, John found his passion for guitars starting to smolder again. In mid-2006, he sat down at his drawing table and designed a new guitar, the P-1. "It was a combination of all the things I had wanted to do in prior years but hadn't gotten to," he explains. "Since it was my guitar, I could design it my way, not Fender's or any other company's way." Thus was John Page Guitars born. Since then, John has designed three more guitar models and a bass. "I also figured, Why not throw my art smack-dab in the middle of the guitars, too? So I have created, and am still creating, some very special art guitars—some by myself, and some in collaboration with my good artist friends Pamelina H., John 'CRASH' Matos, and Vince Carl.

"I'm back," John concludes. "The passion is back, and the guitars are back. I build a very small number of guitars per year, by hand, by myself, the way I think they should be built. I put an enormous amount of time into each instrument, and give it all the time it needs in between each operation to be built the way I think it should be. I have always tried to let my art lead me in the direction I should go, because I can always trust the art."

P-1 (#034), 2009. PAINTED BY CRASH.

As this brightly painted example attests, the Page P-1 does not have to be restrained in appearance. CRASH, whose given name is John Matos, is a New York–based painter, muralist, and graffiti artist whose first painted guitar was a Fender Strat he gave to Eric Clapton in 1996. He has since created several dozen specially commissioned Fender "Crashocasters," and he and John have collaborated on several recent P-1s.

P-1 (#017), 2009.

While at Fender, John designed and built hundreds of guitars and worked with some of the finest musicians in the world, until he got burned out on the industry and walked away in 1998. The P-1 marks John's return to guitar building after a twelve-year hiatus, and is the first line of guitars he has built under his own name in nearly thirty years. The P-1 has a multichambered body, a five-piece laminated neck of Eastern hard maple and Honduran mahogany, and a contemporary six-section bridge. John says it was designed to produce "a more adult tone than a traditional solid-body electric," and this elegant example matches its visual aesthetic to its sound.

CLAUDIO AND CLAUDIA PAGELLI

"I surely didn't get it from my parents," says Claudio Pagelli of his interest in music. "They were all farmers and bricklayers on my mother's side, and factory workers on my father's side." But his older brother, who worked as a DJ, infected him with the rock-and-roll virus when they were growing up in Switzerland. "When I hit my David Bowie phase, things got difficult—white boots with four-inch heels, makeup, and drugs didn't go over well in the conservative province where we lived," Claudio recalls. "But it got me in with the right crowd. Music was everything to me."

The budding musician got his first guitar at eight and really started to play at ten. At fourteen, he placed second in his first battle of the bands contest, though he had to be accompanied by his "manager"—his father—because he was too young to enter the club by himself. "Since there was no music stand, I had to hold up a piece of paper with the lyrics to the song I was singing. Maybe that's why I placed so well. I sang 'Rock Me Baby' with a voice in the middle of puberty, and I had a harmonica hanging around my neck. I thought I was the greatest—until a really good musician won the contest and put me in my place," says Claudio with a laugh.

He cites Frank Zappa, King Crimson, Jimi Hendrix, Robin Trower, and the Beatles among his earliest musical inspirations, then later the early George Benson and Barney Kessel. He says there is not much he likes today, but "Los Lobos is great, Latin Playboys even more so. I loved the last James Bond song from Jack White, and, of course, Gringobeat—my band! Spontaneously, off the top of my head, I also would mention Bonnie Raitt, Prince, John Scofield, Marc Ribot, Ry Cooder, Beck, Eddie Harris, Johnny 'Guitar' Watson, and Keith Jarrett, but also heavy stuff like Queens of the Stone Age, Audioslave, and so on. And one of the records I would take to a desert island would be the Bulgarian Voices—so intense and beautiful."

Claudio first got the itch to build guitars after seeing the local hometown guitar hero scratch, paint, and saw the horns off his Stratocaster to create his own look. "I thought everybody did that," Claudio says. "And when he gave me that guitar as a present, there was no turning back. Pickups out, new ones in, etc. That's how I got started, and I've never stopped. I made my second guitar out of plywood with a blue Formica top. It was more chopping board than guitar. One thing was clear, though: I would become a guitar builder."

The only question was where to learn. Because there were no teachers in Switzerland, except for a few classical luthiers, Claudio ended up spending four years learning how to build and tune pianos. After he finished his apprenticeship, he started repairing and restoring stringed instruments for music stores in Switzerland—"zithers, lutes, classical guitars, harpsichords, contrabasses, electric guitars, anything that had strings. I got a lot of work from the companies that imported Gibsons and Fenders. That was like being thrown into cold water without first learning how to swim."

After a falling-out with a supervisor, Claudio founded Pagelli Guitars in 1979. "Since I was young and self-confident, I (illegally) wrote to all my old clients, and was immediately flooded with work. Of course, that required more employees, who all earned well—except for me, the guy who had to make sure that enough work came in. That was the beginning and the end of Pagelli as boss." Working on his own, Claudio built some guitars himself, and traveled to the U.S. to buy old instruments he could repair and resell at a good profit in Switzerland. He also was playing guitar whenever he could, and was hired by the Swiss New Wave band Stitch. "From then on, I ran a double life—work and play, concert tours all over Europe. That was quite cool!"

Push ultimately came to shove, however, after he met his wife, Claudia, and got involved in work as a studio recording engineer. "I ended up being an owner and recording engineer in my own new studio. After a year came the big question: studio or guitar builder? Both together weren't possible, however much I wanted and tried. So Claudia and I took off to L.A., to chase the dream of all producers and recording engineers. I made a demo, played all the instruments myself, recorded and mixed it—a musical business card. And I got a job offer

CLAUDIO AND CLAUDIA PAGELLI OF PAGELLI GUITARS, SCHARANS, SWITZERLAND.

The Pagellis work together: Claudia drafts most of the designs, while her husband, Claudio, does the actual building. Claudio is a luthier's luthier whose work is admired by such fellow master craftsmen as Charles Fox, Nik Huber, and Jens Ritter. Every Pagelli is a one-off, designed and hand-built from the ground up, and the couple has created a wide range of completely original archtops, flattops, Gypsy jazz guitars, solid- and hollow-body electrics, and electric basses over the years. Claudio says, "Life is too short to make uninspiring instruments. When I'm dead, I don't want to look at the thousands of guitars I made, I want to look at guitars that I can be proud of—every single guitar."

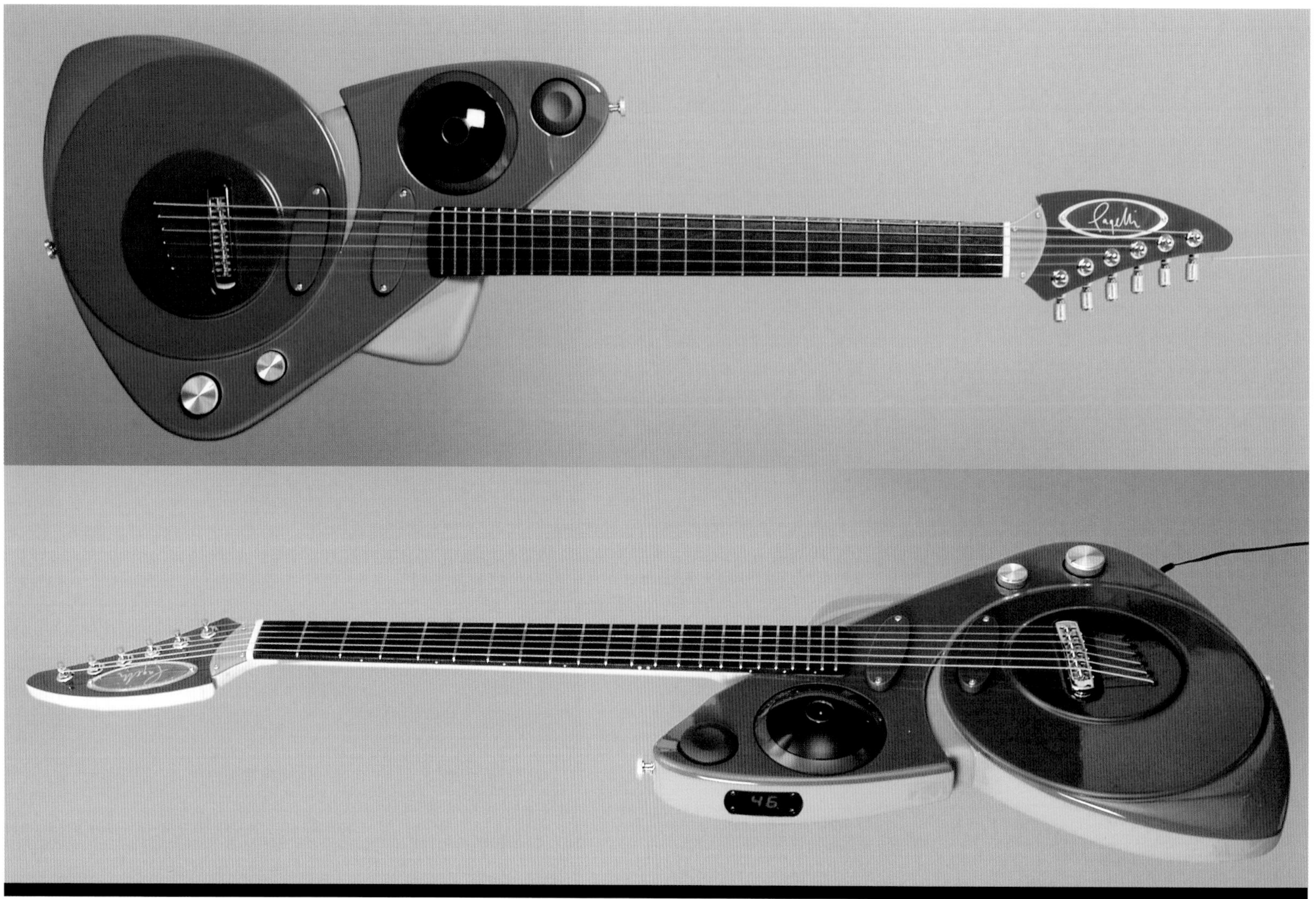

AVANTAIR, 2009.

The Avantair has an alder body and a flame-maple neck with a rosewood fingerboard. In addition to its custom Häussel pickups, it also has a built-in AirFX by Alesis, a device originally intended for DJs. Claudio says he thought it would be cool to add one to a guitar, and explains that "by just moving your hand near the sensor, you can change the parameters of whammy, tremolo, chorus, phaser, flanger, wah-wah, touch wah, seeker, ring modulation, tone generator, and other special effects. No knowledge of programming is necessary. Just plug in and play! For the first time in guitar history, it makes sense to rotate your arm like Pete Townshend . . . it will change the sound every time you cross the lens. Of course, you also can use the Avantair as a normal guitar. Just hit the bypass switch, and it plays like butter, but sounds monstrous!"

Claudio says the guitar was very tricky to build because he and Claudia had to design it around the AirFX unit, so they aimed for a weird, '70s-style design, which he describes as "like a cheap science fiction movie, just without the clouds made out of wool hanging on monofilament."

in the first studio I visited—Paramount! What did I do? I bought the biggest (also the cheapest) Cadillac, a yellow 1970 DeVille, and drove down to Mexico to empty my head, do some thinking, and make some decisions. I decided to go back to guitar building full-time. Unique instruments, of the highest quality I was capable of producing. I guess the American way of life just wasn't my thing."

Then a bout with stomach cancer, discovered two months before the birth of their first child, put Claudio out of work for a year. (Happily, he has been cancer-free since a major operation in 1999.) For a long time, the Pagellis didn't know how they were going to get through from month to month. But things got better. Work came in, not only from private clients, but also from manufacturers like Cort, Burns, Schertler, Eastman, and others. Eventually, word spread about the Pagellis' highly original guitars, and they have been busy ever since. "I'm not really influenced by other makers," Claudio explains. "Of course there are standards like Martin, with their bracing. That's something you

DJAMEL LAROUSSI ARCHTOP, 2010.

Djamel Laroussi is a left-handed Algerian guitarist who combines his Arab-Kabyle roots with Western jazz, rock, and Latin influences. He toured Europe with Stevie Wonder in the summer of 2010. Although he plays left-handed guitars, Djamel strings them in the same configuration as a right-handed guitar, so the bass strings are at top of the fret board and the treble at the bottom.

This archtop is the third guitar he has commissioned the Pagellis to create for him. It has a spruce top on a European flame-maple body and carries a custom pickup made by a friend of Claudio's. Claudio explains that the special trick of the guitar is that its f-holes are hidden under the metal cross—which represents the cross of the desert, an ancient Tuareg symbol—and can be opened or closed when playing by turning screws on the sides of the cross. The cross can be opened or closed when playing by turning screws on its left and right wings. This gives Djamel a number of options for volume and tone, and also allows him to adjust the guitar's bass frequency.

JAZZABILITY CRYSTAL, 2005.

Claudio calls this completely over-the-top and extravagant one-off guitar, which is encrusted with sixty thousand Swarovski diamond crystals, "the ultimate glamour guitar—crazy, exclusive, and perfect for awards galas or a super-stylish punk club."

The guitar, which has an alder back and sides, an Alpine spruce top, and a European flame-maple neck with an ebony fingerboard, was a joint venture between the Pagellis and the Swarovski company, who developed a way to create a "sunburst" color effect with their crystals especially for this project. Claudio notes that the Swarovski development staff also was working on designing crystal-encrusted pants as a costume for the Australian pop singer, songwriter, and actress Kylie Minogue at the same time!

"If Liberace gave Elvis a guitar, would it look like this?" Claudio wonders aloud. Whatever the answer, Claudio says that this creation "shows a lot of Pagelli"—the perfect marriage of fashion, new materials, and heritage craftsmanship. "And," he adds, "the guitar sounds and plays great!"

have to try before you do it differently. Fender, Gibson, and so on—they influenced all builders, and they also serve as a target to improve upon—but there's no one particular builder that I look up to.

"Claudia, my partner for the last twenty years, brought style and a whole new dimension to my guitars. She's largely responsible for the designs. But people should know that my guitars are instruments first and foremost—great to play, with great sound. Looks are third place. With our latest move to Scharans—mountains, peace and quiet, and inspirations—we've found the optimum place for ourselves. And we hope that that's reflected in our instruments."

LARRY ROBINSON

Larry Robinson is widely acknowledged as one of the world's foremost practitioners of the art of hand-cut inlay, to which he has devoted his energies full-time since 1975. Although he began his career as a luthier, most of his artwork graces the bodies, headstocks, and fingerboards of instruments crafted by other luthiers and manufacturers, including Fender, Fujigen, Mark Johnson, C. F. Martin, National, Kevin Ryan, Santa Cruz, and Jeff Traugott. His work comprises some of the most beautifully decorated electric and acoustic guitars ever created. Ranking high among these instruments are major projects commissioned by Martin and Fender: for Martin, Larry provided fantastically intricate inlay for the one millionth guitar to roll off their production line, an undertaking that took nearly two years to complete; for Fender, he covered the fronts and backs of a unique trio of Telecasters—all now in the Fender Museum—with Celtic-, Egyptian-, and Mayan-themed decorations.

The thick-shell technique Larry practices, which is known as *atsugai-hō*, is a traditional Japanese method of decorating the surfaces of wood or lacquer. While the Japanese originally used pieces of pearl and abalone shell, which they glued into incised patterns and then sanded flat, the technique can also be practiced with metal, stone, animal tusks, and/or exotic woods. "Thick" is a relative term; Larry works with material that ranges from three-hundredths to six-hundredths of an inch thick, which he inserts into cuts in the wooden surface he is working on. Larry is renowned for the wide range of materials he employs and his ability to integrate them into a complex and cogent design that takes advantage of the special character of each ingredient without drawing attention away from the whole. He told the on-line magazine *Guitarbench.com* that he tries to do something new on many of his pieces, especially the larger projects, explaining, "If I wanted to do the same thing over and over I'd get a CNC"—a computer-controlled machine that can replicate highly detailed designs with pinpoint accuracy. About his design process, Larry says, "The most challenging inlays are sometimes the simplest ones. With a complex inlay, the viewer's eye is taking in details from many areas at once, but with a simple inlay, any flaws are readily apparent. Geometric shapes have to be accurate, as does lettering, which we see in perfect layout many times every day. If one letter of an inlay is set a half degree off relative to the rest of them, the viewer's eye notices it immediately. This is not to say that the complicated inlays are problem-free. They obviously take longer to execute, but the amount of attention paid to each step of the process is what makes or breaks the finished piece."

Larry has been working with wood since he was six years old, when his father showed him how to use a hammer and saw. He took wood-shop courses in high school, and says he remembers building "some useless ugly stuff" there. He played guitar as a young teenager and got into classical guitar in high school, "mainly to learn to play the Bach bourée popularized by Jethro Tull," he remembers. "So I started taking lessons and had to learn everything all over again, from hand position and posture to growing my fingernails. I still have the nails, which are multifunction tools now—inlay clamps as well as guitar picks, among other things. And, yes, snippets of that technique are firmly embedded in my playing style, even though I spend most of the time on electric bass these days. I got accepted to the Hartford Conservatory and needed to get a real classical guitar before school started, as I was playing a steel-string with nylon strings on it, so I hired a luthier to build me one. Over the course of the summer, as I realized he was taking his sweet time, I kept pestering him to show me how to do various aspects of the process, and by the time school rolled around I had built the guitar myself. Then he asked if I wanted to be his apprentice, and I immediately got my deposit back from the school and never looked back."

After his three-year apprenticeship was completed, Larry moved to California and built guitars for several companies over the next ten years, including Alembic, Turner, and Modulus. He learned how to do inlay work at Alembic after he drilled holes through two expensive

LARRY ROBINSON OF LARRY ROBINSON FINE CUSTOM INLAYS, VALLEY FORD, CALIFORNIA.

Larry Robinson, who has been cutting inlays since 1975, is one of the premier inlay artists in the world. He works entirely by hand, without the aid of computer-controlled cutting machines or other duplicating devices, creating beautifully designed and executed inlays of shell, metal, and wood—and whatever other materials cross his path. His work has ranged from subtle and elegant fingerboard decorations to intricate pictorial inlay that covers the fronts and backs of one-of-a-kind museum pieces, some of which have been commissioned by Fender, Martin, and others.

basses. Rick Turner, who was his boss there, thought he might have more aptitude in another aspect of guitar work, and showed him the basics of inlay. Larry says he has been fascinated by it ever since.

In 1984, he struck out on his own as an inlay artist. Because he had been making fine custom instruments for the famous and not-so-famous players of the world—including studio musicians who were almost unknown beyond the corporate walls within which they worked—he named his business Anonymous Enterprises. Finally, though, realizing that the name was a self-defeating business move, he switched to Larry Robinson Fine Custom Inlays, which has remained his moniker ever since. In 1994, he published *The Art of Inlay*, a book that is now available in a revised and expanded edition, and he has also filmed three instructional videos that have been made into DVDs. Today, his customers include large corporations, small, low-production shops, single-person businesses, collectors, and other people who have heard of his work through the grapevine and want to own a Robinson original.

In recent years, in addition to taking care of his customers, Larry has been collaborating with respected acoustic luthiers in creating artworks that pay homage to particular historical periods. "I buy the instruments and hire the other artists involved, such as painters, jewelers, and engravers," he explains. "I then spend two to three years completing each piece. The first was the China guitar, the second was a salute to the art nouveau period, and the latest project, finished in July 2009, was a copy of a page from an illuminated Celtic manuscript from around 700 CE called the Lindisfarne Gospels. I believe I have a few more of these projects in me before retiring. I'm still just as interested in inlaying as I was back in 1975, and I strive to make each piece better than the last."

"THE MOST CHALLENGING INLAYS ARE SOMETIMES THE SIMPLEST ONES. WITH A COMPLEX INLAY, THE VIEWER'S EYE IS TAKING IN DETAILS FROM MANY AREAS AT ONCE, BUT WITH A SIMPLE INLAY, ANY FLAWS ARE READILY APPARENT."

PAGES 110–111 **FGN VIRTUOSO FLAME** (DRAGON), 2008–2009.

This is one of six unique carved-top electric guitars that Fujigen, Japan's leading guitar manufacturer, commissioned Larry Robinson to decorate in celebration of the company's fiftieth anniversary. Larry says he was asked to inlay pegheads, fingerboards, and archtop bodies for the six custom-shop instruments in September of 2008. "After they okayed my drawings, I received the parts from Japan on October twenty-fourth and had them completed and ready to ship back on December thirty-first." In addition to this and the Nouveau (see pages 112–113) design, Robinson also created inlays for Phoenix, Grapes, and Snake guitars as as a Hokusai guitar, based on the nineteenth-century Japanese artist's famous woodblock print of a crashing wave.

PAGES 112–113 **FGN VIRTUOSO FLAME** (NOUVEAU), 2008–2009.

In order to create the intricate art nouveau inlay patterns for which this guitar is named, Larry first transferred his paper designs onto the bass side of the lower bout, the headstock, and the fingerboard supplied by Fujigen. Then he cut the inlay pieces with jigsaws and fixed them together with adhesives. All the inlay pieces were then numbered, as in a complicated jigsaw puzzle. After the pieces were assembled and bonded into a single design, they were left to dry. Then Larry added ditches for the inlay with tiny knives and a minirouter. Finally, the ornaments were inserted into the fingerboard and body.

All Fujigen guitars employ their patented Circle Fretting System, which features slightly curved frets that enhance pitch accuracy and create a cleaner, longer sustain and truer harmonics. Many musicians have told Fujigen that their guitars sound noticeably cleaner and that note separation is more distinct, contributing to a more balanced and full sound in both solo leads and rhythm passages. According to players, this enhanced separation and clarity is noticeable even when the guitar is used in combination with various effect accessories, such as overdrive, reverb, or chorus. Some musicians have also noted that their fretting hands tend to remain more relaxed because their fingers are not subconsciously searching to compensate for distortions.

SIX FINGERBOARDS FOR FUJIGEN, 2006.

Fujigen cut the slots for the frets on these boards after Larry had completed his work. In some cases, he says he wishes the board did not have to be slotted, because the inlay design is so beautiful by itself.

FUJIGEN

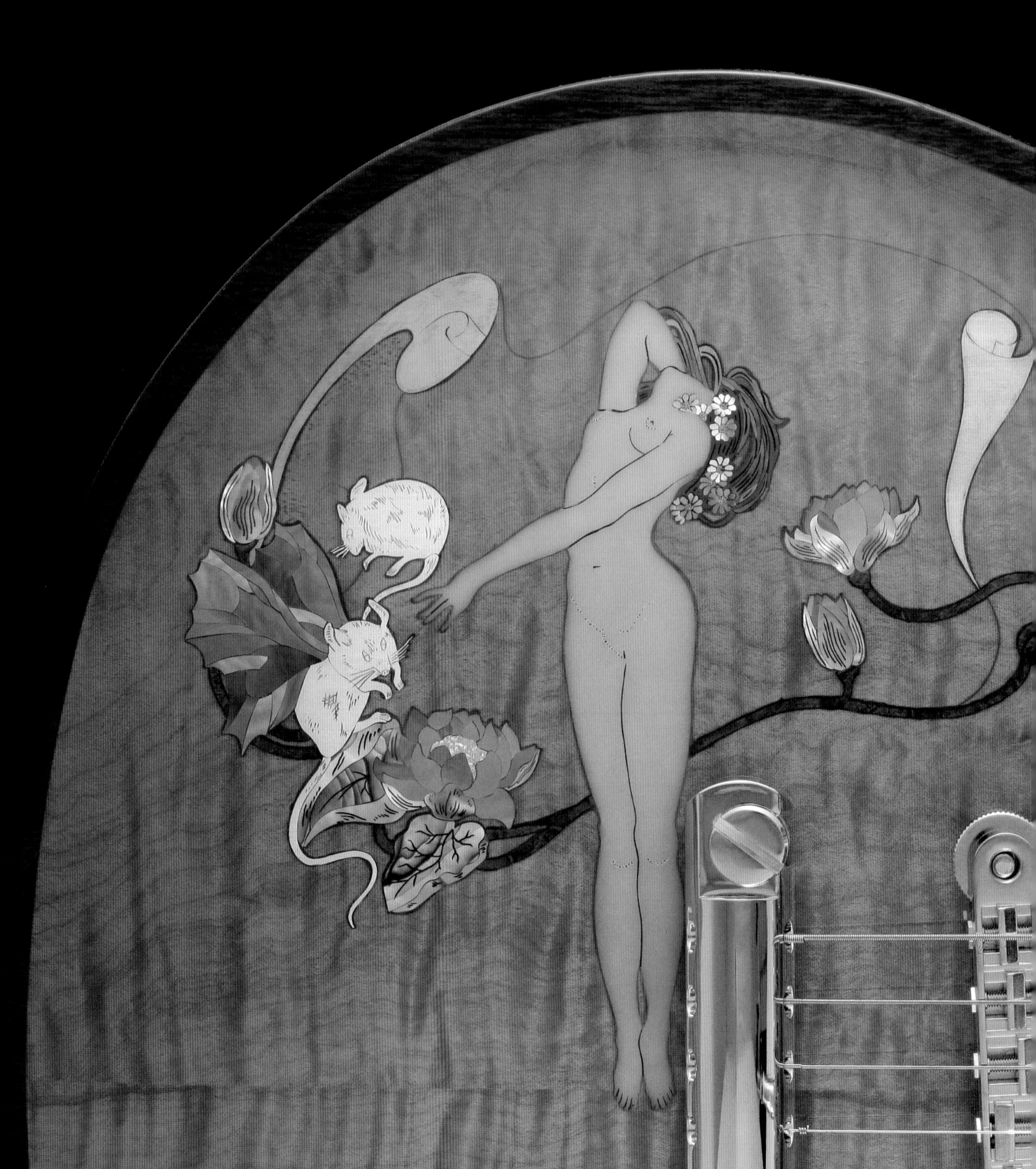

FUJIGEN
Virtuoso FL

Ruokangas

JUHA RUOKANGAS

Juha Ruokangas is one of only six Finnish guitar makers who hold a master luthier certification, and his four-person firm has acquired an enviable international reputation for quality since he founded it in 1995. Juha has designed all Ruokangas guitar models and actively participates in building them along with the other luthiers on his team. So far, Juha has unveiled five original-design guitar models—Duke (1997), V.S.O.P. (2001), Mojo (2003), Hellcat (2007), and Unicorn (2009)—and more than seven hundred Ruokangas guitars have been shipped around the world since the company's inception. Besides making guitars, he serves as the chairman of the board of the Guild of Finnish Luthiers and lets off steam playing guitar in a '70s-influenced rock band. Juha usually plays a Duke or a Unicorn with the band, both of which form the core of his small private guitar collection.

JUHA RUOKANGAS OF RUOKANGAS GUITARS, HYVINKÄÄ, FINLAND.

Juha Ruokangas (at the far left in the photo) has built a worldwide reputation for excellence since founding Ruokangas Guitars as a one-man shop in 1995. "I am fortunate to have now a handful of skilled craftsmen beside me," he says. "Together we stand strong against the tide of the massive guitar-building industry, which sells more in a day than we are able to build within a year. Their main interest is their shareholders' profit, whereas for us this is purely a labor of love." Pictured with Juha are, from left to right: Emma Elftorp, his wife and marketing director; luthier Jyrki Kostamo; and luthier Tomi Nivala.

Juha says he was the kind of kid who enjoyed "all the technical and mechanical stuff, such as miniature cars, bikes, model airplanes, etc." He also was drawn to rock music at an early age, and developed "serious guitaraholism" by the time he was fifteen. "I played guitar day and night, and also got involved in repairing and modifying them. I was determined to become a rock star and played actively in local bands, but about five years later I found my true calling when I had a big realization that my hobby of tinkering with guitars could in fact be a profession." He soon was accepted at a small lutherie school in Finland, where he honed his self-taught tinkering abilities into the skills of a master.

Growing up in the 1980s, Juha was at first seriously involved with British heavy metal—"Iron Maiden and the like"—but was soon investigating progressive rock from the '70s. These days, he says he listens to everything from singer-songwriters such as Jeff Buckley and Ray LaMontagne to Frank Zappa, the Mahavishnu Orchestra, and "harder stuff like Wolfmother or System of a Down." His all-time favorite guitarist is Jeff Beck, but he says "there are loads of others, too, of course. Derek Trucks is an absolutely fantastic player, and Tommy Emmanuel is one of my favorites as well. Tommy is better known for his acoustic guitar playing, but he plays electric as well, and I'm honored

HELLCAT CUSTOM, 2010. COLLECTION OF MATIAS KUPIAINEN.

This guitar was a one-off custom order by Matias Kupiainen of the internationally known Finnish power metal band Stratovarius. It has a Spanish cedar neck-through body with Spanish cedar body wings and a carved Arctic birch top. Noteworthy details include the custom snow-white finish with gold detailing, the beautiful compass-themed white-and-gold mother-of-pearl fret board inlay, and the True Temperament Formula 1 curved frets. The guitar has Graph Tech Ghost piezo/ active electronics and Häussel Tozz XL Custom pickups.

that he bought one of my electrics a couple of years back. Tommy said that the last time he bought an electric guitar was in 1966!"

"Over the years, I've gone through many phases," Juha explains. "I attempted to make more guitars, tried CNC [computer-controlled machinery that makes it possible to duplicate designs exactly], worked with sales reps to grow the business, and so on. But, slowly and surely, I've learned that if you want to continuously build those 'best guitars,' there can't be compromises, and production (I hate that word!) must be very limited. Whenever someone mentions the words 'more effective,' 'better margin,' or 'cheaper' to me, I shiver at the thought.

"From where I look at things," Juha continues, "the best guitars are made slowly enough to give the wood time to react to changes—carving the neck, gluing the fret board, and so on. It's equally important to give the luthier time to react to the wood as well. Also, in order for every Ruokangas guitar to be 'the best,' there can't be too many guitars in the works, because we become bored by the repetition. It's better to have a relaxed process where the luthier can enjoy the ride. A happy guitar maker makes better guitars—that's a fact."

Juha prides himself on using materials that are not easily accessed by other builders. Visually, the most striking thing about his guitars is the figured Arctic birch that he uses for the tops, and sometimes for the fret boards as well. Even though Arctic birch is a local Finnish wood, Juha says he goes to great effort to get it. "I go to the forest with lumberjacks and choose the trees, and they cut the timber for me. Then we dry it outside, seasoning it for several years." He also employs a patented Finnish drying method called thermo-treatment, which releases tensions and hardens the cells of the wood—"pretty much the same thing that happens with natural aging," he says. Another wood Juha works with is Spanish cedar, which is traditionally used in the necks and bodies of handcrafted classical and flamenco guitars. "It's a superbly open-sounding and strongly resonating tonewood," Juha explains, "but it can't be used by the mass producers because there is not enough supply."

Juha is known for his attention to detail, and likes to point out that one of the many small yet extremely important parts of the guitar that he pays particular attention to is the nut. "I have actually found the best nut material to be the shinbones of wild moose," he explains. "These are big and heavy animals with long legs, and the bones have evolved to be extremely dense and strong. We have a lot of wild moose in Finland, and during the hunting season every fall I get moose legs from local hunters. We skin the legs and have a local butcher saw the shinbones into smaller chunks for us. Then we boil the bones over an open fire for several hours to clean them up. The result is the best nut material I can

UNICORN CLASSIC, 2010. COLLECTION OF JUSSI HONGISTO.

Juha says the Unicorn guitar sums up his career so far in many ways. "I'm not the biggest fan of odd-looking guitars," he explains. "I'm the kind of guy who likes guitars when they are . . . well, guitar-shaped. This 'flow' has always shown in my designs. The Unicorn takes off where its role model [the Les Paul Standard] stopped, to evolve tonally, structurally, and aesthetically to be the best of its kind."

This unique custom-made Unicorn was ordered by Jussi Hongisto of the Finnish band Pohjaton. It features an exceptionally figured Arctic birch carved top on its Spanish cedar body, and ebony and pearl details on the control knobs, truss-rod cover plate, and pickup rings.

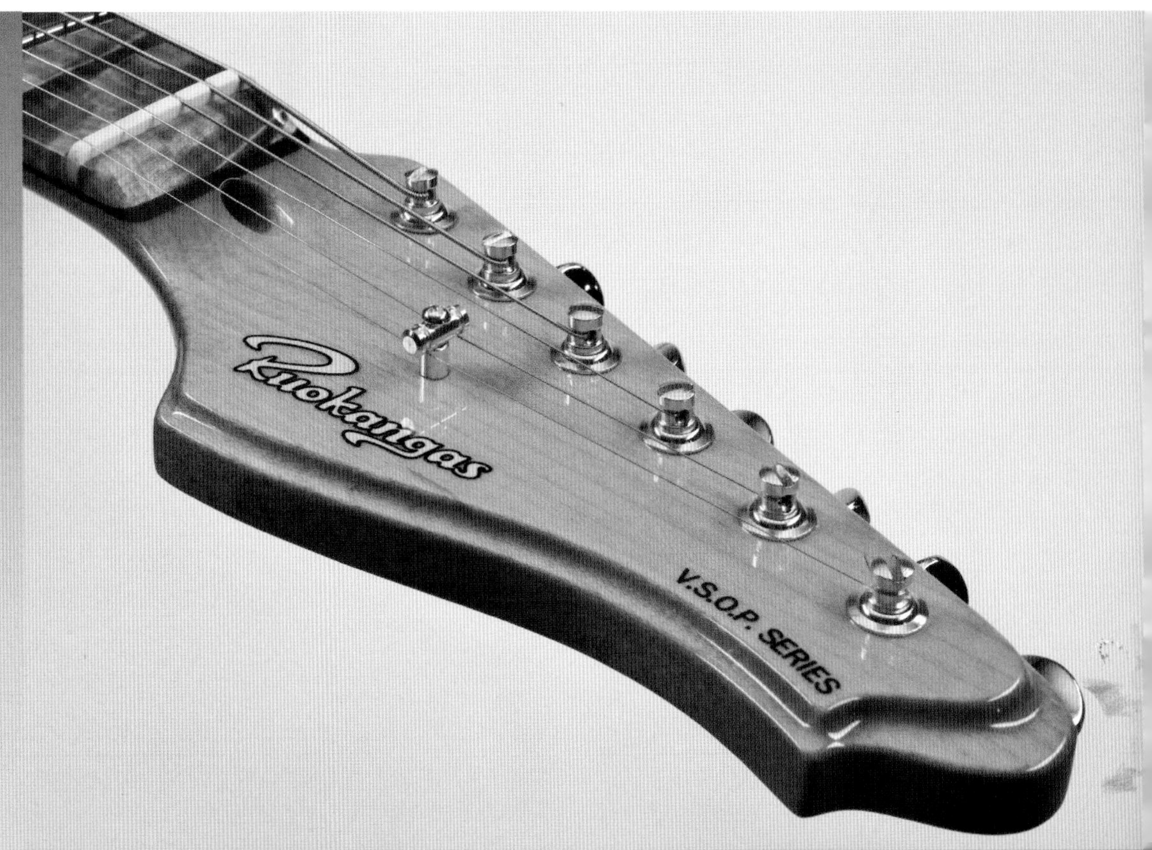

V.S.O.P. DELUXE, 2010.

Juha describes his V.S.O.P. DeLuxe as a guitar that "takes the Strat-type concept to the extreme—from a workingman's simple tool to an elaborately detailed work of art. The harmonically rich, complex tone makes the guitar work beautifully for a great variety of music."

This example was built to be Ruokangas's showpiece at the 2010 Frankfurt Musikmesse. It has a Spanish cedar body and rock-maple neck, while the top, pick guard, and fret board are crafted from differently figured Arctic birch. The figure of the birch used for the fret board is especially rare and choice. As on all Ruokangas guitars, the nut is carved from moose shinbone. The guitar also has Ruokangas SingleSonic pickups with ebony faceplates and pearl inlays, and a Wilkinson by Gotoh VSVG tremolo bridge.

think of. It's great-sounding, dense, and greasy bone that in my opinion works better than fossilized ivory or equivalent materials.

"I've found my own thing to do and place to be, and we're doing really well," Juha says with evident satisfaction. "The demand for my guitars exceeds the supply, and it's most likely going to stay that way, since we're not planning to grow, really. I'm constantly tweaking and refining our tactics, so in five years, my guitars are most likely going to be slightly better than they are now. Maybe the improvements are so small that no one else will notice them except us, but still it's important to be humble enough to realize that there is always room for development."

MICHAEL SPALT

Michael Spalt is a largely self-taught luthier who, like many other builders, got started in what has become his trade by adjusting and modifying instruments rather than building them. His parents bought him a classical guitar when he was around thirteen years old, and he took some lessons, but says he thinks he drove his teachers to desperation by "not practicing and not really exhibiting much of an aptitude for music in general. This is something that has bedeviled me always. I guess I can 'play' the guitar—maybe not make music, but feel and hear the instrument, and coax sounds and notes out of it. I have a good ear, maybe a very good one—but no musical memory. It's not that I'm tone-deaf, but for some reason I just can't remember a tune, not even a simple one. I think the fact that I was forced to approach guitars from a 'sound' point of view rather than a 'melody' point of view led to a deeper sensitivity to the tonal qualities of the instrument. I spent literally hours tuning my '60s Martin D-28, listening to the notes decaying, warbling, trying to get the damn thing to ring as harmonically and sweet as possible. I didn't know much about the inherent intonation problems the guitar exhibits, and it frustrated me to no end."

Michael, who is a native of Austria, first came to the U.S. in the 1970s to study film, photography, and painting at the San Francisco Art Institute. Later, while working as a photographer, he studied painting at the University of Applied Arts in Vienna. His main interest was film, however, which eventually led to a move to Los Angeles in 1986. There, he found work in special effects, set construction, and a variety of other film-industry capacities. Beginning around 1990, Michael—who was then writing screenplays—felt a need to do something physical to counterbalance his cerebral work, and took up guitar building in earnest. He read everything he could, attended guitar shows, and worked on increasingly ambitious projects. Over the course of a few years, he says, guitar building "slowly edged out my film work and became my main occupation, draining whatever financial resources I had in the process, but also giving me great satisfaction. I'm glad that I didn't know then what was in store for me, or I would have never attempted this. The vintage craze was starting up and any new design or newly built guitar had the chips stacked against it. It was ten years before I was able to make a living at this."

MICHAEL SPALT OF SPALT INSTRUMENTS, VIENNA, AUSTRIA.

Michael Spalt, who returned to his native Vienna in 2009 after many years in Los Angeles, is an academically trained visual artist whose output of guitars and basses is among the most varied and innovative in the world. "To me," he says, "the shape of a guitar body is archetypal, a dynamic canvas with erotic overtones." To that canvas, he has brought influences from art deco, Dada, surrealism, collage and assemblage, pop art, conceptual art, and occasional doses of pure kitsch, as well as celebrations of the organic shapes and textures of wood and metal—"the interplay between hard and soft, warm and cold."

624 BT, 2008.

Michael's 624 line of guitars was inspired by his earlier Ruby 624 line, which in turn had been inspired by an old decorative piece of aluminum he had collected that had been stamped Ruby *624 on the back. He started the 624 series by making a custom mold of the aluminum element and having it cast. All the 624 guitars have chambered mahogany bodies and deep-set neck tenons. The slightly asymmetrical shape, perfect for a stage guitar, is designed to look best slung low on the player's body. The top, fingerboard, and headstock overlay for this guitar were all made from bloodwood, a strong and heavy South American hardwood prized for its rich red color. The back is old-stock mahogany with a center stripe of laminated flame maple and rosewood. The 624 BT is fitted with a Bigsby B-16 vibrato and two of Michael's own BoneTop pickups, along with Gotoh vintage-style locking tuners.*

He started out fairly conventionally, building the guitars he had always wanted as a teenager and improving the designs where he felt the originals were lacking. He also did a lot of repairs, working on some of the thousands of vintage and classic guitars in L.A. "I was able to examine them and learn from them and about them firsthand as a good number passed through my shop."

But his background and interest in art eventually led Spalt down his own path as he sought to combine his visual ideas with what he calls a three-legged approach to musical-instrument building: reliability, playability, and tone. Of his working method, he says that he approaches every instrument as a singular project. "I'm not trying to emulate any

"I HAVE NO REAL PATIENCE WITH REPETITION. I NEED NEW CHALLENGES AND NEW THINGS TO DO, AND I'D LIKE TO KEEP EVOLVING."

given type of sound. I don't follow a given formula—I guess you might be able to find some common markers, but most of my instruments have their own personality and sound. I don't think you can go out and say, 'This is the Spalt sound.' As far as the 'art' part is concerned, I approach it as any artist approaches a canvas—you work off an idea, an inspiration, and toward a unity and finality that allow you to leave the work behind and move on to the next one. I try and improve my craft—it's wonderful how many-faceted and never-ending this process is. But I have no real patience with repetition. I need new challenges and new things to do, and I'd like to keep evolving."

Michael explains that a lot of what he does is inspired by and can be traced to earlier work done by collage and assemblage artists—Joseph Cornell, Kurt Schwitters, Max Ernst, Man Ray, Louise Nevelson, Marcel Duchamp, Robert Rauschenberg, and others. He also cites the colors of Matisse, Picasso, and de Kooning, and adds, "I love a lot of the Arts and Crafts objects, buildings, furniture, etc. Vienna, where I live now, is an incredibly rich repository of it, with an incredibly sophisticated tradition of craft and design work."

Upon Michael's move back to Vienna, he began the process of setting up shop and getting his bearings. "The traditional level of the craft is very high here," he observes. "Vienna was a seminal location from which a lot of what influences contemporary acoustic guitar building has emerged. Luthiers here are still making violins and cellos alongside their electric guitars. What I bring to the table is a maybe more 'industrial' approach—the American heritage of a factory-made (albeit high-quality) instrument, evolving to suit a rapidly changing market while making use of new technology. The electric guitar is an American artifact, and I am curious to see what the collision of these two different attitudes will produce.

"I'm working with a luthier here, Andreas Neubauer of Neubauer Guitars, on launching a line of instruments that embody the Viennese tradition of fine craft while combining it with the innovative impulses coming from L.A. I'm also working with Thomas Nordegg, who was the guitar tech for Zappa, Steve Vai, and others, and who is also originally from Vienna. Thomas has a passion for every advance in guitar technology imaginable and joins us as consultant. I do plan to continue making instruments myself, though, and maybe push the envelope a bit more while I'm at it."

APEX Q1202 CUSTOM, 2008. COLLECTION OF JARED MEEKER.

Michael does all the metal and wood work on hybrid guitars like this one by hand. He says the hybrid concept arose from his desire to reduce a guitar to its essentials and to create a modular system that would allow the easy exchange of parts. He also wanted to take advantage of aluminum as a building material because of its stability, tonal clarity, and sustain. "However," he explains, "I felt it was important to retain the comfort and feel of a wooden neck, and this led to a design based around a central mounting plate (the 'body'), to which all the other parts are bolted. The wooden neck dials in the tonal color and is comfortable to play, while the aluminum imparts a warm tone and clarity to the sound."

This double-neck guitar was commissioned by Jared Meeker, a classically trained electric guitar virtuoso who incorporates complex two-handed tapping techniques into his performances, sometimes playing one part with his right hand and another with his left. The guitar combines a thirty-six-fret, 25½-inch-scale neck on top with a 27-inch-scale baritone neck on the bottom. String mutes can be mounted at the nut to facilitate Jared's tapping. The top neck has piezos and a Graph Tech Ghost MIDI system with a thirteen-pin output. The bottom neck is equipped with a Sustainiac, an electronic device that creates intense, predictable, infinite feedback sustain, and two Bartolini humbuckers to supply the magnetic signal. The body parts are made of flame koa, and the necks are made of flame maple.

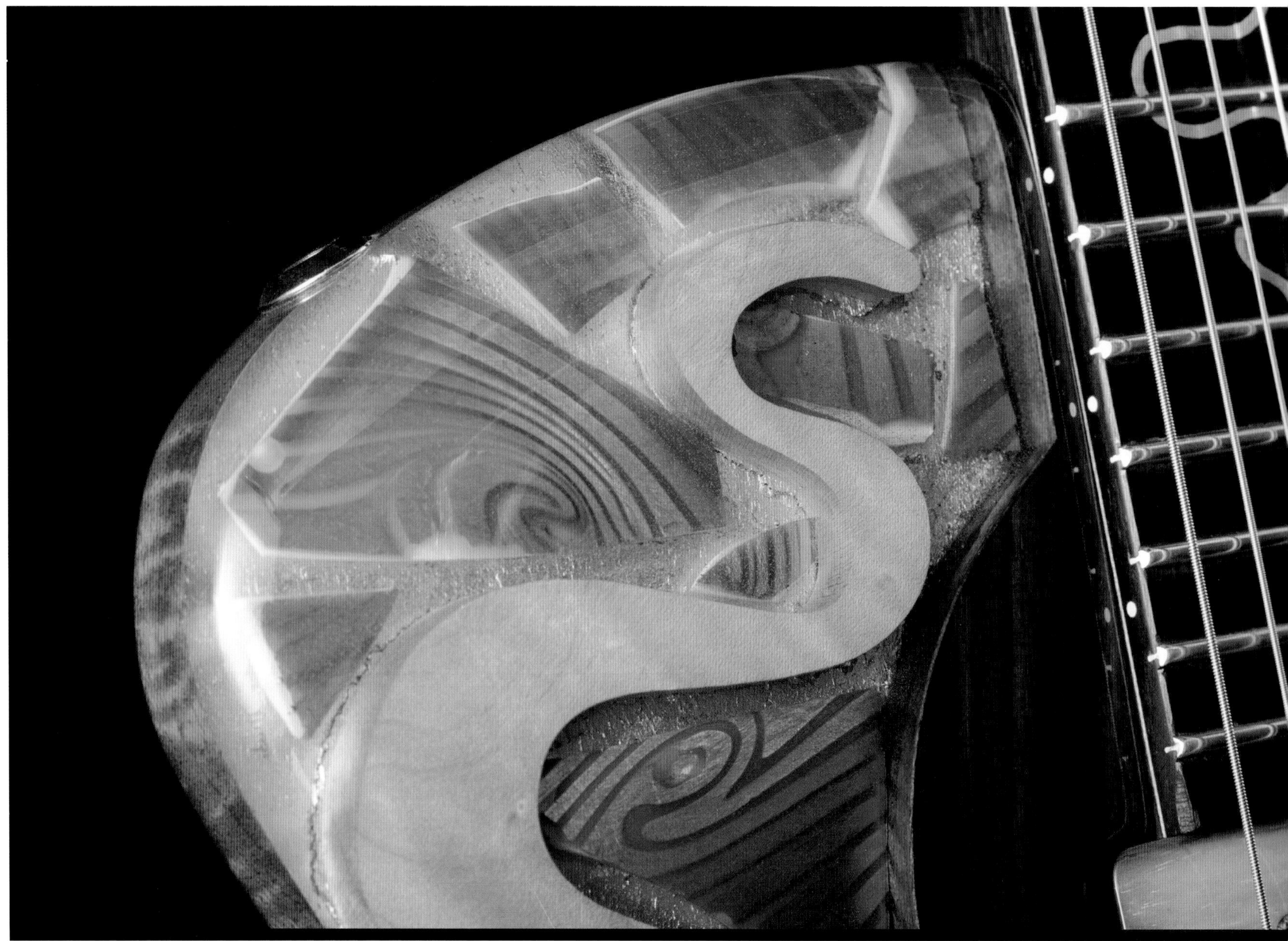

NOUVEAU #11, **LOETZ GILDED SERPENT**, 2009. COLLECTION OF DR. FRANK GUERRA.

The Nouveau series is a special project Michael developed in conjunction with Paul Schmidt, the author of books on the innovative California luthier Steve Klein and archtop masters John D'Angelico and James D'Aquisto. Each of the twelve unique guitars in the series is based on an acoustic shape originally designed by Steve Klein and has a collaged "Resintop" that incorporates art nouveau artifacts from Schmidt's collection. Michael explains that after experimenting with various types of resin, he developed a process that allowed him "to assemble objects and assorted bric-a-brac into a homogenous guitar body. The resin that tops the body is formulated to accommodate the thermal expansion and contraction of the wood and also is sonically transparent. The wood used for the back supplies the basic tonal characterstics and structural stability, while the wood choices for the neck allow me to dial in the coloration of the sound. The resin adds sustain, and its tonal effect is similar to a maple cap over a mahogany body."

All the Nouveau series guitars have aged Indian rosewood necks and centerpieces with body wings of figured old-growth Honduran mahogany and African ebony fingerboards built on a slightly extended scale to give the strings more tension. The pickups were designed around a P-90 architecture, and each pickup was handmade and wound by Michael, with colors matched to the individual guitars. Michael adds, "We used a slightly underwound coil with ceramic magnets to retain clarity in the neck position, while the bridge was fitted with alnico magnets for warmth and sparkle. I also searched for knobs to match the artwork and had custom cases made."

The Loetz Gilded Serpent pays homage to the Johann Loetz glass factory, the premier Bohemian glass manufacturer of the art nouveau period. The Loetz glass Schmidt chose for this instrument features contrasting iridescent-to-opaque hues of gold and flowing organic shapes. Schmidt explains that the serpentine shapes in the glass "invited the blond flame-maple serpent images on the body." Michael artfully rendered all the inlays in silver and pearl, and the knobs and switch are resin and Catalin (a highly collectible form of cast Bakelite) respectively.

S
GUITAR
PARKING
ONLY

MICHAEL STEVENS

Michael Stevens, who grew up on a quarter-horse farm in Ohio, has been a horse trainer and a cattle-ranch hand, a shooter on two championship smallbore rifle teams at Ohio State University, a student of metal welding and casting under the sculptor Harry Geffert, the youngest foreman of a crew digging the BART transit system under San Francisco Bay in the late 1960s, a backup guitarist for Steve Young and Ramblin' Jack Elliott, the composer of a tune used as a theme song by Earth First, the designer of an album cover for the Austin Lounge Lizards, and the president of the Texas Cowboy Poetry Gathering. He is also one of the world's finest builders of electric stringed instruments.

Asked how he got into horses, Mike replies, "I was born. My earliest horse memory is the sound of the milk truck and the garbage truck in my hometown, both of which were horse-drawn. My brother and I grabbed our stick horses and rode around, imitating the sound effects!" His father was a cowboy for a cattle company in Midland, Texas, before World War II, and, with his father and brother, who is now a farrier, Mike trained horses, rode trails, entered competitions, and roped calves until college and the armed services took the brothers away from home. In high school, Mike says he also loved wood shop, "a lot. The school system was so small that they paid me eighteen dollars a day to teach the class if the teacher wasn't there. I scored very well in mechanical drawing, and taught that, too."

He learned to play guitar while a freshman at Ohio State, where, he says, he intended to be a painter—the next Andrew Wyeth. "They beat that out of me, and I transferred to Texas Christian University because they had a rodeo club and what seemed like a good art department. But the rodeo club was gone when I got there." After working as Harry Geffert's casting assistant, he headed to Berkeley, where, while "making a fortune working on the subway," he played in bands and began repairing guitars in his spare time. He never intended to work on guitars for a living, but after the tunnel work ended, fate threw him together with a fellow art-school refugee named Larry Jameson. "We were dating the same woman. Larry was starting a guitar repair shop in the Tenderloin area of San Francisco. Synopsis: He got the girl, I got a job. Less than six months later, we moved to an old meat market in Berkeley, and the real Guitar Resurrection was born."

Mr. Larry, as he was called, didn't know much about power tools, but he knew all about guitars and setting them up—"fret work and pickups and wiring, all of that," Mike recalls. "He was into electrics, and I was into acoustics." Michael brought his knowledge of tools and an understanding of mechanical drawing to the team, and very soon, they were turning out first-rate repairs and meticulous customizing at a competitive price. Guitar Resurrection became "the" guitar shop in the East Bay, and the pair did work for Bob Weir of the Grateful Dead, Country Joe and the Fish, Commander Cody and His Lost Planet Airmen, and other bands on that side of the bay.

In 1974, Michael decided to leave Guitar Resurrection to pursue a career in his first passion, horses. He trained Arabian show horses for five years, developing an abiding taste for hackamores, spade bits, and rawhide before burning out on the show circuit and reuniting with Jameson in 1978 at the new Guitar Resurrection in Austin, Texas. Soon after, Michael opened his own shop in Austin and got his first big job building a Strat-shaped double-neck guitar for Christopher Cross, who was then a huge star. He also did repair and custom work for the likes of Stevie Ray and Jimmie Vaughan, Albert King, Otis Rush, Hubert Sumlin, Lonnie Mack, Ray Benson of Asleep at the Wheel, and George Thorogood, and became friends with Junior Brown, the "wild man" of country music. Mike built the first Guit-Steel, a combination Tele and steel guitar, at Brown's request, and the two have since trademarked the instrument's name.

By 1986, Mike's work had attracted the attention of Fender, and, when they made him an offer that was too good to turn down, he moved back to California to cofound the new Fender Custom Shop with fellow designer and luthier John Page. (The move also gave him the opportunity to spend time in the ranch country north of L.A.) He and Page designed and built many of the instruments that Fender's endorsement artists have played, and Mike also became the first person in the history of Fender to sign the instruments he built—

MICHAEL STEVENS OF STEVENS GUITARS, ALPINE, TEXAS.

Michael Stevens, seen here on horseback outside his studio in southwest Texas, is not only one of the most accomplished guitar builders in the world, but also a cowboy who can hold his own with seasoned ranch hands. Mike's skills as a luthier have been refined to a remarkable level through years of hands-on work and study in his craft. Although he is a great admirer of classic guitars, his designs are, as he puts it, "informed, but not constrained, by the great instruments of the past."

starting with the Stevens LJ, which was then available in Fender's Designer Series. The Eric Clapton Stratocaster was the shop's first project, and Mike says during the two weeks he spent copying Clapton's legendary Blackie, the guitar "never left my sight unless it was locked in my office in Corona or stashed under my bed, in which case I slept with a pistol under my pillow."

In 1990, Mike moved to Alpine, Texas, a small university town at the edge of the Chihuahuan Desert between Big Bend National Park and the Davis Mountains, where he continues to build electric guitars, basses, and mandolins for players all over the world. Now that Mike is again living in ranch country, he is being tutored by some great cowboys in range skills and etiquette. He says that one of his proudest moments was hearing a mentor tell him, "You made a hand today."

Mike considers designing and building guitars an art, and although he is known as a perfectionist who won't leave something alone until it is exactly right, he says the real challenge for him is in the "paper work" of the initial design. Although he customizes the particulars of his guitars to suit his clients' tastes and needs, he shapes the basic body forms of his instruments from templates that are held in place by locator pins as he works. "Each template has the locator holes in the same place," he explained to Joe Mendel of Mel Bay's *Mandolin Sessions*, "but each one has a different shape and different cutouts from the previous one. The first template is for the outside shape of the body. After routing that shape, I remove it and put the next template on. That one might have the pickup and control cavities, and the next one might be the neck pocket. It usually takes three or four templates to completely rout out a body. Since all the templates use the same locator holes, once you get the templates right, everything is repeatable and can be done very quickly."

Asked if he has ever considered using CNC machining instead, he answers in his typically straightforward manner. "If I was in a factory setting, cranking out lots of instruments, I would probably go that route. But the learning curve is so steep that it's not worth it at the rate I'm building. I could build a lot instruments in the time it would take to get up and running with CNC. Nothing against it, I just don't have the time."

NEO CLASSIC, 2009. COLLECTION OF ROBERT HANSEN-STURM.

This prototype for Mike's Neo Classic model has a chambered, semihollow one-piece Honduran mahogany body, topped with carved Eastern red maple, and a quartersawn one-piece Honduran mahogany neck. Both the fingerboard and the peghead veneer are Brazilian rosewood. The guitar has a 24.625-inch scale, twenty-two frets, and is equipped with a pair of humbucking pickups built by Tom Holmes. Robert Hansen-Sturm, who commissioned this guitar, is a professional photographer who owns several of Mike's guitars.

CLERKENWELL LJ, 2009. COLLECTION OF JUSTIN MOODIE.

Michael Stevens's LJ model is named in honor of the late Larry Jameson, who was Mike's partner at Guitar Resurrection in Berkeley and Austin. This LJ has a chambered korina body topped with Western flame maple, a laminated three-piece korina neck with a wenge center, and a Madagascar rosewood fingerboard and headstock veneer. The pick guard and body binding is ivoroid, a type of plastic. Mike says that businessman and publisher Justin Moodie, who commissioned the guitar, asked if Mike could put an asymmetrical end on the fingerboard. "I did, and I rather like it," Mike adds, "but I'm unsure if I will change the model over."

Justin lives in a London neighborhood called Clerkenwell, which is named after Clerks' Well, where priests of London Parish would perform religious plays in medieval times. He says it is an amazing place, "home to Oliver Cromwell, Fagin and the Artful Dodger, Daniel Defoe, Lenin's newspaper, distilleries, breweries, and some of the world's greatest watch- and clock makers. It's still home to the Order of Saint John, Sadler's Wells theater, Smithfield Market, Exmouth Market, Fergus Henderson's St. John restaurant, and many of the city's architecture and design firms. My two children were born here, and it's here that I ordered and designed the guitar. And it's also here where it's played, enjoyed, and admired. And so, after all that, I really couldn't imagine a better name for my Stevens than the Clerkenwell LJ."

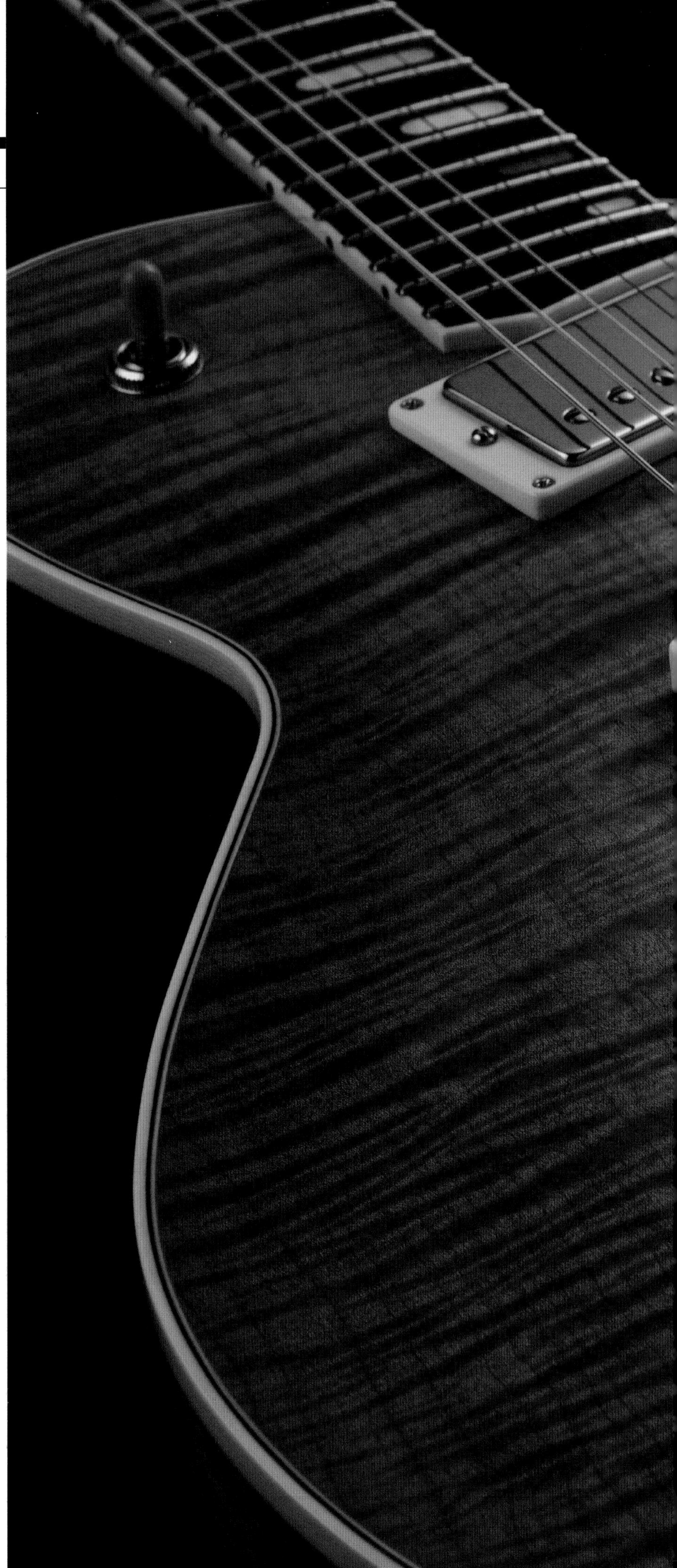

JUNIOR BROWN GUIT-STEEL (OLD BUD), 2010. COLLECTION OF JUNIOR BROWN.

This is the latest in a series of custom-built hybrid instruments conceived by the virtuoso alt-country guitarist Junior Brown—seen opposite page, left, with Old Bud in his cabin in the Texas hill country—and brought to reality by Mike Stevens. "Lots of things grow out of customer requests," Mike explains. "They ask; I go to the drawing board and see what happens. I never would have come up with the Guit-Steel concept on my own, but it wouldn't look like it does if Junior had designed it."

Old Bud combines a 25 ½-inch Eastern curly-maple guitar neck with a standing single-neck, ten-string pedal steel, enabling Brown, who is a master of both instruments, to switch back and forth over the course of a song, easily moving from twang to slide. The pedals on the steel are connected to combinations of strings preset by Brown, and allow him to raise and lower their pitch while he is playing. He uses picks to play on both necks, and stores his metal slide bar in the recessed head of the pedal steel when he is playing the guitar neck.

Duane Marrs, who worked for Sho-Bud, a manufacturer of pedal steels in Nashville, for many years, built the pedal steel for Junior from 1970s Sho-Bud parts that Junior had lying around. He and Junior furnished Mike with diamond marquetry so that Mike could match his portion of the instrument to the Sho-Bud, but, sadly, Marrs died shortly after Junior got the steel. "It was quite a puzzle to pull it off," says Mike. "I had to cut the shelf the guitar part sits in, and, in doing so, beef up the underside with a large block of sugar maple for strength. That is what the big flat bolts and wing nuts go through to hold the neck on and support the rest of the steel. I did modifications on the steel, and designed the small box that holds the volume pot. I also designed the padded cutout for the peghead to drop into." Mike designed all the metal parts, too, which were machined in Alpine by craftsman Jim Collins, and the bridge was built by the Gordon-Smith company in the UK. The pickups, Mike notes, are "top secret."

JUNIOR BROWN PLAYS HIS FIRST GIG WITH HIS NEW GUIT-STEEL, OLD BUD, AT THE LEGENDARY CONTINENTAL CLUB IN AUSTIN, TEXAS, ON MARCH 28, 2010.

ULRICH TEUFFEL

The German industrial designer and guitar maker Ulrich Teuffel sees himself as following in the footsteps of Leo Fender, whose minimalist electric guitar designs were also considered radical and even ridiculous by early observers. Like Fender, he is trying to create something new under the sun and to build instruments that will free contemporary musicians from the past the way Fender's Tele and Strat freed guitarists in the 1950s and '60s.

"I'm trying to prove that the evolution of the electric guitar hasn't yet come to an end," Ulrich explained in a video interview with Gourmet Guitars. "There are many paths we've never tried . . . I wouldn't call my guitars modern instruments. If you take a closer look, you'll see that someone could have built them in the '50s or '60s. There's nothing that's on the technological cutting edge," he added with typical straightforwardness. "As a matter of fact, I only used classic materials. But I redefined the form."

Ulrich says that he was probably fated to do creative work, citing his many artistic forebears as evidence. "My great-grandfather was an engineer, my grandfather was an engineer, my father is an engineer; my other grandfather was a cabinetmaker, my uncle is a cabinetmaker, my granduncle was a painter; so what can I say? Becoming an accountant has never been my ambition. An inventor is a bit more my style."

He built his first guitar, which he describes as a "desktop-wood guitar" built from the cheapest possible materials, when he was a child, and then, after graduating from high school, he began an extended apprenticeship in metalwork and construction at Mercedes-Benz. "During that period," he says, "I learned that you can't call a thing exact if it isn't accurate to one-hundredth of a millimeter." He adds, "Today I think that the figure is actually more like one-thousandth of a millimeter. But everyone starts out as a beginner."

After building his first legitimate, non-desktop-wood acoustic guitar, he came across a book by Donald Brosnac called *The Steel String Guitar: Its Construction, Origin, and Design*. The book not only explained how to build an acoustic guitar but also showed gorgeous pictures of instruments built by luthier Steve Klein. "I started at once to try to replicate a Steve Klein acoustic," Ulrich recalls. "But the guitar looked more like a Canadian hunting lodge with carvings and a sound hole on it, so I skipped it. The first real guitar I built was an homage of my own to Steve Klein—or at least it was a replication of his form, because I had no idea of his construction, which the pictures didn't show."

In the following years—and especially after he founded his company, on June 1, 1988—Ulrich spent his time building electric guitars and basses. "In those years," he recalls, "I designed my first guitar series, called Dr. Mabuse, and a line of basses called JFK, both of which were based on traditional examples—glued-in necks, mahogany bodies, flame- or quilt-maple tops, Brazilian rosewood fingerboards, pickups, tuners, vibrato from wholesale suppliers, glossy finish—the usual things." But as his somewhat weary recitation of "the usual things" suggests, he found himself dissatisfied with his work a year before he started to market his designs. "The series had been developed completely, the results were good instruments, and today they are even collectible," he explains. "But I had been looking for a wider challenge."

To assist in his search, Ulrich studied industrial design from 1992 to 1996, an experience that he says was formative to his approach to guitar building. He found the key he had been looking for when he realized that his industrial-design experience taught him to look at his work from a distance, to go back to first principles of form and function. So he took a step back, which led to a radical rethinking of the way a guitar could look and sound. "At the end of the process," says Ulrich, "I resumed my work and came back with the birdfish guitar, which was introduced in 1995. Two years later, I created the coco series, then the tesla series, and, in late 2007, the niwa." All of them are as utterly distinctive and original as the Steve Klein acoustic that first inspired him as a builder. The birdfish, which the British magazine *Guitarist* picked as one of the most important guitars of the twentieth century, may just as easily be seen as one of the most important guitars of the twenty-first century, and certainly ranks with Ken Parker's Fly as the most complete reexamination of the electric guitar since the instrument was codified by Leo Fender in 1950.

ULRICH TEUFFEL OF TEUFFEL GUITARS, NEU-ULM, GERMANY.

Ulrich Teuffel, seen here in his studio, is a former industrial designer who has conceived and built some of the most unusual and innovative electric guitars in the world. The birdfish, his most radical design, contains neither a traditional body nor a head, and his tesla, which glows in the dark, allows the player to produce retro distortion sounds that belie the instrument's space-age looks.

BIRDFISH, 2009.

The birdfish, which was originally introduced in 1995, is the most radical of Ulrich's designs. The instrument, which has been played by the likes of David Torn, Henry Kaiser, Billy F. Gibbons, and Page Hamilton of the band Helmet, has won three design awards, and examples are owned by several museums.

Ulrich's original idea was to construct a solid-body guitar with the fundamental elements—the tonewood and pickups—intact, but put together in a modular fashion so they can be moved at will. So the birdfish's body consists of two wooden tone bars that are screwed onto aluminum bird- and fish-shaped elements. The neck is bolted onto the upper element, the "bird"; the lower element, the "fish," carries the electronics control box. A rail between the bird and fish holds three slideable pickups, whose positions can be rearranged within seconds.

The pair of tone bars defines the basic sound of the guitar, just as the body wood on a traditional solid-body guitar does. They also are interchangeable, which allows the birdfish to alter its basic musical character. The tone bars are made of traditional tonewoods: one is made of American alder and the other is crafted from specially selected Michigan maple. Ulrich manufactures all the hardware (including some of the screws) in his workshop to guarantee that all the parts harmonize perfectly. Only the Gotoh and Schaller Tune-o-matic bridges he uses come from outside Ulrich's workshop.

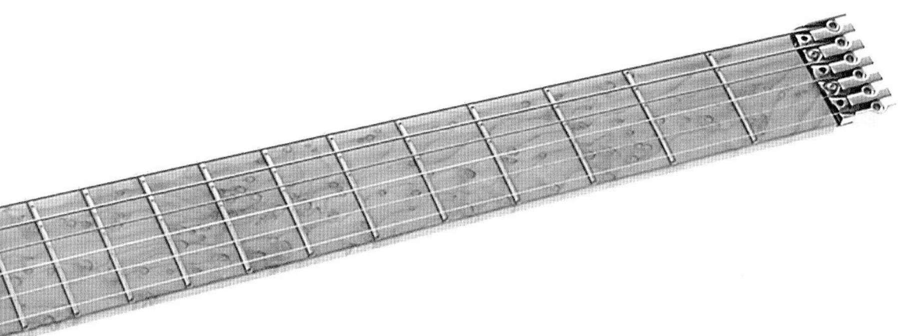

TESLA TREM, 2010.

Ulrich's tesla created a sensation when he introduced it at the 2000 NAMM (National Association of Music Merchants) show. Among the first buyers were Henry Kaiser and David Torn, two of the most acclaimed experimental guitarists at work today.

Ulrich designed the tesla to produce both modern guitar sounds and the primitive background noises—feedback, loud humming, signal interruptions, and so on—that have been refined out of other contemporary guitars. The tesla has three buttons that allow the player to add noise to his playing whenever he wants and make it possible for the player to control and combine them in entirely new ways. The left button causes a sixty-cycle hum, the middle switch interrupts the signal, and the right button activates a small microphone beneath the neck pickup, which produces the unmistaklable sound of screaming microphone feedback. This new tesla trem model adds a floating headless vibrato that can be locked with a lever.

NIWA, 2009.

The curved body of the niwa is shaped to "cuddle" against the player's waist, so the guitar follows his or her moves instead of swinging around as a flat-backed solid-body does. The body is cut out of a four-inch block of American alder, one of Ulrich's favorite tonewoods. The neck is also alder; the fingerboard, headstock, pickups, and control knobs are rosewood; and all the metal parts are chrome-plated.

TEYE

The Netherlands-born flamenco guitarist and luthier who goes by the single name of Teye calls his instruments "unapologetic, big chunks of guitar," and they are surely that. As Teye freely admits, his highly ornamented designs, with surfaces covered with flashy shell mosaics and intricately etched metal, are clearly inspired by the work of Tony Zemaitis, but he also has borrowed techniques in construction and finish from classical and flamenco guitar making and rolled them into something quite his own. Zemaitis made two guitars for Teye in the 1990s, which, he says, "opened my mind to the importance of balance in electric guitars. Zemaitis's instruments were as lively, vibrant, and responsive as the best flamenco instruments by Manuel Reyes and Lester DeVoe: no other electric guitar had ever done this."

As a former full-time professional musician, Teye is first and foremost a player, one who brings his extensive stage and studio experience to every instrument he builds. "I do not have formal training as a guitar maker, and as such I am neither helped nor burdened by my training. I design my instruments as a player, not as a builder," he explains. "My guitars are often complimented for their exteriors, but underneath all the adornment and beauty, they are really powerful and versatile performance tools. All materials other than the inlay and the knobs are used specifically to help the sound. My goal is to build guitars that sound strong and resonant before you plug them in, because electronics can only pick up the voice that is already there."

Teye grew up in the Netherlands of the 1960s, during the days of pirate radio. "We listened to Radio Veronica in the daytime and Radio Luxembourg at night," he remembers. "I was taking classical guitar lessons when I first heard the legendary '60s and early-'70s guitar-oriented music that turned me to the electric guitar. I have vivid memories of my light blue bell-bottom trousers, maroon platform boots, and my first electric guitar—a fabrication in plastic and plywood of the lowest possible quality—which still resides in my collection."

Teye's ambitions quickly outstripped that instrument's capabilities, and, because he could not afford the guitars and amps he really wanted and his otherwise supportive parents did not want him to pursue a career in music, he was left to fend for himself. "That meant I needed to either modify my existing gear," he recalls, "or build new gear from scratch. So I chose the latter, and my father, who was an electrical and mechanical engineer, did help me enormously with that. In the end, the guitars and amps I made consistently sounded better than the ones they were modeled after."

In his late teens, Teye moved to London "to become a famous guitar player." He played and toured with numerous bands over the next few years before returning to the study of classical guitar at the Royal Conservatory in The Hague. Then, chasing a Spanish girlfriend, he hitchhiked into what he describes as his new life—flamenco. The reclusive flamenco Gypsies welcomed him into their circle and taught him their style of flamenco guitar playing, an unusual opportunity because of the mistrust, almost racism, that exists between Gitanos (Gypsies) and payos (non-Gypsies). "For the next twenty-five years, I devoted my life to flamenco guitar," he recounts. "During long stays in Andalusía, I studied and played with the absolute masters of flamenco, including my mentor Juan Muñoz-Planton, and financed it all with an endless series of performances." Ultimately, Teye was granted a green card and U.S. citizenship on the basis of his musical ability, and, after moving to Austin, Texas, toured for five years with Joe Ely's powerful country-rock band, with whom he played flamenco guitar.

After twenty-five years of playing and touring full-time, Teye wanted to settle down and start a family with his wife, the flamenco dancer and rock drummer Belén. While he was asking himself what else he could do to make a living—something that would offer more security and stability than performing; something that would allow him to "have a life" again—an electric "dream guitar" he had just built for himself caught the attention of several players, and they encouraged him to try his hand at lutherie. He says that guitar was

TEYE OF TEYE GUITARS, AUSTIN, TEXAS.

Teije Wijnterp, who goes by the single name Teye, is a Dutch-born professional flamenco guitarist who spent years studying with Spanish Gypsies and touring the world as a performer before turning to guitar making in 2006. "It sounds kind of strange, quitting a 'day' job as a guitarist, but that's how it is," he told Vintage Guitar *magazine. "You can't pursue a dream halfway. After a quarter century of playing guitars professionally, I'm pursuing the dream of building them."*

His extravagantly decorated instruments combine a unique personal visual style with innovative wiring, specially designed, handmade bridge and tailpiece systems and pickup rings, and other musical advances based on his vast experience as a working musician.

the result of experimenting with different parts and materials "to achieve my long-desired goal of being able to switch between fat '70s rock sounds—the wail of Jimi, the twang of Marty Stuart and Pete Anderson, and the sonic richness of Brian Setzer—without a guitar change. I was driven to make an instrument that would satisfy me." Teye says his Electric Gypsy guitars combine everything he has always liked about guitars—"three pickups, simple switching, a vast array of 'real' sounds at my fingertips, a twenty-four-fret heelless neck, the direct response of a flamenco guitar, and playability."

Asked about his favorite guitarists, Teye quickly responds: "Paco de Lucia, Vicente Amigo, Ry Cooder, David Grissom [an Austin stalwart who played lead for Joe Ely for many years], Jimi, and Mick Taylor." In 2010 he developed a prototype for a new, one-pickup guitar that retails for a tenth of the cost of his high-end models. This new guitar, although not inexpensive, comes from his heart, he says, for all the struggling players out there. The economic turndown almost forced Teye to close his doors in 2009, but then things began to look up, and he is hopeful about the future. He says he wants to stay small and continue building "top-quality instruments that make people's eyes light up when they play them. My great passion has always been the guitar," he says unequivocally, "and I feel privileged to devote my life to her."

ELECTRIC GYPSY A-SERIES #023 (LA INDIA), 2009. COLLECTION OF CALVARY KENDRICK.

La India was the first model developed by Teye. It features a fully hand-engraved aluminum plate on the front that is outlined with a hand inlaid stabilized turquoise mosaic and a mahogany body. Like all Teye guitars, it carries three special high-clarity Jason Lollar humbucking pickups. Teye explains that he chose these pickups because "I want lots of low end from my bridge pickup, and lots of clarity from the neck one, so that when I switch, I don't need to rush over to my amp to quickly correct the sound." All three pickups are housed in a unitary pickup ring that Teye designed and that is machined and hand-engraved in-house. The bridge and tailpiece are also Teye's own, designed to provide ample focus and sustain.

ELECTRIC GYPSY A-SERIES #019 (LA CANASTERA), 2008. COURTESY OF GEORGE BORST.

All Teye guitars carry names influenced by Spanish Gypsies, with whom the luthier lived for many years. As was the case with English working-class people in centuries past, who often based their surnames on their professions—a practice reflected in names like Cooper (barrel maker), Smith (blacksmith), and Wagner (wagon maker)—many Romany people named themselves after the traditional trades they practiced. This was especially true in Spain after 1492, when Romanies there were forced to assimilate and banned from using their own language. Canastero, meaning basket maker, became such a common surname that the plural, canasteros, is often used today to refer to Gypsies in general or Gypsies from northern Spain in particular.

Spanish Gypsy women have always been partial to coral jewelry set in gold, so Teye chose that color combination to decorate his La Canastera guitar. The instrument has a red coral border with detailed inlays, a hand-engraved front plate made of gold and anodized aluminum, and gold-plated hardware. The back of the mahogany body is finished with a hand-rubbed caramel-colored violin finish.

ELECTRIC GYPSY A-SERIES (EL DORADO), 2010. COLLECTION OF KONSTANTINE ZAKZANIS.

The El Dorado is Teye's top-of-the-line model, and, fittingly, he also calls it fuera de serie*—out of the ordinary. The flamboyantly decorated guitar is named for the fabled city of gold that Spanish explorers sought in vain for centuries. It has a black korina body with a hand-inlaid zircote top surrounded by a mosaic of rare purple abalone and ebony. Continuing the theme, the walnut neck has an ebony fingerboard inlaid with mother-of-pearl, and the hand-engraved aluminum plate on the back includes images of an Arabian oud (a lute-like stringed instrument that is an ancestor of the guitar) and a type of rifle used by Bedouin camel riders.*

Teye's guitars do not use preamps or active electronics. He says that in devising his proprietary wiring system, he ignored everything about existing guitar wisdom except the idea of feeding high-quality pickups straight into an amp. "With all knobs on ten," he explains, "filtering is not engaged. However, at lower settings, when the filters do engage, I achieve a palette of sonics that is unheard-of. There are many sounds that can be produced only on this instrument."

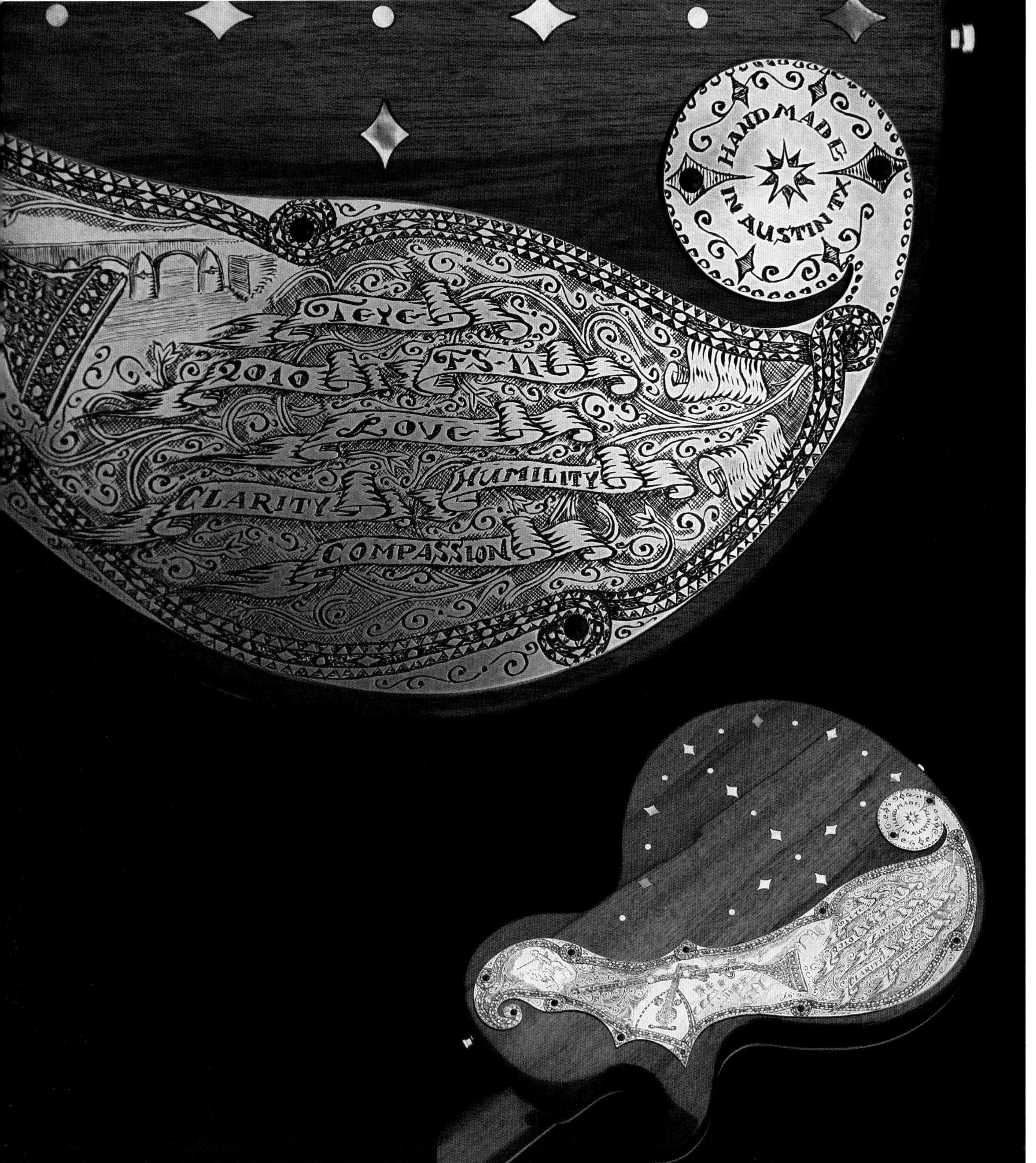
HANDMADE IN AUSTIN TX
TEYC
2010
FS-11
LOVE
HUMILITY
CLARITY
COMPASSION

JAMES TRUSSART

Unlike other, more traditionally inclined, electric-guitar makers, James Trussart uses steel as his primary building material, and his maverick approach allows him to produce guitars that are as distinctive in appearance as they are in tone. "I don't make 'em to please anyone. I make them to please myself. Maybe that's why they're so different," James told *Wired* magazine, which described his trademark SteelCaster model as "equal parts Frank Gehry and H. R. Giger."

James is a Parisian native, a musician turned luthier who began his career as a fiddler, accompanying Cajun singer-songwriter Zachary Richard in the late 1970s. In 1980, he turned his attention to crafting violins and, later, guitars, and eventually began shifting his attention from wood to steel as his medium. Then, in 2000, he moved to southern California, where, from his home workshop, he began crafting custom-made steel-bodied guitars, basses, and violins in a dazzling array of finishes—from elaborately engraved surfaces reminiscent of the shiny metal-bodied resonator guitars of the 1930s to others resembling rusty, weathered, or even discarded machinery. The tone of his instruments—which James, in typically laconic fashion, can only describe as "interesting"—is so distinctive that Trussart guitars have become "must-have" instruments in the arsenals of many influential artists. "I've discovered over the years that there was something magic about it," says James of the tone.

Trussart aficionados like former *Guitar Player* magazine editor and guitarist Joe Gore are far more expansive and precise: "I literally believe [James's SteelCaster] makes me play better," he explains. "I love the [SteelCaster's] combination of ultra-articulate attack and full-bodied sustain. It's almost as if one is playing through a high-quality compressor, only without sacrificing a shred of transient impact. The subtle metallic resonance—that extra midrange peachiness—telegraphs articulation details. I play predominantly with my bare fingers, and I've never before encountered an electric guitar that communicates the texture of skin, nail, and combinations thereof with such breathtaking immediacy. I also find myself better able to 'shape' notes. I think that's a combination of the guitar's innate sustain, the perfect fretwork, the way subtle neck bends complement finger vibrato, and the gratifying 'feedback loop' created when the metal body hums against your chest."

Owners of Trussart guitars include Paul Simon, Eric Clapton, Billy F. Gibbons, Joe Walsh, Jack White, Charlie Sexton, Robert Cray, Daniel Lanois, Marc Ribot, Sonny Landreth, Joe Perry, Tom Morello, Billy Corgan, the Roots, and many, many more—all of whom, James is quick to point out, paid full freight for their Trussarts. "I can't afford to give them away," he explains, and his counterintuitive nonendorsement campaign has produced the kind of advertising that money can't buy.

Trussart guitars are entirely handmade down to their pickups, which are custom-wound by Arcane, Inc., to James's exacting

JAMES TRUSSART OF JAMES TRUSSART CUSTOM GUITARS, LOS ANGELES, CALIFORNIA.

James Trussart, who was born in France, is a former professional fiddler who is renowned for his metal-bodied guitars, many of which he leaves outside to corrode before further distressing, patinating, painting, engraving, and otherwise finishing the surfaces to achieve a host of different effects. The guitars sound as wonderful as they look, a fact borne out by the list of major rock and blues guitarists on James's client list. James is seen here playing one of his flamboyantly painted and etched SteelCaster models.

STEELCASTER (RUSTOMATIC), 2009.

The Trussart RustOMatic finish was named by Billy F. Gibbons of ZZ Top. Gibbons is just one of many prominent musicians to play a SteelCaster; others include Joe Walsh, Robert Cray, Tom Morello, Billy Corgan, Marc Ribot, and Joe Perry.

STEELCASTER (3-TONE GANJA, PERFORATED FRONT), 2007. COURTESY OF GEORGE BORST.

The SteelCaster is James's most popular model, and is offered in a wide array of finishes, including Antique Silver Paisley, RustOMatic Roses, Antique Copper Gator, and this colorful tribute to Rastafarianism's sacred herb. This example has a perforated "holey" front, another of James's many unique options. Every Trussart instrument comes with a slight element of neglect or decay on its surface, giving it a personality of its own.

STEELCASTER (PINK-ON-CREAM PAISLEY), 2008.

The Trussart SteelCaster produces a uniquely enunciated sound that, when played through the instrument's resonant hollow steel body, can range from sweet and crystal clear to aggressive and scream-like. The construction of these instruments is only half the story, however: the other half is the finish. This Pink-on-Cream Paisley is one of James's more elegant offerings.

specifications. The hollow bodies are stamped in France from one-millimeter-thick steel and shipped to L.A., while James buys neck blanks from other area luthiers and shapes and hand-finishes them himself. Every one of the three hundred or so instruments that come out of his shop each year is different, a true custom creation. "I've always liked the look and feel of old guitars, believing them to have a life beyond that of their creator," says James. "You learn from everything that's come before. These guitars are the best of everything I know about my favorite models," which include Teles, Strats, and Les Pauls. "I wanted to somehow emulate the effect of age and history on my own guitars. I wanted to make a guitar that came with a slight element of neglect, of decay, so it had a personality of its own."

James's signature RustOMatic technique (a term coined by the irrepressible Billy F. Gibbons) involves leaving the metal guitar body and hardware exposed to the elements for several weeks, allowing them to corrode before treating them to arrest the natural process. Since every rust pattern is different and basically uncontrollable, this assures that the results are unique. James and his small team of assistants then complete the treatment with paint, engravings, or just sandpaper before finally covering the guitar with a clear satin-finish coat. In addition to a variety of RustOMatic finishes, James offers antique copper, antique silver, shiny nickel, two-tone green, three-tone ganja (red, yellow, and green), butterscotch on black, cream on red, and other color combinations, and many Trussarts

STEELDEVILLE (RUSTY GATOR), 2009.

The SteelDeville has hollow steel body with a single cutaway and a bolt-on maple neck with a recessed steel head cap. The added weight of the steel head cap increases the guitar's sustain.

STEELTOP (ANTIQUE SILVER AFRICAN MAHOGANY), 2009.

The chambered-body SteelTop, which is James's only wooden-bodied guitar, is available with either an alder body and maple neck or a mahogany body and neck. The engraved steel top is recessed into the body. The fret board is rosewood, and the guitar has a 24¾-inch scale length.

are further decorated with engraved or imprinted patterns on their metal bodies, the pick guard, or the headstock. Skulls, roses, dragons, paisleys, and tribal art are among the common themes; others include textural motifs such as snakeskin and alligator skin—for which James literally sandwiches a piece of gator hide between layers of metal and lets the structure sit in water for several days. Another exclusive Trussart option is a perforated "holey" body, pierced with an overall pattern of small, round holes like those found on the inside of a clothes dryer.

Along with the Tele-shaped, single-cutaway SteelCaster, which is his most popular model, James also builds a Strat-like double-cutaway called the SteelOMatic; the lightning bolt–shaped, Explorer-like SteelX; and several other guitar and bass models. He also offers one wood-bodied guitar, the SteelTop—his own take on the Les Paul—which has a chambered alder or mahogany body topped with a steel plate that is recessed into the wooden body. The SteelTop's wooden headstock also carries a recessed steel plate that James says improves the guitar's sustain. Both recessed metal parts can be engraved, perforated, or otherwise treated, and the back of the wooden body, neck, and headstock can be painted China red, satin black, or see-through green—or simply treated with a mahogany stain.

"People realize how much work goes into each guitar, and they realize it's worth the price," Trussart told *Wired* magazine. "It's a passion. If you want to make money, I don't advise you do what I'm doing."

GALLERY OF ELECTRIC GUITARS

A SHOWCASE OF AXES FROM AROUND THE WORLD

LEFT **AIR MAIL SPECIAL.** JEAN-YVES ALQUIER. PERPIGNAN, FRANCE, 2009.

After seeing this one-of-a-kind instrument at the 2009 Montreal Guitar Show, Guitar & Bass *magazine described it as "a jaw-dropping '50s-inspired hollow-body tour de force in eye-aching red with auto-style aluminum binding, a single Charlie Christian pickup, and the appearance of being sucked rather than carved from wood. From the fearless concept to the tiniest detail of the handmade hardware, it was killer." Luthier Jean-Yves Alquier conceived the Air Mail Special as a tribute to the seminal electric guitarist Charlie Christian, and named it after a tune that Christian and Benny Goodman wrote and recorded with the Benny Goodman Sextet in 1941.*

RIGHT **PAPALEOCADA.** JEAN-YVES ALQUIER. PERPIGNAN, FRANCE, 2010.

This tricone electric lap steel guitar and matching amp is the second in an annual series by luthier Jean-Yves Alquier—the first being his Air Mail Special (left). The striking design includes a special custom magnetic Benedetti pickup and a custom Jégou KT66 valve amp, which Alquier designed and had made by a specialist specifically for this guitar.

Alquier explains, "The Air Mail is the first part of a concept story: Papaleocada is the second part of this story, and for me it's very important for people to know that I make a concept year after year with all the same elements—red color, same contour, same philosophy, using the same metals [titanium and stainless steel], maple, and mahogany—to make totally different electric or electro-acoustic guitars."

The guitar's name came from Alquier's infant daughter. He was in Canada for the Montreal Guitar Show, and, when he called home, his wife asked their then-year-and-a-half-old daughter where her papa was. She said, "Papa lé au Cada," *which is baby French for* "Papa, il est au Canada" *(Papa is in Canada). "I thought that sounded Hawaiian," says Alquier, "and I had just conceived of my tricone two days before, so that became its name. I like to take all the anecdotes around my life and include them in my work. It's strange, but it's my way of inspiration. In French we call that* 'faire les choses sérieusement sans se prendre au sérieux'*: do things seriously without a serious mind, or with a fun attitude . . . or something like that."*

LEFT **BEN HARPER SIGNATURE MODEL SERIES II LIMITED EDITION.** BILL ASHER. VENICE, CALIFORNIA, 2010.

With its classic flame-maple top, this collaboration between luthier Bill Asher and lap slide master Ben Harper combines the look and tone of a '59 Les Paul, the unique vibe of a vintage Weissenborn acoustic Hawaiian guitar, and the feel and sustain of Asher's own highly regarded lap steels. Its solid African mahogany neck runs through a mahogany body with cylindrical tone chambers; a pair of Seymour Duncan'59-style humbuckers completes the picture.

RIGHT **ANNA.** JERRY AUERSWALD, AUERSWALD INSTRUMENTS. KONSTANZ, GERMANY, 2009.

Jerry Auerswald is probably best known for the Symbol Guitar he built for Prince in 1993, but he has created many other visually unorthodox guitars over the years. He says his basic idea is that the instrument is a tool and a transport medium for the artist's creativity. "For that reason, I lay great stress on his individual prerequisites. Everything has to be in just the right place and harmonize with the musician's physique and ergonomic needs."

Auerswald is a perfectionist who builds very slowly, producing only about a half dozen instruments per year. He is currently working on a special-commission piece that will sell for more than one hundred thousand dollars. He holds a patent on the sustain bow, the stabilizing arm seen on this instrument, which connects the head and body. The sustain bow provides extra support to the upper neck and produces longer sustain.

ABOVE **PADAUK-AND-SATINWOOD CUSTOM**. ANDREW WRIGHT, AW CUSTOM GUITARS. ALOHA, OREGON, 2009.

Andrew Wright of AW Custom Guitars built his first guitar in 1996 with no intention of starting a business. "Being a player myself," he explains, "I was just seeking a higher-quality instrument than was readily available on the market."

Wright, who has a BA in music from California State University, Fullerton, where he studied with jazz guitar great Ron Escheté, says his goal is to help put the art of lutherie back into electric guitar building, which he feels has long been overshadowed by the art of manufacturing. "All AW Custom guitars are built to the exact specifications of my customers. I often find that a musician has a particular tonal, visual, or functional aspect that he would like incorporated into his instrument. It is these types of challenges that make my work interesting." With the exception of its ebony fingerboard, this AW Custom was built entirely of nontraditional tonewoods. Andrew says it sounds as unique as it looks, with "a rare combination of warmth, depth of tone, and incredible sustain."

ABOVE RIGHT **JBD-300**. BRUCE BENNETT, J. BACKLUND DESIGN. CHATTANOOGA, TENNESSEE, 2009.

Master luthier Bruce Bennett and entrepreneur Kevin Maxfield formed J. Backlund Design in 2007 to bring the retro-futuristic guitar designs of illustrator John Backlund from concept to reality in the form of world-class instruments. The company has produced five models that are based on Backlund's illustrations, and is developing a number of others.

John Backlund is a self-taught artist and designer who has worked as a commercial illustrator and a fine artist. Of his delightful guitar illustrations, he observes, "I like color in my designs. I like bright things. I like two tones that complement each other. I like a splash of chrome for contrast, and I like it all integrated into a flowing form that is balanced, well proportioned, and pleasing to the eye. Solid-body electric guitars are a tempting and wonderful subject for my style of design, and, because I have been a guitar player for many decades, it's only natural that they figure prominently in my efforts."

This JBD-300 has an African mahogany body and neck and a bird's-eye maple fingerboard with ebony dots and side position markers. The body and neck are painted in a three-stage "Heritage Cherry" paint scheme with a custom "Marble Tortoise" pick guard. The guitar is equipped with both top-mounted and pick guard–mounted electronics, as well as a Lace Music Products Alumitone humbucker in the bridge position.

RIGHT **B3 WATER.** GENE BAKER. ARROYO GRANDE, CALIFORNIA, 2010.

Gene Baker, whose alter ego is a shredder known as Mean Gene, is a master luthier, author, columnist, CAD/CAM engineer and programmer, entrepreneur, and working musician—in other words, a man who lives, eats, and breathes guitars. After graduating from jazz guitar great Howard Roberts's Guitar Institute of Technology (now the Musicians Institute) in 1986, Baker tried and failed to become a rock star, then taught thousands of lessons, built guitars under the Mean Gene name, and produced an instruction book and video called Mean Gene's Insane Lead Guitar. *Baker now builds his own b3 designs as well as instruments by other designers, including Swiss nuclear physicist Luca Zanini and the Premier Builders Guild collective.*

The b3 guitar comes in what Baker describes as five "flavors"—Earth, which is a flattop; Metal, a neck-through; Fire, a carved-top solid-body; Wood, available with either a chambered or a hollow body; and Water, the top-of-the-line hollow-body model, which has a carved top and back. Combinations of elements, such as an Earth-Wood model (a flattop with a hollow body) or a Fire-Metal model (a carved-top neck-through), are also possible. Baker does not take orders, but instead builds on inspiration and the raw materials at hand, and then distributes the results through a network of dealers. "Because of this," he explains, "we are able to offer a wide variety of models and options. You'll see a vast array of woods, various control layouts, inlay features, color schemes, scale-length choices, and an assortment of hardware and pickup combinations."

QUILTED MAPLE MODEL 15. VICTOR BAKER. BROOKLYN, NEW YORK, 2009.

Victor Baker is both a master luthier and a professional jazz guitarist who describes himself as a "total guitar maniac." He began playing guitar in 1980, when he stole his sister's cheap acoustic out of her room, and says he soon developed a tendency to tear apart and reassemble every guitar he came across. He attended Berklee College of Music on a partial scholarship after performing "a crazy stunt-like eight-finger string-tapping Bach invention for a professor." After a variety of touring and gigging experiences, he studied privately with jazz legend Pat Martino and "switched up" to playing jazz full time.

Baker branched into building guitars in the late '90s and quickly found himself completely obsessed with the craft. Since then, he has built more than two hundred instruments and relocated from Philadelphia to New York City, where he continues to balance a busy life of lutherie and jazz. This is the last guitar Baker built before moving his studio to Brooklyn. The back, sides, neck, and headstock are all made from spectacular quilted maple, which provides a powerful contrast to the solid-color top.

ELECTRO RESONATOR. STEVE EVANS AND BILL JOHNSON, BELTONA RESONATOR INSTRUMENTS. WHANGAREI, NEW ZEALAND, 2009.

Luthier Steve Evans and engineer Bill Johnson introduced the world's first metal hollow-body electric resonator guitar in 1995. This new model, by contrast, is created from glass and carbon fiber, a construction approach that Beltona pioneered. The result is a small, lightweight instrument that, like Beltona's original design, combines magnetic and piezo cone pickups. The guitar can be played without amplification, and its small body belies its acoustic tone, which is full, sweet, and punchy. Under amplification, the magnetic P-90 pickup in the neck position and piezo resonator pickup on the cone combine to give a wide variety of tones. The pickups are wired together into an onboard preamp with a volume control for each pickup and a mono line out.

NUCLEUS 003. ANDREW SCOTT, BLINDWORM GUITARS. COLORADO SPRINGS, COLORADO, 2009.

Andrew Scott's guitars are made from a wide array of unusual materials, which he chooses for both their visual appeal and sonic qualities. His Nucleus 003 has a body of slightly figured poplar, a roasted-maple neck with padauk stripes, and an Osage orange fingerboard. The planet-bearing tree-of-life inlay on the fingerboard was cut from box-elder bark and has jade foliage. Scott explains that it stands atop "a turquoise earth with continents made of dinosaur bone and diamond dust. The tree grows planets of purple shell, red and blue tigereye, purple beetle-kill ponderosa pine, and picture jasper. As the tree's planets mature, they fall to the sky, toward the camphor burl sun." The term "beetle-kill" comes from the fact that ponderosa and other pines are sometimes killed by beetles that burrow into the trees to lay their eggs. The beetles carry a variety of fungi with them into the tree, which stain the wood as the tree dies.

The guitar's nut was carved from a single meteorite collected in northwest Africa, and the side fret markers are inlaid dinosaur bone circled in Osage orange, with jade, turquoise, and meteorite at the twelfth and twenty-fourth frets. Last but not least, the control knobs, which are also Osage orange, are topped with "planets" of labradorite and spotted maple with blue tigereye.

LEFT **ELECTRIC GUITAR 3** (LUST GODS AND CHILD TIME). BLUEBERRY GUITARS. VILLE SAINT-LAURENT, QUEBEC, 2010.

Blueberry guitars represent an unusual marriage of East and West, combining the skills of North American and Balinese wood-carvers. This solid-body electric guitar, which has a 25½-inch scale length, was made under the supervision of master Balinese wood-carver and luthier Wayan Tuges. The body is solid mahogany, and the neck is a combination of ebony and maple. The fret board and headstock are Macassar ebony, and the inlays are a combination of mother-of-pearl and a light-colored wood that Tuges purchased in Bali. The carving on the headstock is done with the same Balinese wood, which was stained and then inlaid into the block of Macassar ebony that comprises the entire headstock. The carved dials are made of solid Macassar ebony.

The intricate carvings on the top of the guitar tell a Hindu legend. The Hindu god Shiva and his wife, Uma, are depicted on the upper part of the top. They were promiscuous gods whose seed fell to earth and produced a child named Kala, who is depicted on the lower part of the top. Kala, who, as the god of time—and, therefore, death—has power over all living beings, is one of the most powerful and frightening gods in Hindu mythology. He was born in part to remind his parents that all things, including lust, have a proper time and place.

RIGHT **F4C.** BORN TO ROCK DESIGN. NEW YORK, NEW YORK, 2006.

Conventional guitar necks have to be rigid to keep the strings straight and prevent the neck from warping. The decidedly unconventional Born to Rock guitar (U.S. Patent 4,915,009) was invented by a guitar player who realized that the tension of the instrument's strings could be used to position its neck and keep it straight. The Born to Rock F4c is crafted of lightweight aluminum tubing with a wood-backed aluminum fret board. The neck, bridge, and pickups are a floating unit suspended from the headstock and body by pivoting joints, and string tension is conveyed from the headstock to the body via a piece of tube that is designed to bend as it takes up tension, without affecting the neck.

BORN TO ROCK

LIQUIDWING CUSTOM. SIGGI BRAUN FINE YOUNG GUITARS. GÖPPINGEN, GERMANY, 2009. COLLECTION OF ALEX HÄRTEL.

Siggi Braun is a mechanical engineer and guitar player who built his first guitar in his father's basement workshop. He founded his company in 1993, and now works with a small production team. As a player, Braun was always frustrated by the neck-body joint on his guitars, which he found either clumsy in feel or not stable enough. To remedy this problem, he invented his proprietary CNS System (Comfortable Neck Segment System), which is cut from a solid piece of wood and combines the advantages of a bolt-on and set-in neck in a single unit.

This one-off Braun custom was built for Alex "Lahnsteiner" Härtel, who plays bass in the metal band Arma Gathas. It has a master-grade quilt-maple top on a korina body with a five-millimeter-thick mahogany "backtop," a black walnut neck, and an ebony fret board. It carries a pair of humbuckers designed by Braun himself.

LEFT **MARK I CUSTOM**. BREEDLOVE GUITAR COMPANY. BEND, OREGON, 2009.

The Breedlove Guitar Company, which grew out of surfer Kim Breedlove's decision to turn his attention to lutherie in the 1970s, has built a strong reputation for its high-quality acoustic guitars over the course of four decades. Breedlove himself designed the asymmetrical body shapes that are his company's trademark, and was a trendsetter in the use of sustainable native Pacific Northwest tonewoods, such as walnut, Oregon myrtle, Western red cedar, Sitka spruce, and redwood.

Breedlove's new electric guitars share the ergonomically designed, asymmetrical forms of their acoustic predecessors as well as the company's commitment to quality materials and workmanship and environmentally friendly practices. This top-of-the-line custom-built Mark I has a shallow (1¾-inch), two-piece chambered Honduran mahogany body with a sharp right-hand cutaway, a carved figured redwood top with dark "burst" edges, and gold hardware. The mahogany set-in neck has a hand-rubbed finish, and the guitar is equipped with a pair of Lollar Imperial humbuckers.

RIGHT **ARTISAN SERIES #3, CLARO WALNUT APOLLO.** JACK BRIGGS. RALEIGH, NORTH CAROLINA, 2009.

Jack Briggs worked in the printing industry for a decade before opening his own guitar business in 1999. He is an accomplished musician who first picked up a guitar in 1971, and says that his thirty-year experience as a professional musician gives him a shortcut to the builder—namely, himself.

On this guitar, "the only non-wood parts are the mother-of-pearl nut, the electronics, the hardware, and the strings," Briggs declares emphatically. "No plastic parts at all! To say that the instrument has a 'woody' tone would be an understatement." It has a one-piece Spanish cedar body with a carved, flame-claro-walnut top and a one-piece Madagascar rosewood neck with an African blackwood fingerboard that is inlaid with light-colored African blackwood sapwood on its face and heartwood on its side. All the bindings are also African blackwood sapwood, and the pick guard, tuner buttons, headplates, pickup rings, switch tip, control knobs, and cover plates are blackwood heartwood. And, Briggs points out, "the guitar features a rear headplate/skunk stripe/heelplate. I had never seen these parts made as a one-piece continuous part, so I thought it should be attempted!" As for the metal parts, the pickups are Tom Short TomBuckers, and the hardware is nickel.

LEFT **HAMPDEN SKYLINE.** BEN BRUTON, BRUTON STRING WORKS. SPENCERPORT, NEW YORK, 2010.

Ben Bruton is a former professional musician who earned an MFA and worked as a furniture maker before he began his touring career. He says he is still an "aspiring guitarist." He laments that he was never able to find a guitar on the market that fit his specific criteria for tone, responsiveness, and ergonomic function, so he eventually ventured into building his own. After several years of apprenticeship under master luthier Bernie Lehmann, Bruton founded Bruton String Works, where he combines his considerable experience as a practical working musician with his experience as a skilled woodworker.

The Hampden Skyline is Bruton's most recent model. Its asymmetrical body is fully chambered on the bass side and has three additional chambers on the treble side, so it is light and easy on the shoulders. The Skyline comes with a lipstick pickup on the neck and another single-coil pickup on the bridge. Ben notes that "from neck to bridge position you can go from creamy to as much spank and honk as you can handle, and if that doesn't satisfy your palate, you've got the option of dual P-90s or dual Humbuckers."

TOP RIGHT **NELSONIC TRANSITONE.** DEAN CAMPBELL, CAMPBELL AMERICAN GUITARS. WESTWOOD, MASSACHUSETTS, 2008. COLLECTION OF BILL NELSON.

Dean Campbell touts his company's commitment to old New England craftsmanship and ingenuity, and his decidedly retro-looking guitars offer an unusual mix of Fender and Gibson influences without obvious visual reference to either company's classic designs. The space-age "Rocket Ship Red" Nelsonic Transitone, which was built with input from the multitalented English guitarist and artist Bill Nelson, has a solid Honduran mahogany body equipped with a pair of Seymour Duncan humbuckers and a 25 ½-inch-scale-length ebony fingerboard with two red coral "atom" inlays at the twelfth fret. Guitar Buyer *magazine summed up the appeal of the guitar in its review: "The Nelsonic's sounds and playability are both so good that this guitar feels almost addictive. It's very hard to put down once you start playing it, and when you grow used to the fact that beneath the quirky image lies an achingly gorgeous and highly usable guitar, there's almost no going back."*

ABOVE **WORMY MAGPIE.** SAM EVANS, CARDINAL INSTRUMENTS. AUSTIN, TEXAS, 2010.

Luthier Sam Evans's Cardinal Instruments is dedicated to producing unique musical instruments using a socially and ecologically responsible approach. The company specializes in building with locally harvested and salvaged woods, including not only traditional tonewoods such as walnut, cherry, and ash but also such local Texas woods as mesquite, pecan, persimmon, Texas ebony, bois d'arc, and Eastern red cedar. Evans is a big fan of vintage Danelectro guitars, and his bare-bones designs reflect that aesthetic, which he has brought into the twenty-first century and adapted to reflect contemporary concerns about sustainability and the integrity of local work.

The body of this wild-looking guitar was made from a single piece of worm-eaten sinker cypress—wood that has been submerged for nearly a century, then milled and air-dried for another ten years. The guitar has a one-piece bocote neck and fret board, and carries a Lollar P-90 bridge pickup and a Cardinal custom-wound H/O pickup in the neck position. Of this guitar's name, Sam says, "I studied birds quite a bit as an undergrad. Corvidae have fascinated me for years, and the magpie is as smart as the crow and raven. They're clever, resourceful, and tough. Not to mention pretty!"

RIGHT **BARITONE ACOUSTIC-ELECTRIC.** HARVEY CITRON. WOODSTOCK, NEW YORK, 2010.

Harvey Citron is a guitarist, bandleader, and former architect who has been building guitars, basses, and pickups since 1974. He built his first baritone guitar for his friend and neighbor John Sebastian, who fronted the Lovin' Spoonful in the '60s. Citron recalls, "John had been playing Fender six-string basses tuned down a fifth and strung with strings gauged from .016 to .080. The sound was amazing, and enchanting. He used to capo at the second fret or so to make the reach a little bit more manageable. My then-partner, Joe Veillette, and I built him a 28¾-inch-scale baritone that worked very well for him."

Citron's own baritone model was also originally designed for Sebastian, who called it the best baritone he had ever heard. The Citron acoustic-electric baritone is tuned B–B, a fourth lower than a standard guitar, and has twenty-four frets. It has a 2½-inch-thick hollow mahogany body with a maple top (spruce is also available), a one-piece maple neck, and a pao ferro hardwood bridge with an extra-thick compensated bone saddle. The guitar carries two Citron custom-blended humbuckers, which Guitar Player magazine said produce huge, deep sounds that make the instrument "a thing unto itself." The humbuckers can be run alone or in tandem with the EMG under-the-saddle piezo pickups, which add acoustic tones to the mix.

OPPOSITE PAGE **COLLINGS 360.** BILL COLLINGS, COLLINGS GUITARS. AUSTIN, TEXAS, 2009.

Founded by luthier Bill Collings in the mid-'70s, Collings Guitars has grown steadily over the years, from a one-man operation to a twenty-two-thousand-square-foot shop with more than fifty full-time employees. Collings built his reputation on his high-quality acoustic flattop guitars, which have been played by everyone from Joan Baez, Emmylou Harris, and Joni Mitchell to Keith Richards, Pete Townshend, and Steven Spielberg. Then, after thirty-two years of building acoustic instruments, he decided to try electric guitars, a move that he saw as a natural extension of his carving experience. He says he thought making electric guitars was going to be easy, but he discovered he was dead wrong. It took more than seventy prototypes to arrive at a guitar he felt comfortable putting his name on, which turned out to be "an electric that is acoustic enough to add some complexities to the sound rather than relying on the pickups to do it all."

The 360, which is named after Loop 360, a scenic highway that winds through the hills of western Austin, Texas, is loosely based on a Les Paul, although its body shape is somewhat stretched in comparison, and it is thinner and lighter than a classic LP. This custom-made left-handed 360 has a solid one-piece Honduran mahogany body and a fully carved, premium quilt-maple top, both of which are finished with a crimson high-gloss nitrocellulose lacquer. The mahogany neck has a 24⅞-inch-scale length, an East Indian rosewood fingerboard, and an ebony peghead veneer. The neck is hand-set, with mortise-and-tenon joinery, and the guitar has black pickup rings and knobs. The 360 is equipped with custom minihumbuckers by Jason Lollar and has what Collings calls "'50s-style wiring," by which he says he means that "the tone circuit is attached to the wiper, or output, of the volume pot instead of the input side, where the pickup comes in. This makes the tone circuit less sensitive, so it doesn't get muddy when the volume decreases. It helps maintain clarity by not bleeding off the highs as the volume decreases."

LYRIST. BILL COMINS (PAINTED BY ANNIE HASLAM). WILLOW GROVE, PENNSYLVANIA, 2009. COLLECTION OF BOB MILES.

Bill Comins started playing guitars as a kid and majored in jazz guitar performance at Temple University. He worked in a violin shop for several years and also maintained his own repair business. After building several instruments on his own, he sought out master archtop luthier Robert Benedetto and, under his tutelage, built his first archtop guitar in 1992. He opened his own shop in 1994, and got his first big break a couple of years later when the late Scott Chinery invited him to participate in his Blue Guitars project. (Chinery, who had collected a remarkable group of historic archtops by Gibson, John D'Angelico, Elmer Stromberg, Jimmy D'Aquisto, and other luthiers, invited eighteen contemporary archtop builders to create a unique guitar, specifying only that its lower bout be eighteen inches wide and that it carry a deep blue finish developed by D'Aquisto.

The Lyrist, which Comins describes as possessing "an unpretentious yet poised aesthetic, evocative of the violin world," is his only solid-body electric model and features a carved maple top on a mahogany body. This unique Lyrist was painted by Annie Haslam, who, while best known as the lead singer of the English progressive rock band Renaissance, is also, as this guitar attests, an accomplished visual artist.

SIDEWINDER CUSTOM. BILL CONKLIN. SPRINGFIELD, MISSOURI, 2009.

Bill Conklin is known for his unusual and dramatic combinations of woods. This one-of-a-kind Sidewinder has a hand-carved, spalted-maple top with a matching headstock cap, a carved curly-Spanish-cedar body, and a three-piece multilaminated hard-maple neck with a cocobolo fingerboard.

The guitar is also loaded with state-of-the-art electronics, including Lundgren humbuckers, RMC piezo saddles, and an RMC thirteen-pin polyphonic output. This allows the guitar to be connected to a pitch-to-MIDI converter, a device that turns single-note lines into streams of MIDI data that can drive a synthesizer and produce any sound the synthesizer is capable of. Separate outputs for the piezo and magnetic pickups give the instrument even wider possibilities.

LA PALOMA. ERIK SMITH, CROW HILL GUITARS. CEDAR RAPIDS, IOWA, 2010.

Erik Smith of Crow Hill Guitars says that the ultimate focus of his work is, and has always been, comfort and playability, and his attention to these factors extends to the hand-carved wooden and buffalo-horn picks he makes for his customers. "I cradle and caress each instrument I build to ensure absolute comfort, whether the player is standing or sitting," he explains. "The size, weight, and shape of the body are designed and monitored throughout the building process to create the proper overall balance, and the electronic controls are positioned so that they are easily accessible while playing." Smith carves his necks asymmetrically, so they fit the curvature of the hand, and also carefully carves and shapes the neck heel, the forearm cut, and the belly contour on the back of the guitar.

This guitar is a chambered semihollow-body electric that has a body of Nicaraguan cocobolo on top of African wenge, African mahogany, and Nicaraguan cocobolo, with curly-maple veneer accents. The seven-piece neck-through design is made from African wenge, Brazilian macacauba, and purpleheart with curly-maple and wenge-veneer accents, and the fingerboard is Indian rosewood. Smith added black and white mother-of-pearl and abalone inlays on the neck, fingerboard, and body, and fitted the guitar with a pair of Nordstrand NDC pickups and a three-way toggle switch.

GRETCHEN. PETE SWANSON, DAGMAR CUSTOM GUITARS. NIAGARA-ON-THE-LAKE, ONTARIO, 2010.

Pete Swanson has pioneered a new approach to guitar construction that started when he was working for a custom yacht manufacturer and saw a senior woodworker construct a wooden urn by gluing thin strips of wood at specific angles to form a tube shape. Pete first used the technique to make wooden bicycle fenders, which he shaped in a reverse S curve so they swooped up at the rear. Once he was successful at reversing the curve, the idea of building a guitar came almost immediately.

One of Swanson's realizations was that a guitar rim shaped like one of his wooden bicycle fenders would have a kind of "amphitheater" effect on the sound. After all, Swanson's voice rang loud and clear in his own ears when he talked into the concave bicycle fender to amuse his kids. He also realized that a guitar rim made in this new way—void of any straight, hard edges—would be comfortable for the player. So he developed a procedure for shaping the guitar rim ergonomically, then reinforced it with carbon fiber, and added a top, a back plate, and a bolt-on neck.

Swanson developed this guitar's double-cutaway body with the help of a grant from the Ontario Arts Council. Gretchen's rim is a checkerboard of cooked flame maple and flame maple; the top is mahogany, and the back is flame claro walnut. The guitar's laminated neck is made of cooked flame maple and carbon fiber cloth. The neck pickup is a TV Jones Power'Tron, and the bridge pickup is a Power'Tron Plus.

TELSTAR. GENE BAKER AND CHAD UNDERWOOD, DESTROY ALL GUITARS. FUQUAY-VARINA, NORTH CAROLINA, 2008. COLLECTION OF CHARLES DAUGHTRY.

The Telstar is a collaborative venture among session guitarist Matte Henderson, luthiers Gene Baker and Chad Underwood, and guitar consultant and marketer Cliff Cultreri, who heads the consortium and builders' guild Destroy All Guitars. As its name suggests, the Telstar is intended to marry the best of Fender's flagship models, the Telecaster and Stratocaster, in a single modern instrument. Cultreri says that the heart of the Telstar is its versatility. "There's no such thing as one Swiss Army knife that does everything," he explains, "but there certainly are some instruments that do more than others. Guys who play Strats and Teles can now get it done with this [one guitar]. You don't need to bring two."

The Telstar embodies DAG's twin slogans: "Modern Vintage Mayhem" and "Schizophrenic Mojo." Matte Henderson, who developed the concept for this guitar, says, "Part of 'schizophrenic mojo' is balancing aesthetics and functionality. I wanted this to have that classic '50s Leo [Fender] aesthetic, but I wanted any modifications we made to enhance the playability—to scream out when you play it, not when you look at it."

The Telstar is now being made by Lance Lerman's LsL Instruments, which has been able to drive the price point down by consolidating the work that Baker and Underwood were doing separately.

16-INCH HOLLOW-BODY. ROB ENGEL. STAMFORD, CONNECTICUT, 2010.

Rob Engel calls his guitars "not your average hollow-body," and is proud of the fact that they produce little or no feedback, even at high volume levels. The electronics on this guitar include two Lindy Fralin humbuckers on a four-conductor cable wired in series, parallel, and single-coil formation so that each pickup can produce three different sounds.

The top of this guitar is quilt maple, and the sides and back are butternut. Butternut (Juglans cinerea) *is a member of the walnut family that grows throughout the eastern United States and produces sweet, oily nuts that give the tree its common name. The tree's soft, coarse-grained wood works, stains, and finishes well, and is often used for cabinetry, furniture, and wood carving. Engel, who is one of the few artisans who use it regularly in guitars, says "butternut is great stuff. It has a really good acoustical response, plus it is light in weight—about twenty-six or twenty-eight pounds to the cubic foot. I use it for backs and sides on my electric guitars, and it is actually my favorite wood for the solid-bodies I make." The neck and headstock veneer also are quilt maple, and the fingerboard is ebony.*

LIGHT BODY GUITAR. DAVID ENKE. LA VETA, COLORADO, 2005. COLLECTION OF JEFF DOCTOROW.

David Enke's Light Body Guitar, which is designed to use acoustic strings and can be played as a standard acoustic guitar, carries twelve sympathetic strings in its neck—an idea Enke borrowed from early instruments in the violin family. The Light Body produces an extremely natural and convincing acoustic tone when plugged into an amp or PA system, and the sympathetic strings add another dimension of overtones and richness that is typically the exclusive domain of acoustic instruments. Electric sounds can be mixed in from the magnetic pickup, allowing the guitar to be driven into distortion and feedback modes without getting out of control.

The Light Body's hollow neck is made from precisely mitered staves of wood joined in opposing grain orientations to increase stiffness and stability. The guitar is indeed very light and comfortable to play, regardless of whether the player is sitting down or standing up. Enke's clever design leaves a full twenty-seven frets clear of the body joint, which allows not only extraordinary access to high notes but also a variety of options for the use of capos. When a capo is put on the twelfth fret, for example, the instrument essentially turns into a piccolo guitar. A specially designed three-position mute allows the player to choose whether the sympathetic strings ring open, are muted, or buzz like those on a sitar or tamboura.

MR. EUGEN CUSTOM. HENRY EUGEN. BERGEN, NORWAY, 2009.

Henry Eugen has been building high-quality custom guitars and basses since 1979, and now builds exclusively to order. "My philosophy is to combine excellent craftsmanship with a sensitivity to my customers' needs, creating instruments that will bring out the true musician in you," he explains. "Each instrument is crafted by hand from the ground up, based on the customer's preferences, so every Eugen guitar or bass is a truly one-of-a-kind instrument."

This 25 ½-inch-scale Mr. Eugen Custom, his top-of-the-line model, has a one-piece mahogany body with a two-piece AAA-grade flame-maple top and a mahogany set-in neck with a pao ferro fingerboard. The body is designed with a three-inch neck joint, which assures solid set-in construction, and the guitar is equipped with a Rio Grande Genuine Texas pickup at the neck and a Rio Grande BBQ pickup at the bridge.

'50S TELECASTER RELIC LTD (PAINTED BY SHEPARD FAIREY). FENDER CUSTOM SHOP, FENDER MUSICAL INSTRUMENTS CORPORATION. SCOTTSDALE, ARIZONA, 2005.

The Telecaster has been in constant production and demand since its official introduction in 1951, and Fender has created myriad special and limited-edition variations of the basic design over the years. Each guitar in this particular limited edition of thirteen—no two are alike—is decorated with unique custom art by Shepard Fairey, whose purposefully contradictory work straddles the worlds of street art, propaganda, and commercial advertising. Fairey first gained notoriety in 1989, when his "Andre the Giant has a Posse" stickers hit a nerve and mysteriously began appearing in public spaces all over the world. Fairey went on to create his own business and viral marketing campaign called Obey Giant, and also designed the well-known "Hope" campaign poster for Barack Obama in 2008.

SHAKES 1 QUART
GOLD FROZEN
1947
Cars
Cars

BELOW **GEO BLUE**. HARRY FLEISHMAN. SEBASTOPOL, CALIFORNIA, 2010. COLLECTION OF RICHARD MERMER.

Harry Fleishman has been building and designing highly creative and innovative basses, guitars, pickups, and sound reinforcement systems since 1969, and figures he has hand-built some three hundred and forty instruments since then. He says that he was inspired and obsessed with music and art at a very early age—"if you can call surf music 'music' and model cars 'art' "—and that he has always loved fixing things, "even when it meant breaking them first." In addition to building custom-made instruments, he designs guitars for several companies, most notably Fender, and spends about half of his time teaching guitar making and directing the Luthiers School International, the training program he founded in Sebastopol.

Although Fleishman's focus over the years has been primarily on basses and acoustic flattop guitars—he designed and built the first fretless upright electric bass and has pioneered asymmetrical design in both basses and flattops—he occasionally turns his attention to electric guitars as well. This is his most recent design, made as a showpiece for the 2010 Newport Guitar Festival in Miami Beach and for luthier and collector Rich Mermer. Fleishman explains that the guitar has an alder body and a maple neck with a blue finish. It also incorporates, in his words, "blue Plexiglas for the flat layers and stucco for the sides. The pickups are custom-made, with odd-shaped covers, and, when you turn a pickup on with the PUSH button, an LED lights up next to that pickup. The trem is a Trem King, which is a hardtail when you are playing, but becomes a trem as you use it. It stays in tune, and sounds great. I designed this guitar using Photoshop and Microsoft Word, which changed the entire way I thought about the aesthetics and the structure."

RIGHT **STAG LEAP**. CHARLES FOX. PORTLAND, OREGON, 2010.

Charles Fox is a pioneering luthier, designer, and educator who has been building guitars since 1968 and is currently director of the American School of Lutherie. His original design concepts, such as the "thin-line" acoustic guitar, as well as his building techniques and production devices, such as the universal side bender, are widely used by guitar builders and factories all over the world, and he has mentored hundreds of young luthiers over the years. In the late '70s and early '80s, Fox's GRD Guitars, based in Vermont, helped define the market for high-end electric guitars. He has focused primarily on acoustic guitars since moving west in 1983, but he is easing back toward electricity with this new design.

Fox says the solid-body Stag Leap, which is named for a modern dance move of the same name, is "an exercise in lyricism and muscularity that aims to capture the dynamic gesture of free expression." He adds, "I hand-carve each instrument—no CNC [machining], mechanical duplicator, etc., is involved. There's nothing practical about doing it this way, but the result is a unique sculptural statement that represents this artist's personal vision, judgment, taste, and skills at a moment in time." Although the Stag Leap's dramatic appearance qualifies it as an "art guitar," Fox says that it also sounds as good and plays as well "as any guitar possibly can." The Stag Leap's on-board electronic setup offers a broad soundscape of electric guitar voices for everything from clean, quiet jazz to mind-bending, overdriven lead work. The Stag Leap's neck is figured hard rock maple, and its body is alder—a classic formula for a classic feel and sound.

LEFT **MARNIE STERN'S PINK PAISLEY SF3-CLF.** SCOTT FRENCH. AUBURN, CALIFORNIA, 2008. COLLECTION OF MARNIE STERN.

Scott French says that his decision to become a luthier was inspired by his mother, who at some point asked what he would do if money were no object. "I thought about it a while," French recalls, "and said I would probably go to school and learn how to build the instruments I had been planning and thinking about for years." After discovering that his grandmother had left him some money for his education, he enrolled in the Roberto-Venn School of Luthiery and ultimately landed an apprenticeship at the First Act Studio for Artists in Boston. After that, he moved back to California and opened his own shop.

The SF3 is French's flagship model. The design incorporates a refined treble-side horn and a "reverse" rear line that French says "puts more meat on the bass side, where some players are used to resting their wrists." Marnie Stern is a New York guitarist, singer, and songwriter best known for her virtuoso, rapid-fire, two-handed string-tapping technique. This is her main stage guitar.

BELOW **50TH ANNIVERSARY KORINA TRIBUTE.** CUSTOM, ART, AND HISTORIC DIVISION, GIBSON GUITAR CORPORATION. NASHVILLE, TENNESSEE, 2008. COLLECTION OF MATTE HENDERSON.

In addition to making dead-on copies of its original models, Gibson's custom shop has also created some creative original variations on their own themes. This one, a korina-bodied mashup of a Les Paul Custom, a Futura (the fork-headed precursor of the Explorer), and an ES-5 Switchmaster, celebrates the fiftieth anniversary of Gibson's original korina guitars, the Flying V and Explorer.

The Korina Tribute was the brainchild of Edwin Wilson, program manager of the company's Custom, Art, and Historic Division, and is considered by many players and builders to be one of Gibson's best ever. Session guitarist and Gibson endorser Matte Henderson, who owns one of the one hundred Korina Tributes in the limited-edition run, says, "It's cool to see such a 'reissue/glory days–heavy' company have a little fun. This has an element of nonconformity that is still steeped in the traditional. There's also an elegance in the simplicity of the execution—no flame-maple top, no fingerboard binding, just good old white limba, doing what it's supposed to do. I've had forty-five historic Les Pauls since I signed on with Gibson in '94, but this takes the cake."

GS CUSTOM. PATRICK GIGLIOTTI, GIGLIOTTI CUSTOM GUITARS. TACOMA, WASHINGTON, 2009.

Patrick Gigliotti has a patent pending on his unique Gigliotti Voicing System, which combines a chambered wooden thin-line body with a brass or aluminum top. The metal tops are cut and finished with a water jet to create their distinctive patterns, then mounted flush to the face of the guitar so that they "ring like a bell." Each Gigliotti instrument is built entirely to order, and buyers can choose from a host of options, including sixty different clear, satin, solid, tinted, dyed, and "sunburst" finishes. Blues-rock guitarist Joe Bonamassa, who is the instrument's best-known player, affirms Gigliotti's claims about the instrument's tonal versatility and tuning stability, and says he gets so many comments about the guitar's looks after shows that he made printed information cards to hand out to interested fans.

POPPYGIRL. CHRIS LARSEN (PAINTED BY JANET MILLER), GIRLBRAND GUITARS. TUCSON, ARIZONA, 2005.

Janet Miller recalls her first conversation with Chris Larsen, the mad genius behind GirlBrand Guitars. "I had just started painting on glass, and I got a phone call from some wacko saying he had started building electric guitars and if he could work out how to cut tops out of glass would I consider painting them? I said, 'Uh, sure, buddy, call me when you get that together.' I figured I'd never hear from him again. But he called me back after a year or two and said he had cut tops out of Plexiglas, and would I consider painting on that? It sounded like fun, so I said yes."

PoppyGirl is a prime example of their playful collaboration, with a bright top depicting opium poppies, painted by Miller with sign-painter's enamels, and elaborate complementary neck inlay by Larsen. The toggle-switch options are WANT *and* NEED, *and the guitar is equipped with a pair of Larsen's own VOLCANIC single-coil pickups.*

Janet Miller lived and worked in West Africa for most of the early 1980s and first encountered reverse glass painting, a process of painting backward on the wrong side of clear glass, in Senegal, where it is a traditional art form. "The synergy of paint and glass has a depth and luminousness I've not seen in any other medium," she explains. "I am often asked if it's tedious or frustrating working inside out and backward, but I'm left-handed and dyslexic, and for me it feels natural and comfortable."

ROLLERCOASTERGIRL. CHRIS LARSEN (PAINTED BY JANET MILLER), GIRLBRAND GUITARS. TUCSON, ARIZONA, 2005.

GirlBrand guitars are not only hysterically funny but also smartly and differently built. Why the name "GirlBrand"? "I usually say that it's because guitars, like boats, are always female, and one can take that pretty far," Larsen explains. "But really I think that 'girl' is just such a terrifically loaded word—a word that's so general and yet so powerfully specific."

Larsen says that RollerCoasterGirl is his favorite Janet Miller top. "The heart on a plate, the roller coaster with the stars in the sky, the fishnet stockings—wow!" Miller explains that the image came from a painting she originally did on flat glass and reproduced on Plexiglas at Larsen's request. "The image came from my dating experiences after being in a twenty-year relationship. The thrill! The ouch! I felt very vulnerable, but was ready for whatever happened next. It was also inspired by the Giant Dipper in Santa Cruz, California, where I grew up. It's a fabulous 1920s wooden roller coaster, a jarring, rattling, creaking, bone-shaking, noisy ride. It's a glorious artifact of monumental foolishness and beauty. When I was young, I never considered riding it; I was afraid of it. During this particularly fragile time in my life, I started to ride that roller coaster and came to love it. So the painting is about embracing fear and calling it by another name, about enjoying the wild ride instead of avoiding it." Note that the toggle-switch options are THROB *and* ACHE.

For all his guitars, Larsen hand-built the pickups from scratch, crafted bodies of anodized aluminum over a wooden core, and made the backs from either phenolic resin or Formica over birch plywood. However, Larsen was, unfortunately, forced to stop building in 2008 because of extreme reactions to all the chemicals he was using. He says he is hoping to go back to it, "though not in quite so intimate and poisonous a way." As of 2010, Janet Miller tells us, he has moved on to reviving the lost Mexican art of making colored cast-concrete floor tiles, using ancient machinery he salvaged from a warehouse in Mexico. "If Chris ever gets back into making guitars," she adds, "I would jump at the chance to work with him again. It was hilarious, joyful play."

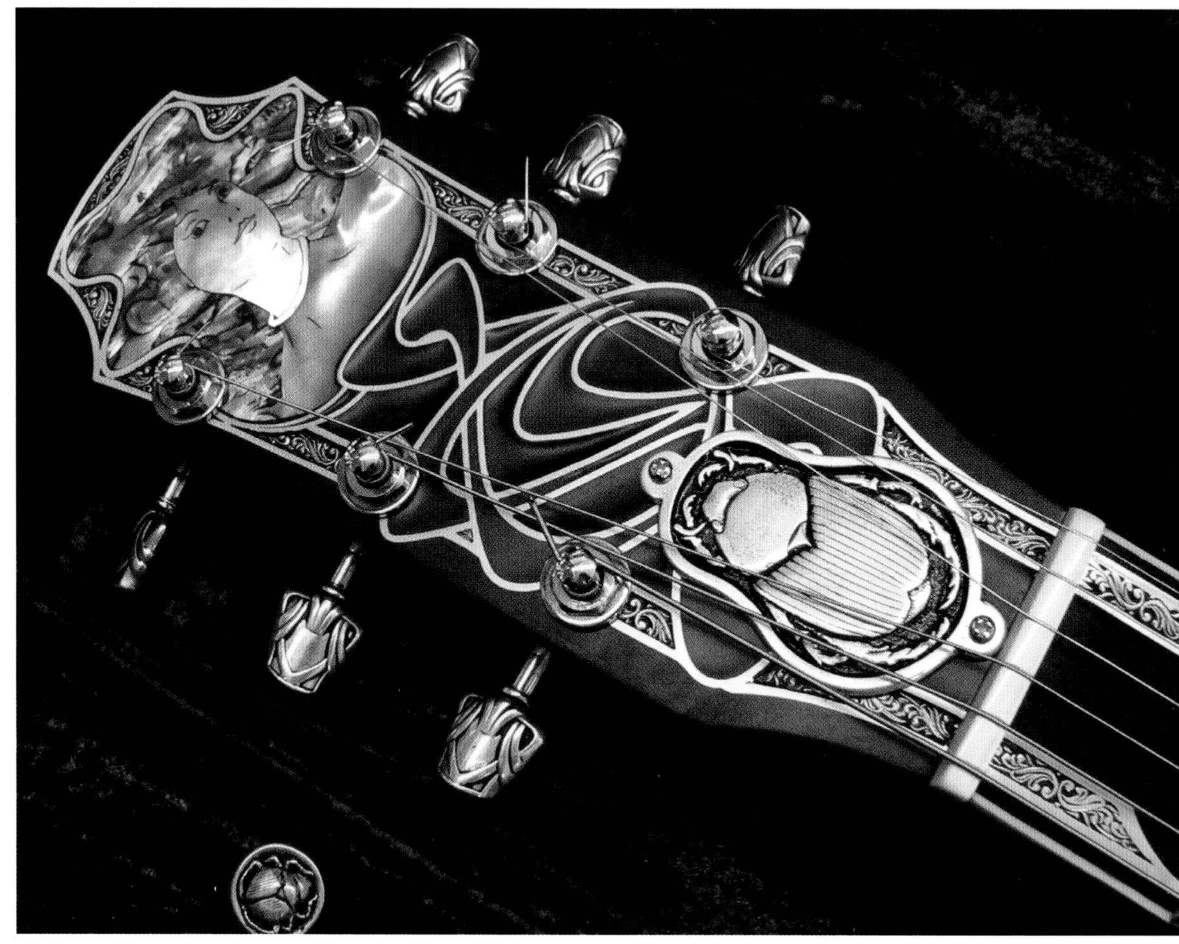

LEFT AND ABOVE **LENORE**. SAM "SANDY" WINTERS AND DANIEL BAUGHMAN, GOLDBUG PRODUCTS. DELAVAN, WISCONSIN, 2009.

GoldBug Products, which was founded by professional musician and instrument maker Sandy Winters in 1977, is best known for its handcrafted sterling silver ornamental tuning knobs, bridge pins, and other cast-metal hardware, which have been used on high-end guitars built by Gibson, Martin, and a number of independent master luthiers. The company, which takes its name from a famous story by Edgar Allan Poe, is now moving into building its own guitars, and the Lenore, fittingly, is a limited edition of forty guitars built to commemorate the two hundredth anniversary of the poet and short-story master's birth. Named after a typically tragic Poe poem—an "anthem for the queenliest dead that ever died so young"—the Lenore has a South American mahogany body and neck and a solid flame-maple carved top complemented by solid sterling silver hardware, inlays based on Poe's works and themes, original GoldBug-designed Tru-Tap pickups, and a hand-rubbed antique violin finish.

CUSTOM ALUMINUM GUITAR. ANTHONY GOULDING, GOULDING GUITARS. ESSEX, ENGLAND, 2010.

Anthony Goulding and his team of craftsmen make the bodies of Goulding guitars from a two-inch-thick billet of aluminum that is machined from the rear to make it hollow. The front is machined to mimic the look of a carved wood top, and the neck is also made from solid aluminum. Goulding offers customers a wide variety of options; he designed this guitar's gold-plated brass tailpiece and pickup surrounds as well as the knobs and strap buttons. The guitar carries a pair of Seymour Duncan humbuckers and an active L. R. Baggs piezo bridge pickup.

RESERVE PLEXIJET #059-09 (6120 ORANGE). DON GROSH, GROSH GUITARS. BROOMFIELD, COLORADO, 2009.

Don Grosh grew up helping his father build sets for Hollywood film productions, so it isn't surprising that he eventually became a master carpenter. He is also a long-time guitar player, and in 1985 he joined Valley Arts, a famous guitar-building shop in North Hollywood, California, that is now owned by Gibson. With Don as shop foreman, the company quickly grew to employ thirty-five workers, who created guitars for such elite musicians as Larry Carlton, Leland Sklar, Vince Gill, and Lee Ritenour. Don founded Grosh Guitars in 1993, and his company now offers seventeen different models in a vast array of colors and custom options.

The Grosh Reserve is a collection of premier guitars designed and specced personally by Don Grosh and his shop crew and released on a periodic basis either as one-of-a-kind guitars or in very limited numbers. All Grosh Reserve guitars feature master-grade, old-growth body and neck woods from Don's personal reserve, and offer configurations and features not available in his other guitars. This unique Reserve PlexiJet has an alder body painted in 6120 Orange—named after the Gretsch 6120's distinctive color—a maple neck and rosewood fingerboard, a pair of TV Jones FilterTrons, a Gotoh 510 vintage-style tremolo bridge, and a translucent silver Plexiglas pick guard.

MODEL 228. CHIHOE HAHN. GARNERVILLE, NEW YORK, 2009.

Chihoe Hahn has been a working musician for more than thirty years. He has been "fixing, tweaking, and modifying guitars" for more than twenty years, and has been building guitars in his one-man shop for five years. "Every screw is put in by me, and every point is soldered by me," he says. He also makes most of the parts he uses, including the bridges, saddles, knobs, and neck and control plates. "Basically, I began making guitars out of my desire to find an ultra-responsive, clear, articulate guitar that sounded like the old country, soul, and rock records that I love." Hahn's stated aim is to "make a simple guitar, the right way." He adds, "I am building the guitar that you would have bought as a pure production model in the '50s. The sound of a Hahn guitar is unmistakable—it's new, but it sounds old. You can break it in or relic it yourself by playing it!"

Hahn's inspiration is Leo Fender's original Telecaster, which he describes as "probably the most basic design in a guitar that you can have." As he explained to Premier Guitar*, "You can't even break it down beyond how it has been broken down. So that is really what I try to stay true to: the absolute simplicity of the design. And I sort of stay away from anything that is either ornate or tone-sucking. I just keep it as plain as it can be."*

SWITCHBLADE CUSTOM. WILLIAM HARNDEN, HARDEN ENGINEERING. CHICAGO, ILLINOIS, 2010.

Bill Harnden of Harden Engineering (whose last name is slightly different from the name of his company) says that his pickups are really the heart and soul of his guitars. "I spent many, many hours wasting wire," he explains, "until I achieved the right combination of magnetic field and turns of wire. My guitars are a marriage between a pickup and the wood that surrounds it."

Harnden dreamed of being a musician and supported himself doing a variety of jobs, working as a machinist and cabinetmaker before landing a gig as a repairman for another Chicago-based luthier. There he started forming his own ideas about guitar design, and after eight years of experimentation, came up with the design for the Switchblade. His company, Harden Engineering, which creates guitars, pickups, and "Flaming Skull" booster/distortion boxes, is "dedicated to creating one-of-a-kind collectible instruments that retain all the high points of American guitars of the '50s and '60s." All the work is done by hand by Harnden and a single apprentice—although, Harnden says, "occasionally my thirteen-year-old pitches in!"

Every Switchblade is customized with the customer's choice of woods, inlay, pickups, and neck shape and size. This Switchblade has a chambered korina body, a pao ferro fingerboard, aged-copper hardware, and a bleached-white body finish. The pickups are Harnden's humbucking models, and the neck is carved in an offset V profile similar to high-end Gretsch guitars of the '30s and '40s, which Harnden describes as "very resonant."

FAR LEFT **S2.** GRAHAM AND PARIS HENMAN. HOLLYWOOD, CALIFORNIA, 2010.

Henman guitars represent a fusion of minimalism, craftsmanship, art, and old-school quality. The S2's body is one-piece African mahogany with a figured North American maple top and headstock. The 25 ½-inch-scale neck is three-piece African sapele with a figured Macassar ebony fingerboard. The three-piece neck is a unique design that reduces string tension by up to eighty percent over traditional guitars. Truss-bar adjustments, while rarely necessary, are performed by removing a plug on the back of the guitar and simply inserting a supplied Allen driver and making minimal turns in the desired direction. The neck pickup is a WCR Crossroads humbucker and the bridge pickup is a WCR Godwood humbucker. Both are hand-wound and tappable, so they offer a range of tones not often found on a single guitar.

Since January 2011, all Henman guitars have been built by master luthier Rick Turner and are offered with a variety of new options. The S2 has been renamed the Mod.

LEFT **327.** SAUL KOLL AND JEAN-CLAUDE ESCUDIE, HOTTIE GUITARS. PORTLAND, OREGON, 2010.

Jean-Claude Escudie's Hottie Guitars has built a name for itself for its retro-sounding humbucking pickups and its powerful little solid-state amps, which come housed in vintage American toasters for visual effect. The company has now stepped into guitar building with the help of independent master luthier Saul Koll. Guitar Player *magazine described the new Hottie 327 as "strutting onto the scene like a dressier Les Paul Junior back fresh from the city with a new sharkskin suit and a crisp, flattop haircut." The no-nonsense guitar has a solid mahogany body, a mahogany set-in neck, an ebony fret board marked only with side position dots, and a single Hottie humbucker—which, on this example, is painted with symbolic flames.*

LEFT **STANDARD.** IAN ANDERSON, IAN A. GUITARS. SAN DIEGO, CALIFORNIA, 2009.

Ian Anderson started his professional career in the early '90s with luthier and restoration expert Scott Lentz. His ideas of what makes a great guitar have been informed by Lentz's influence and by hands-on experience with the hundreds of historic Fenders and Gibsons that have come through the Lentz shop.

While continuing his work with Lentz, Anderson launched his own business in 2008. He describes his Standard model as "an instrument for the modern world, a guitar inspired by the 'holy-grail' instruments of the 1950s and built with materials and techniques from generations past." It has a hand-carved, slip- or book-matched Eastern red-maple top on an old-growth Honduran mahogany body, and a mahogany neck with an old-growth Indian rosewood fingerboard. The Standard's 24.625-inch scale length is modeled after '50s Gibsons. Anderson reinforces his necks with old-style single-action truss rods, uses hot hide glue to hold things together, hand-builds his own pickups, and mixes his own nitrocellulose lacquer colors.

RIGHT AND FAR RIGHT **MODEL 1925.** JOSEPH JESSELLI. HUNTINGTON, NEW YORK, 2010.

Joseph Jesselli designs and builds cutting-edge acoustic and electric guitars inspired by the art deco and art nouveau movements of the early twentieth century. He proudly calls his work "something of an anachronism; modern technology seamlessly blended with an elegant and classic aesthetic." He told The New York Times *that he also is inspired by gun and furniture makers and by "skilled artisans who served true apprenticeships and know how to use their hands," a group he believes is a dying breed. "To me, an artisan has to chop stuff, really do a good job, like a wood-carver," Joseph says. "A guy who inlays, a guy who gilds, a guy who finishes. These take lifetimes to really master."*

This art deco–influenced guitar, named after a central year in the history of the art deco movement, has a Circassian walnut body cut from Jesselli's private stash of choice woods, pieces he calls the "filet mignon of the tree." Unlike most luthiers, Jesselli insists on compete control of his materials and makes or casts every part of his instruments' hardware himself, including this guitar's elegant art deco tuners.

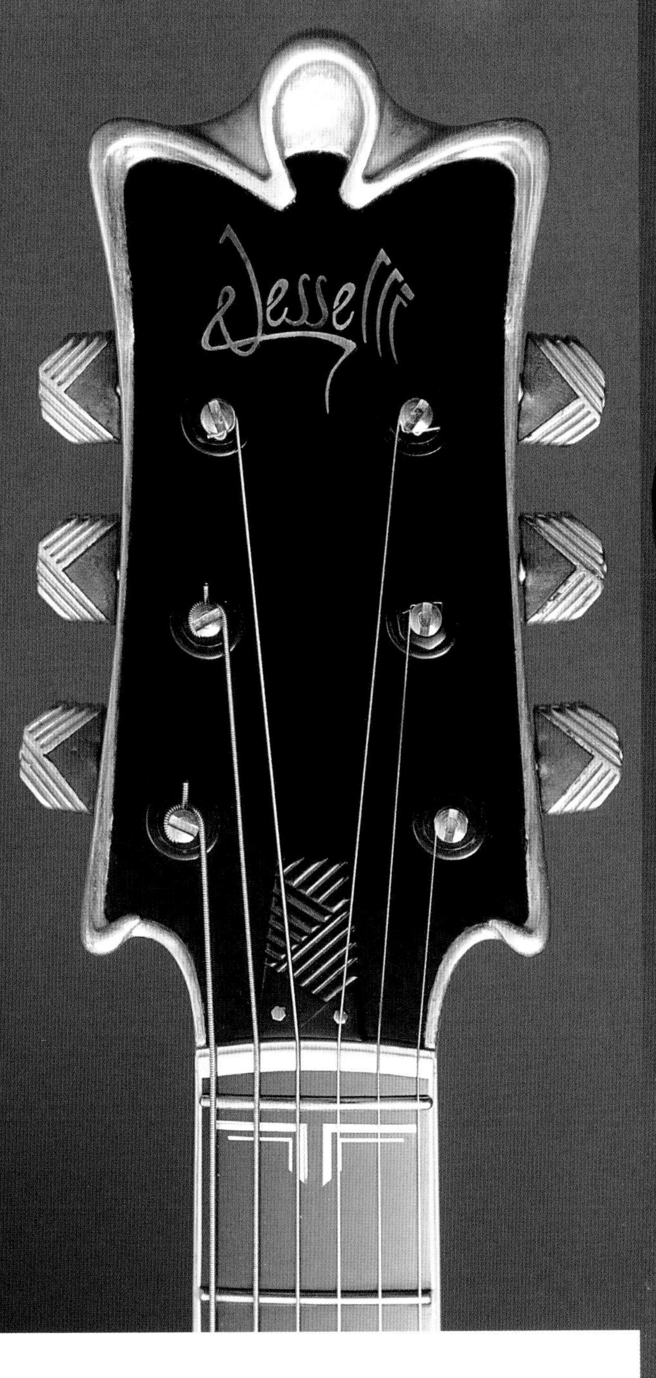

LEFT **GOLD MODERNAIRE**. JOSEPH JESSELLI. HUNTINGTON, NEW YORK, 2009.

After apprenticing with a wood-carver, for whom he made and gilded frames for paintings and mirrors, Joseph Jesselli served a second, multiyear apprenticeship with James D'Aquisto, whom many experts and fellow luthiers consider the greatest guitar maker of all time.

Jesselli crafts only a handful of guitars each year, taking five to six months to complete each one. "A lot of people design their guitars for a market niche—Les Pauls do this and Fenders do that," he told The New York Times. *"Well, I don't do that. I make my guitars for me, so that people who are like-minded, they're going to die for these guitars." Keith Richards, who is among the like-minded owners of Jesselli guitars, played one on the Stones' video for "Undercover of the Night."*

This understated art nouveau–influenced guitar, which showcases Jesselli's combined skills as a woodworker and metalsmith, has gold-plated hardware that he designed and cast himself, including an elegant stylized tailpiece reminiscent of a long-tailed butterfly.

RIGHT **SPECTRA-SONIC SUPREME.** THOMAS V. JONES, TV JONES, INC. POULSBO, WASHINGTON, 2009.

Tom Jones has built an enviable reputation for the pickups he has designed for Brian Setzer, Gretsch, and many other companies and players over the past two decades. He founded TV Jones, Inc., in 2001, and subsequently began building his own guitars while continuing to offer a variety of high-quality pickups.

The Spectra-Sonic Supreme is an upgraded version of a Jones design that was originally distributed by Gretsch. The TV Jones–branded version has a semihollow chambered alder body with a maple back and a figured-maple top, and carries a pair of TV Jones TV Classic pickups and a Bigsby vibrato. Jones explains that he "went with a new design, which features an ebony fingerboard and custom 'shoestring-potato' inlays, which are similar to what I used back in the '90s on a lot of my custom guitars. I also thought it would set it off [visually] if the whole instrument were bound—the headstock, fingerboard, and the body . . . I also thought it would be a great idea to use TV Classic pickups, which give great clarity in the low end, instead of the Power'Trons, which were used in the Gretsch models. Also, the finish is lacquered, which was really important to me."

BARN BUSTER. RON KIRN. JACKSONVILLE, FLORIDA, 2010.

Ron Kirn modestly describes himself as "just this old guy that makes guitars." But he knows as much about vintage Fender Strats and Teles as anyone on the planet, and builds some of the most exactingly crafted guitars available today, all based on Leo Fender's classic designs. Kirn began experimenting with making his own guitars in the late 1970s. "With the awful stuff Fender was putting out then," he says, "it was almost necessary if you wanted a decent Strat. I got pretty good at it and wrote a few books to help others who wanted to give it a try." Based on his detailed studies of vintage Fenders, he also created templates for his designs, which have been used by hundreds of amateur builders.

As a student of classic Fenders, Kirn believes that "it doesn't matter what wood you choose—a Strat is still going to sound Strat-like and a Tele will always sound like a Telecaster. It really comes down to parts and quality of construction." That said, this guitar is one of a group Kirn built from loblolly pine salvaged from a barn that was built in 1898. Loblolly pine (Pinus taeda) *is the same lumber Leo Fender used for the very first guitars he made, and many Fender fanatics consider those the finest-sounding instruments of all. "What makes such aged lumber superior?" Ron asks rhetorically, and then explains: "Prior to use, lumber is dried, but drying only addresses water moisture. The resins, however—what we called sap as youngsters—take many more years to fully crystallize. I am among those who feel that those resins inhibit the resonance of the body. It takes about fifty years for crystallization to occur, and that is often touted as the reason that older guitars sound so wonderful."*

The Barn Buster's body is shaped to 1950 Broadcaster specs and finished with genuine nitrocellulose satin lacquer in a natural amber tint. The pickups are Kirn's own custom-wounds ("alnico V, Formvar-coated copper, Forbon bobbins, beeswax and paraffin, scatter-wound by hand, vintage-style"), the knobs are Bakelite top hats in triple-chrome-plated solid brass, the pick guard is genuine lacquered Bakelite, and the guitar weighs in at about seven and one-half pounds.

CHILI AND SQUIGGLEY. MARK KNOWLTON. TIGARD, OREGON, 2010.

Mark Knowlton gives each of his unique creations a nickname—examples include Bluto, Mr. Big, Zoot Suit, Mr. Peabody, Rochester, and Rocky and Bullwinkle. All the guitars in his 2750G-6 line—including Chili and Squiggley—feature book-matched tops and backs that surround a hollow core. Chili and Squiggley have hollow cherry cores and oil finishes; Chili (on the left) has a Peruvian walnut, maple, and mahogany top and back, and Squiggley has a flame-maple and walnut top and back. Each carries a single Bill Lawrence L-600 pickup and a single volume knob.

CUSTOM SEVEN-STRING. SAUL KOLL. PORTLAND, OREGON, 2003. COLLECTION OF JEFF DOCTOROW.

Saul Koll says that he has had an interest in how things are made and what makes them work since his childhood in southern California, and freely admits that "while other kids were playing sports, I was in the garage taking expensive toys apart and gluing the components into weird new contraptions." He started playing the guitar when he was twelve, studied art in college, continued making "contraptions" ("under the guise of sculpture," he says), and played and sang in several bands, most notably the Charms, a highly regarded pop-rock outfit he describes as "very successful artistically; a profound failure commercially." He began building and repairing guitars in the mid-'80s, and after being mentored by Jon Peterson and Glen Mers at World of Strings in Long Beach, California, he launched the Koll Guitar Company in 1990.

Koll is a fearless and open-minded builder who has made everything from traditional acoustic archtops and straight-ahead Strat-style solid-bodies to "multistring extended-range freak-outs" that may be related to his ongoing love of contraptions. He has created guitars for a number of today's most innovative and discriminating players, including Matte Henderson, Henry Kaiser, Lee Ranaldo of Sonic Youth, Elliott Sharp, and David Torn. This prototype for a carved-top seven-string was built for Henderson, who, as Koll notes, has probably owned more custom instruments from more custom shops than anyone else on the planet. This was the first guitar that Henderson specced out with Koll. It has a 1 3/4-inch white-limba back and a half-inch-thick carved Eastern blister-maple top, a one-piece pernambuco neck with a skunk stripe, Michael Stevens rod-magnet seven-string P-90 pickups, and a Hipshot seven-string tremolo.

CLASSIC. MARK LACEY. KINGSTON SPRINGS, TENNESSEE, 2009.

Mark Lacey is an English-born luthier who has built and repaired instruments for dozens of prominent musicians, including Aerosmith, Howard Alden, Jackson Browne, Duran Duran, Herb Ellis, Pink Floyd, John Fogerty, Leo Kottke, Paul McCartney, Terje Rypdal, Sting, Andy Summers, Tiny Tim, U2, and Stevie Ray Vaughan. He first studied musical instrument technology at the London College of Furniture, and then spent four years in Oslo working as a repairman for Norway's largest importer of musical instruments before vintage expert and dealer George Gruhn lured him to Nashville to work in his repair shop. There, he was exposed to older archtop and flattop guitars for the first time, and had the opportunity to examine the D'Angelicos, D'Aquistos, and Gibsons that became his standard of excellence. After subsequently working for pickup designer Bill Lawrence in Los Angeles and for Guild in Westerly, Rhode Island, Lacey returned to L.A., and in 1988 opened the Guitar Garage just off Sunset Strip in Hollywood. He hired two men to help with the workload, and within a short time they were inundated with repair work, which allowed him to devote his time exclusively to building. Since then, he has concentrated on archtops, and in 1995, he returned to the Nashville area, where he continues to work in his home shop.

Lacey's Classic model, which he designed for jazz and R & B players, has a fifteen-inch-wide mahogany body that he routs out on both sides to create sound chambers, leaving a solid center core. The top is hand-carved spruce, which, when combined with the maple, results in an incredibly warm tone that retains some of the acoustic properties of a full-size archtop and also reduces feedback. The neck is mahogany with an ebony fingerboard, and the optional brass tailpiece is hand-engraved and plated in eighteen-karat gold. Two Gibson '57 Classic humbucking pickups, combined with a three-way selector switch, two volume controls, and one tone control, complete the electronics. Mother-of-pearl inlays and ivoroid bindings add the finishing touches.

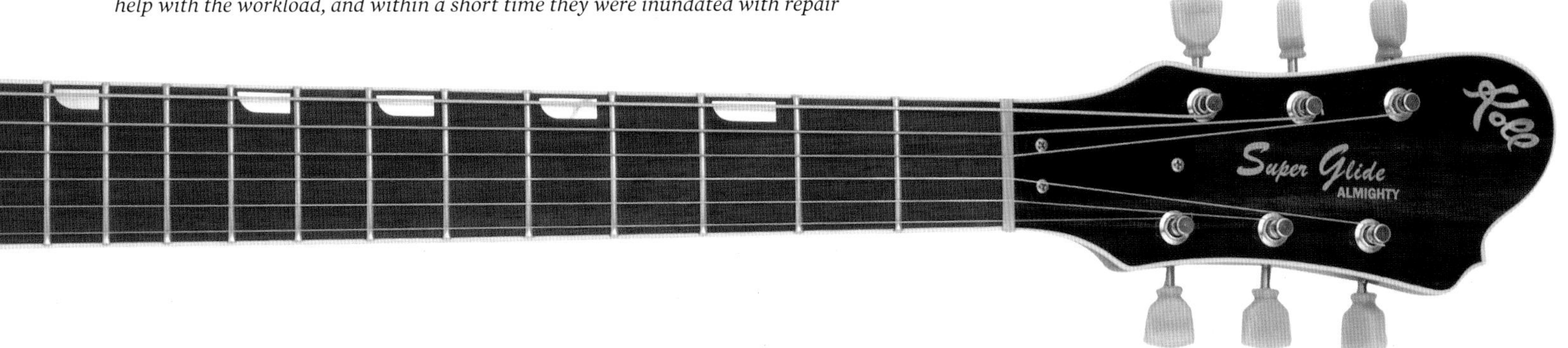

SUPER GLIDE ALMIGHTY. DESIGNED BY SAUL KOLL (PORTLAND, OREGON) AND BUILT BY GENE BAKER (ARROYO GRANDE, CALIFORNIA), 2010.

Saul Koll's Glide series is based on an original design that he describes as "new yet familiar." He offers the Glide in a variety of configurations, with many pickup, binding, and trim options. All the Koll Glide models are designed by Koll and built by Gene Baker at the Premier Builders Guild workshop.

The Super Glide Almighty is the flagship Glide, the top of the line, boasting every conceivable feature, including a chambered mahogany body bound in ivoroid and a hand-carved flame-maple top. This "Fiesta Red" example has a 24.625-inch-scale mahogany neck with a rosewood fingerboard and mother-of-pearl thumb inlays, a headstock with bound ebony veneer and a mother-of-pearl Koll logo, a Bigsby B3 tremolo, and a pair of Lollar humbuckers.

Koll calls the Super Glide Almighty the ultimate electric guitar, and suggests that guitarists "bow down; repent; submit; order."

LANGCASTER. JOH LANG. AUCKLAND, NEW ZEALAND, 2009.

Joh Lang is a Dutch-born inventor who builds the bodies of his guitars from the oldest workable wood in the world: thirty-five-thousand-year-old swamp kauri, milled from logs that have been found just under the surface of farm fields and ranch lands in northern New Zealand. Kauri (Agathis australis) *is a conifer that has grown in New Zealand and other countries around the Pacific Rim for some 175 million years. New Zealand's remaining preserves of living kauri trees are now protected. Swamp kauri is similar to cherry in density and to basswood in texture, but its grain and color are unique.*

Although the use of swamp kauri certainly affects his guitars' sound, Lang asserts that the pickups on any electric guitar are far more important than its wood or design. And, because he could not find pickups that satisfied him, he invented his own extremely low-impedance pickups, which he has coupled with a built-in overdrive preamp, also of his own invention. To prove his point about the importance of pickups, Lang attached a Langcaster neck and pickups with overdrive to a retrofitted beer crate, à la Les Paul and his Log. His videos of the "beer crate guitar" are both funny and convincing; without question, it rocks.

BLOND SOLID-BODY. HOWARD ROBINSON, LINDSAY WILSON GUITARS. BARNSTAPLE, ENGLAND, 2010.

Howard Robinson is a former rock-and-roll guitarist and road manager who began building guitars after his thirty-year career in custom-fitted period furniture design and manufacture was destroyed by the worldwide recession. Although he still makes built-in cupboards and cabinets for a select group of clients, he has now launched a second venture as a guitar maker. Under his Lindsay Wilson brand, Robinson builds about six unique instruments per year. Lindsay and Wilson are the middle names of Howard and his wife, which he says he picked because it sounded good and very American, pointing out that "Lindsay can be a bloke's name, and where guitars are concerned, America has it covered, much as I hate to admit it."

In making built-in furniture, Robinson explains, "I had a lot of freedom to add my own style. Whereas freestanding furniture is usually made by cabinetmakers, fitted furniture is more often made by joiners and carpenters, a distinct difference. I think it is the same difference as that between a luthier and a guitar maker: I see a luthier as someone who makes acoustic instruments and a guitar maker as someone who makes solid-body electrics—again, different skills. I love warmth, soul, balance, good proportion, harmony, shape, and texture, so I like my guitars to be like cherished pieces of furniture. I can't stand the over-lacquered, crisp, sharp factory instruments. While they may be incredibly accurate, they lack the warmth and soul of one person putting his effort and passion into one single instrument."

This example of Robinson's work has a solid body of reclaimed English elm that he bleached and limed, a solid maple neck, and a flame-maple headstock. The ebony fingerboard is inlaid with a Japanese-influenced birds-in-peony decoration made of mother-of-pearl, abalone, reclaimed stone, acrylic, and briar.

LMG "T." LIQUID METAL GUITARS. VANCOUVER, BRITISH COLUMBIA, 2010.

Liquid Metal's motto is "Fighting global warming by making extremely cool guitars," a mission the company accomplishes by crafting the bodies of their instruments from aircraft aluminum. The body is machined from a solid block of aircraft-grade 6061-T6 aluminum to a proprietary thickness. The top and sides are contiguous, so the body is quite rigid, and because the aluminum shields the electronics, the guitar produces little or no hum. In addition, aluminum is far more dense than wood, so the energy of sounded strings stays intact much longer, ultimately making for a clearer, purer sound. The tool marks on the outside of the body are left in place for an industrial look, and the body is coated with a scratch-resistant clear finish developed by AkzoNobel for use on luxury cars, giving the machining a sense of depth and adding overall luster to the surface. The neck is Canadian hard rock maple with an ebony fingerboard.

Pickup maker Seymour Duncan was so intrigued by the sonic possibilities of LMG instruments that he designed special pickups for them. The Seymour Duncan LMG Custom Wind Phat Cat pickup in the neck position creates what the company describes as "a beautiful buttery tone," and a Seymour Duncan Little '59 pickup on the bridge takes full advantage of the body's unique characteristics.

RADIOSTAR (BARITONE GUITAR). LEONARDO LOSPENNATO. BERLIN, GERMANY, 2010.

Leo Lospennato, who is the author of a book on electric guitar and bass design, describes his instruments as "retro-futuristic designs," adding, "They look as if someone designed them back in the '50s, trying to anticipate the looks of a guitar from the twenty-first century. . . . My main influences come from the '50s and the '60s, cartoons like The Jetsons *and those fantastic concept cars that never made it into production." His RadioStar baritone guitar has a subtly carved solid mahogany body, a bolt-on flame-maple neck, and a third control knob that acts as a blender, allowing the two pickups to be mixed any way the player chooses.*

T-BONE (VINTAGE CREAM). LANCE LERMAN, LSL INSTRUMENTS. VAN NUYS, CALIFORNIA, 2009.

Lance Lerman's LsL Instruments has built its reputation on its T-Bone model, which re-creates the look, feel, and sound of vintage '50s Telecasters. This T-Bone has a lightweight, handmade swamp-ash body, a fully handmade, C-profile maple neck with a walnut skunk stripe, and LsL's own custom hand-wound vintage-style pickups. All the metal parts are manually aged for a vintage look and feel, and each guitar's fingerboard is manually worn in patterns copied from photographs of actual vintage instruments.

LEFT **BLU MEANIE**. SCOTT MACDONALD. HUNTINGTON, NEW YORK, 2009.

This one-of-a-kind custom-built guitar has an African mahogany back and a maple top with figuring that "rolls down the sides like a waterfall," as luthier Scott MacDonald puts it. The Yellow Submarine–themed fingerboard inlays for which the guitar is named were sketched by MacDonald and brought to life by inlay master Larry Robinson. MacDonald and his client chose custom-made Lindy Fralin high-output humbuckers to complete the guitar and provide what MacDonald describes as "a powerful voice great for blues and rock, full and warm, with punchy crisp highs and no muddy mids."

RIGHT **LAPRO ELECTRIC RESONATOR GUITAR**. DAVE BEGALKA, MANKATO WOODWORKS/LAPRO GUITARS. NORTH MANKATO, MINNESOTA, 2009.

Dave Begalka's Lapro is a new spin on an old concept that combines elements of square-neck resonator and lap-steel guitars. Begalka explains that he was turning maple burls one night when he noticed that a half-finished bowl sitting upside down on his workbench had the same overall size and proportions as a biscuit-style resonator cone. "It occurred to me that it might be possible to make an electric guitar with a turned-wood resonator cone," he recalls. And it was.

The Lapro's maple resonator cone carries a piezo transducer that provides a bright, responsive, yet feedback-resistant tone, and the instrument's body-mounted magnetic pickup produces a full-bodied electric sound. The sound samples on Begalka's Web site back up his claim that the instrument can "cover territory from clean traditional bluegrass to thick electric blues to ethereal and experimental" types of music.

ABOVE **TAOS GLOSS SPECIAL**. ANDREA BALLARIN, MANNE GUITARS. SCHIO, ITALY, 2010.

Andrea "Manne" Ballarin founded Manne Guitars in 1987 and has built an international reputation for his high-quality, handcrafted, solid-body electric guitars and basses. The Taos Gloss Special, which is based on an original design that Guitar Player *magazine called "as bold and purposeful as a Ferrari," is the company's top-of-the-line model. It has an African korina body topped with hand-selected, deeply figured Italian burled poplar and a set-in, rock-maple neck with a thin and fast fret board molded from synthetic phenolic resin, which produces a precise attack without dead notes. The neck has a multilaminated core of European beech, a unique Ballarin invention, and its asymmetrical shape ensures playing comfort. The guitar is equipped with two Manne blade minihumbuckers and a Manne blade bridge humbucker.*

Ballarin decided to switch to resin fret boards when he discovered that after a long day under the lights at a guitar show, all his instruments needed to have adjustments made to their wooden necks. "As I watched the other exhibitors," he explains, "it was clear that maintaining good instrument action would require much morning and evening work! My thought was, 'I can do better than this!'" It took five years to find the right supplier with the right material, but Ballarin swears by his fret boards now. "Our necks sound much more like maple necks than phenolic necks," he explains. "I would say they are just a little less glassy than all-maple necks, but they have better durability and stiffness."

Ballarin uses a number of European woods in his guitars, including beech, ash, alder, and Italian yew. Of the burled poplar that tops his Taos Gloss Special, he says he and his team inspect about one hundred cubic meters of poplar trunks, boards, and even freshly cut trees each season, looking for the right consistency, color, and wood grain. "The species we look for," he explains, "has yellow and pink striped sections with striking flames and curious textures."

LEFT **CREMONA DELUXE 90** (LEMONBURST). GEORGE GORODNITSKI, MASTER HANDMADE GUITARS. LOS ANGELES, CALIFORNIA, 2008.

George Gorodnitski is a versatile builder who makes—by hand—an extremely wide variety of acoustic and electric instruments, ranging from archtops to solid-body electrics and even a bowable guitar/violin/cello he calls an arpeggione. Gorodnitski says his semihollow Cremona was designed for jazz and blues players, but to his surprise it also has been highly praised by hard rockers and alternative-style players. In fact, Gorodnitski notes, "Wes Borland of Limp Bizkit ordered three Cremonas and used them for the Chocolate Starfish and the Hot Dog Flavored Water *album. He even posed on the cover of* Guitar World *magazine with a Cremona in his hands, and in an interview in that issue said, 'George's guitars are the best I've ever played.'"*

This Cremona DeLuxe 90 has a Honduran mahogany body topped with 5A-grade curly maple. The neck is also curly maple and is faced with an African ebony fingerboard with abalone purfling and inlay. The tailpiece is hand-carved African ebony.

RIGHT **CURL M20 CUSTOM.** JOHNNY MØRCH, MØRCH GUITARS. ØRSTED, DENMARK, 2010.

Johnny Mørch started to manufacture electric guitars in 1970, in cooperation with his father, Arne. Originally, the Mørches' guitars and basses were made in a sort of cottage industry assembly line of artisans: a carpenter made the body, a painter did the lacquer work, an engraver cut out the pick guard, and the rest was done by Mørch himself, who assembled and adjusted the instruments and delivered them to music shops for retail. Since then, the firm has expanded, in that they're making more instruments, but also consolidated, in that the entire production now takes place exclusively in Mørch's workshop. Throughout, there is close contact between the musician and the craftsman, and all Mørch instruments are handmade and adjusted to the needs of the individual musician.

Mørch says, "We recognize the fact that people are different and have different needs. That's why we can't present any 'models' for you, other than the Curl. In short, whatever shape, color, or sound you want, we'll build it for you." The Curl, which is named for its scrolled upper bout, was designed by guitarist Thomas Puggaard-Müller, who was involved with the firm for many years. This example has a quilt-maple top on a mahogany body, a mahogany neck with an ebony fret board, and Mørch pickups.

BELAIRE. MARK FUQUA, MOTORAVE GUITARS. DURHAM, NORTH CAROLINA, 2009. COLLECTION OF PATRICK MONTPETIT.

Mark Fuqua has been building and repairing guitars since 1990, and worked for both Terry McInturff and James Trussart before opening his own shop in 2002. As befits the name of his operation, Fuqua says he likes guitars "that look like they go fast and that play beautifully," and his BelAire does both. The base model, which Fuqua constructs with hot hide glue, has a mahogany or Spanish cedar body, which he routs to leave a four-inch center core, half-inch sides, and a quarter-inch top. The quarter-inch back is book-matched. The neck is quartersawn mahogany, which Fuqua attaches to the separate headstock with an interlocking scarf joint for strength and increased stability at that most vulnerable juncture. He further strengthens the neck with two carbon-fiber bars that run along either side of the truss rod. The 24.625-inch-scale fingerboard can be either rosewood or ebony, and comes with real clay dot inlays. The pick guard, truss-rod cover, and jack plate are made of aged brushed aluminum, and the guitar is equipped with the customer's choice of either TV Jones FilterTrons or Wolfetone Dr. Vintage pickups.

This custom BelAire, which is one of Fuqua's personal favorites, differs from the base model only in that it has a handmade string-through tailpiece instead of the standard Bigsby B7. "That's part of what I like about it," he says—"the fact that it's so simple. The string-through is made in my shop, too, which sets it apart from the Bigsby models a little bit. A touch more class!"

STACKPOLE. MATT PROCTOR, M-TONE GUITARS. PORTLAND, OREGON, 2010.

Matt Proctor is a long-time guitar player and former professional sculptor who worked with steel, cast metals, and wood for more than fifteen years before he started making guitars. As a visual artist, he is especially sensitive to the surfaces of his instruments. Because he does not like the look or feel of plastic, he hand-cuts his pick guards and control-cavity covers from sixteen-gauge steel and patinates them individually to complement the painted surface of the instrument. He explains that his colors actually consist of many thin layers of color, "alternately sprayed on as solid layers, then misted on as millions of tiny dots. Each guitar is then carefully hand-sanded to reveal just the right amount of color from the layers below. More color is added, followed by more sanding. When the color balance is just right, a few thin layers of clear coat are sprayed on, and the guitar is buffed to a deep mirror finish."

This Stackpole has a mottled-green alder body and Lindy Fralin P-92 pickups. The neck is made of goncalo alves, a highly figured tropical hardwood commonly known as zebrawood or tigerwood.

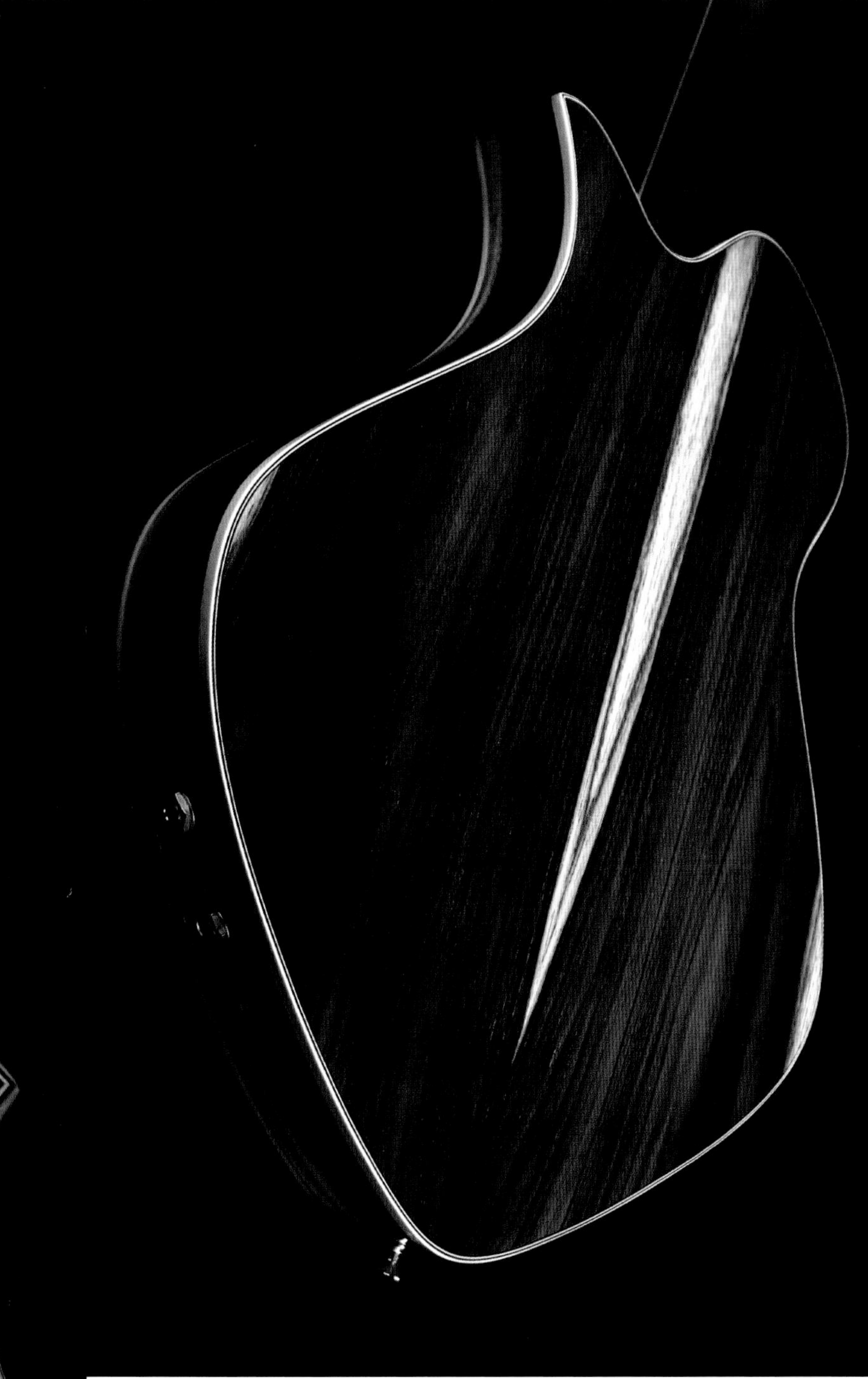

FLARETONE ACOUSTIC/ELECTRIC. DESIGNED BY ROB TAYLOR AND ENGINEERED AND BUILT BY DAVID MYKA. SEATTLE, WASHINGTON, 2008. COLLECTION OF ROB TAYLOR.

The Internet has been the dominant force fueling the explosive growth of independent lutherie during the first decade of the twenty-first century, allowing small builders to reach players all over the world without a huge investment in advertising and marketing. Rob Taylor, the Connecticut-based musician who commissioned and designed the Flaretone guitar, says, "It wasn't until I typed 'custom guitars' into the search engine on my very first Internet-connected computer that I realized there were luthiers out there who could build whatever instrument I could imagine!"

David Myka works alone and entirely by hand. "By that," he explains, "I mean that every tool I use is directly controlled by me without the use of automated machinery. In this way I can produce a much more integrated guitar in terms of overall tone and workmanship." He has built a wide range of unique guitars and other stringed instruments over the years, including hollow- and solid-body electrics, archtops, and acoustics.

After realizing that Myka could indeed make a dream guitar into reality, Taylor drew up full-scale plans for a new breed of Les Paul Goldtop he called the Sungazer. His and Myka's collaboration on that instrument proved so satisfying that they were eager to work together again. So he went back to the drawing board—or, more accurately, to the computer. Here's how he describes his design process on the new guitar, which he named the Flaretone:

"I began designing a hybrid acoustic-electric based on the Sungazer shape—a stage guitar that, at high volumes, would not be limited by typical feedback problems. It would also be able to stand alone as either an electric or amplified acoustic and, when needed, switch between and blend the two tones. It fascinated me to channel the soul and vibe of classic archtops, with multiple bindings, a pick guard, sound holes, and an ornate headstock. One of my proudest moments as a designer was when I found I could combine the curves of the smaller sound hole, the fret board edge, and the pick guard to create an 'implied' sound hole. Since the Flaretone is a marriage between an electric and an acoustic guitar, I found this element of the design amusing and quite fitting."

As with the Sungazer, Taylor knew exactly what he wanted the guitar to look and sound like, but he needed Myka's expertise in engineering and building to complete his vision. So he sent an e-mail with specs and his own Photoshop rendering of the instrument for the luthier to work from. Myka says it's fairly rare for a client to produce such an exact design for him, but trying to get as close as possible to it presents a unique challenge.

After looking over Taylor's design and e-mail, Myka got to work. He says that he and Taylor both wanted to capture the natural voice of an acoustic instrument as well as provide decent feedback resistance and a good semihollow electric tone. "So," he explains, "the design was essentially a hybrid. The body of the instrument was designed identically to how I would build a fully hollow acoustic flattop guitar with the addition of a solid center block of Honduran mahogany. This block would provide the solid core of the instrument and offer excellent feedback resistance by limiting the movement of the soundboard and back.

"The electronics on this guitar are very simple and straightforward," he continues. "With a single magnetic bridge pickup for the electric guitar tones and a single acoustic pickup (three separate transducers make up a single pickup source), we needed only to provide a simple set of switches. The magnetic pickup has a volume and tone, the acoustic pickup has a volume, and to control the amounts of each signal there is a three-way switch and a blend knob for when they are both in use. Each pickup has a separate output for use with an appropriate amplifier. The goal was to have a guitar that could be a main acoustic stage guitar while allowing the player to punch in an electric lead with ease from the same guitar."

Myka sums up the result of his collaboration with Taylor this way: "In my mind, the Flaretone was a complete success. As a luthier, I strive to produce valid musical tools that fit the needs of the musician. In a lot of ways, this was easy, working with Rob Taylor, since his vision was quite clear and complete. It was also an extreme challenge to work within such tight parameters. My engineering skills and craftsmanship were pushed to a new level. This was one of those projects that transcends the expectations of both the designer and builder. The Flaretone represents a versatile, modern guitar with a fresh look and sound. I could not be happier to have been chosen to build it."

CHARLIE HUNTER SWAMP ASH EIGHT-STRING. RALPH NOVAK, NOVAX GUITARS. EUGENE, OREGON, 2010.

Ralph Novak has been a pioneer in the development of fanned-fret guitars, which, unlike traditional parallel-fret guitars, have frets that are wider on the bass side to accommodate the long scale of the bass strings and taper to narrower spacing to accommodate the short scale of the treble strings. Despite their odd, off-kilter look, fanned-fret guitars are actually quite easy and comfortable to play, "especially if you can play without looking at your fretting hand," Novak says. "Because of the ergonomics of fanned-frets," he adds, "the fretting hand can be much more relaxed than on a parallel-fretted instrument, and playing can become much less physically stressful."

Regarding his patented design, Novak explains, "When we look inside a grand piano, or at a harp, we see that the string lengths vary with the pitches of the strings. But fretted instruments are traditionally constructed to a single scale length, negating the benefits of scale length relative to pitch. Since there are relatively few strings on most stringed instruments, compromises are made and string gauges are manipulated for workable results. Players, accustomed to the compromises of single-scale-length construction, are often pleasantly surprised by the richness and clarity of fanned-fret instruments. When the fanned-fret concept is applied to a six-string guitar, for example, the result is a 'focused' sound—clear, articulate, and balanced." As Novak suggests, the utility of fanned frets increases with the number of strings, and is particularly effective on instruments like this solid-body eight-string guitar, which was built as a signature model for virtuoso jazz guitarist Charlie Hunter. The guitar has a swamp-ash body, a maple neck and ebony fret board, and carries custom Bartolini pickups with stereo outputs for bass and guitar.

MILAN ELITE DECO FLAME. PETER OCCHINERI CUSTOM GUITARS. BLOOMFIELD, CONNECTICUT, 2010.

Pete Occhineri is a skilled and imaginative woodworker who builds what he calls "playable pieces of art," and his unique designs and dramatic combinations of exotic woods certainly make a strong visual impression. He also builds protective glass-fronted ash, maple, cherry, and mahogany display cases for his and other guitars, so that players and collectors can hang their instruments on the wall in safety and enjoy looking at them when they are not making music.

This top-of-the-line model has a bocote and flame-maple top on a mahogany body, a flame-maple neck with a mahogany stripe, and a bloodwood fingerboard. The guitar has a 25 ¾-inch scale length and is equipped with Seymour Duncan P-Rails SHPR-1 pickups, a five-way switch, and push/pull knobs.

Seymour Duncan
Seymour Duncan
P.A. OCCHINERI

FACET REDUX. PHILIP SYLVESTER, PHEO GUITARS. PORTLAND, OREGON, 2009.

Phil Sylvester is a fine-art painter, draftsman, and sculptor who attended the Berklee College of Music and the Hayes-Marshall School of Theatre, earned a BA in mathematics at Reed College and an MA in architecture from Princeton, and worked as a professional architect and artist before turning to guitars as his principal art form in 1996.

Sylvester notes that although most guitar makers are obsessive about the perfection of their craft, he is not. At his company, Pheo Guitars, he says, "I strive to build instruments that sound exceptional, play beautifully, and are extremely interesting to look at. The instruments aren't gratuitously tidy or perfectionistic or consistent. I tear them apart and rebuild them until I find them exciting. Perfect guitars are great, but there are plenty of those. I'm searching for something more raw, more direct."

To that end, with the exception of its neck, the Facet is all planes and no curves. Despite the flat surfaces, however, its body is designed to fit the player's body ergonomically. The body is hollow, with a Spanish cedar top, Indian rosewood back and sides, and an internal truss system to provide the necessary rigidity while using the least amount of material. The result, Sylvester says, "is an incredibly light, acoustically alive body. The whole guitar weighs only five pounds and three ounces." The 25 ½-inch-scale neck is maple, and the guitar carries a vintage Gibson single-coil pickup in the neck position and an overwound Fralin P-90 pickup with pole-piece magnets at the bridge.

PRO ONE. WOODY PHIFER. GARNERVILLE, NEW YORK, 2003. COLLECTION OF JEFF DOCTOROW.

Every part of the hand-carved body of Woody Phifer's Pro Series electric guitar is contoured to fit the player's body; only the headstock is flat. Phifer is a meticulous craftsman, and his guitars are full of innovative details and fastidious workmanship. The book-matched headstock and flush-mounted truss-rod cover are cut from the same wood as the top, and the access panels are carved from the same piece as the back. Both the truss-rod cover and access panel are bound and held in place by one set screw, and a raised Plexiglas pick guard shows off the luster of the wood below. Phifer also crafts unique knobs, truss-rod covers, and access panels for each instrument. The three hand-turned knobs on this instrument are made from the same material as the body, and are canted to follow the flow of the top. With mother-of-pearl inlay on top and a rubber grip to help the player manipulate volume swells, the knobs are one-of-a-kind. "Don't worry," Phifer assures customers. "We make an extra one, just in case."

LEFT **MERCURY GT**. MIKE POTVIN. BRAMPTON, ONTARIO, 2010.

Mike Potvin has been building custom guitars since 1993, but didn't introduce a standard model until 2009. This one is a single-pickup "workingman's guitar" intended to bring together the vibe and feel of two vintage workhorse guitars—the Fender Esquire and the Gibson Les Paul Junior—which Potvin describes as "loved for their no-nonsense attitude." The suggestively named Mercury has lines reminiscent of vintage '50s car designs. This snazzy Mercury Gold Top has a one-piece black walnut body with a maple top and a three-piece, 24¾-inch-scale black walnut neck with an Indian rosewood fret board. The GT comes equipped with a pair of Lollar P-90s and a three-way switch.

RIGHT **RAPIDE 5.9**. DAMIAN PROBETT. FARNHAM, ENGLAND, 2009.

Damian Probett builds all his guitars to order, allowing his customers a wide array of personal choices on each of his standard models. Probett's Rapide 5.9 is his top-of-the-line model and represents his rethinking of the Les Paul for modern players. To start with, the body is slightly offset and asymmetrical, to provide improved balance and comfort for the player. The one-piece Honduran mahogany neck meets the body at the seventeenth fret, and an angled lower horn gives easy access to the remaining five frets. The long-tenon neck joint offers stiffness, and the carbon-reinforced neck heel ensures stability.

The body is made from a single piece of Honduran mahogany and has a classic '50s-style carved maple top. The fingerboard is Madagascan rosewood, and the guitar has a 24.625-inch scale length, comparable to a Les Paul.

Probett names all his guitars after vintage British motorcycles, another of his passions. The Rapide was one of the first bikes made by the legendary Vincent company, which later produced the Black Shadow and the Black Lightning, immortalized in song by Richard Thompson.

LEFT **PRIVATE STOCK SC-J #616**. PAUL REED SMITH, PRS GUITARS. STEVENSVILLE, MARYLAND, 2004. COURTESY OF GEORGE BORST.

This first-ever Paul Reed Smith SC-J (Singlecut Jumbo) archtop jazz guitar was built for the 2004 NAMM (National Association of Music Merchants) show and was signed by Smith on the back of the headstock. This is indeed a show guitar, featuring a quilt-maple back, flame-maple binding, and an intensely figured 5A-grade flame-cherry neck and body from Smith's fabled "private stock" collection of rare and choice tonewoods. The inlays on the Brazilian rosewood fingerboard mark the first use of Smith's new "Americana" bird inlay, which depicts a bald eagle in various positions of flight. The pattern was created by Floyd Scholz, a world-renowned bird carver who has spent his entire life watching these graceful, powerful birds and has been carving them in wood for more than forty years. The eagle inlays have solid-shell black-lip and brown-lip mother-of-pearl wings, gold mother-of-pearl talons, mammoth-ivory heads and tails, and orange spiny oyster-shell beaks.

The SC-J was originally only offered as a Private Stock model, but PRS later offered a limited-edition run of three hundred thinlines with figured, select-grade maple tops and backs and mahogany necks topped with Macassar ebony fingerboards and headstock veneers. Both the Private Stock and Limited Edition SC-Js were built around a semihollow mahogany body core.

RIGHT **REVERSE TEARDROP ARCHTOP**. TOM RIBBECKE. HEALDSBURG, CALIFORNIA, 2010. COLLECTION OF JACQUES-ANDRÉ DUPONT.

Tom Ribbecke has been building guitars since 1974 and long ago established a reputation as one of the most skilled and innovative luthiers at work today.

This unique custom guitar, which was built as a gift for Jacques-André Dupont, the founder and general manager of the annual Montreal Guitar Festival, was inspired by a famous teardrop archtop built by the master New York luthier John D'Angelico. D'Angelico put his teardrop on the treble side of the lower bout, facing out from the body of the instrument, so Ribbecke, wanting to modernize and put his own stamp on the form, chose to add a reverse teardrop on the lower left bout, facing in to the center of the body. Putting the teardrop on the bass side also had a practical, acoustic advantage, adding more resonating room where it would do the most good. The bass notes on this instrument boom like those on a grand piano.

Ribbecke adds, "It occurred to me that my Halfling archtop design might be the perfect candidate for a teardrop, because, if I reversed its traditional position, I would be able to use the extra soundboard 'real estate' to enhance the effect of the Halfling design, in which the soundboard is flat on the bass side and arched on the treble side. The Halflings are capable of large full fundamental bass response with the ability to hear and distinguish all the notes of a complex chord when ringing together, thereby combining the best qualities of a flattop and an archtop in one instrument. The aesthetic of putting the tear on the bass side also satisfied my eye for purposeful movement in the guitar's shape. The decision to use a fanned fret design followed, because the longer 26¾-inch bass scale has more power to drive the bass side of the top, while the shorter 24¾-inch scale on the treble side is clear and quick-sounding, and is nice on this instrument's carved treble side. The guitar has a Kasha-style bridge, a spruce top, and bigleaf maple back and sides from my special 'cello' reserve material. All the fittings are ebony. It is X-braced and carries a Bartolini Ribbecke pickup."

ABOVE **PRINCESS ISABELLA BENSON-TRIBUTE**. JENS RITTER. DEIDESHEIM, GERMANY, 2010. COLLECTION OF GEORGE BENSON.

Jens Ritter has built an international reputation for his innovative and stylish bass guitar designs. For the Princess Isabella Baritone, his first six-string jazz guitar, Ritter challenged himself to create a solid-body instrument that would have sustain, attack, and basic sound characteristics similar to a traditional hollow-body archtop jazz guitar.

Instead of using a traditional floating bridge or attaching a bridge to the body with studs, Ritter hand-cast a bridge foot and mounted it into a small hollowed area carved into the body. The foot is held in place by friction, and its only contact is with the two-millimeter-thick elliptical contour ridge along the hollow area, so most of the surface area on the interior side of the bridge foot and the bridge studs "floats" in air.

The Princess Isabella is named for the daughter of a New York friend, who, at age four, resplendent in a white dress, greeted Ritter at the front door to her family's home and told him she was a princess. How, then, could the name be otherwise? This signature model was commissioned by jazz great George Benson, who was amazed when he saw and heard Ritter's Princess Isabella Baritone at a guitar show in Nashville. He could not get over the fact that it was a solid-body guitar and wanted to have one made for him immediately.

Ritter notes that the resulting Benson-Tribute is one of the few solid-body guitars in George Benson's huge personal guitar collection. The 24¾-inch-scale guitar has a light German alder body, a mahogany neck, and a Bavarian maple fingerboard. In contrast to the Princess Isabella Baritone, the Benson-Tribute's pickup, bridge foot, and truss-rod cover are naturally finished, and Ritter also added tone and volume pots to the instrument.

Left **ORIGINAL SERIES HARDTAIL MINIROCKER.** JADEN ROSE GUITARS. CAMBRIDGE, ENGLAND, 2010.

Jaden Rose comes to guitar making with a twenty-year background in bespoke joinery and precision engineering in the UK, U.S., China, and several European countries. As a long-time guitar player, he found himself frustrated by the limitations of production guitars that, in his judgment, just missed the mark, and so he decided to design his own ideal guitar. However, instead of making just one, he set up his own minifactory, complete with brand-new tooling and CNC machinery. Rose produces no more than two hundred guitars per year, and he sets up and checks every one himself.

This Original Series Hardtail has a book-matched mahogany and flame-maple body and a three-piece maple and bubinga neck. The pao ferro fingerboard is marked with offset mother-of-pearl dots, and the headstock is maple with flame-maple laminate. The guitar is equipped with a DiMarzio hot humbucker and a pair of DiMarzio Area T single-coil pickups, and has a three-way DiMarzio toggle switch with split-coil wiring.

Right **JOHN MCLAUGHLIN MODEL.** MIKE SABRE. PARIS, FRANCE, 2004. COLLECTION OF JOHN MCLAUGHLIN.

Mike Sabre comes from a family of musicians and painters and has been a professional luthier for more than thirty years. This thirty-three-inch-long guitar, built for jazz and fusion virtuoso John McLaughlin, is designed so that McLaughlin can carry it with him aboard planes while he's touring, thus avoiding the possibility of damage to the instrument in the baggage compartment. The neck is made of very old mahogany and is reinforced in its center by a piece of rosewood, with two carbon rods inserted against an adjustable, two-way truss rod. The peghead is thicker than usual and is reinforced on its front and back faces by a thick veneer of rosewood, with a hill on the back side. It is glued to the body and bolted with four screws.

The base of the body is also made of mahogany, and the top is an assemblage of curly maple in the center and rosewood on the sides. The entire body is hand-carved, arched on the top and curved on the back for comfort while being played. The guitar is equipped with a jazz minihumbucker at the neck position, which has its own volume and tone controls, and the tremolo bar is mounted with RMC MIDI saddles and a separate volume control. McLaughlin can be seen and heard playing this guitar on three DVDs: Remember Shakti: The Way of Beauty, Santana: Hymns for Peace—Live at Montreux 2004, *and* Eric Clapton: Crossroads Guitar Festival *(2004).*

LEFT **VERSION R OPERA.** TAKU SAKASHTA. ROHNERT PARK, CALIFORNIA, 2006.

The multitalented, versatile, and much-loved luthier Taku Sakashta was tragically murdered in a senseless act of violence in February of 2010. He was only forty-three years old. Sakashta built superlative acoustic, archtop, and electric guitars, and made instruments for Robben Ford, Boz Scaggs, Tuck Andress, Martin Simpson, Pat Martino, and many other musicians. His philosophy was that guitars are an extension of a musician's personality and soul, and that each musician demands different instruments because each has different talents and motivations, not to mention different ideas about sound, looks, and touch.

Sakashta started playing rock-and-roll guitar in elementary school, and decided he wanted to become a luthier after reading about the guitar designer Rick Turner. After working in research, design, and development for a major guitar company in Japan and the United States, he opened his own business in 1995.

The Version R is an original design that Sakashta developed for a new generation of jazz guitarists, one whom he perceived as creating new playing styles but still preferring to play instruments that have traditional specifications and sound. " 'New Age' playing requires immediate full-tone response after picking each note in the initial phrasing," he explained. "In the past, musicians have added effects or overdrive to achieve this, because traditional archtop guitars have severely limited immediate response to support initial phrasing. They also have feedback problems and no sustain." Sakashta also noticed that the sustained tones produced by solid-body guitars played without amplification disappear when the instruments are plugged in. "I thought about this over and over," he said, "realizing the need to capture these lost sustained tones that clearly support current playing styles and music."

His solution to the problem was to add rounded, hand-carved side rims to the body of his standard archtop models. According to Sakashta, the side rims create "first response with sustain, plus they carry reproduction of full overtones even with thin, clear amplifier settings. Sounds thus generated," he added, "have natural overdrive—full, clear tone." The Version R's reduced internal volume efficiently turns limited electric-guitar picking energy into clear, undistorted overdrive, without feedback. The modern-looking shape has no side-rim corners (which impede the efficient transmission of energy) and also is more comfortable to play. The Version R Opera pays tribute to archtop master James D'Aquisto, who invented the soundhole configuration it employs.

SCHAEFER 7. ED SCHAEFER. BASTROP, TEXAS, 2009.

Ed Schaefer comes by his trade naturally: his great-grandfather was a finisher at the Steinway & Sons piano company in Queens, New York, and his father was a pianist who had his own radio show in Baltimore in the late 1940s. Schaefer, who studied classical guitar and began his career as a luthier by building classical guitars, now specializes in archtops, and says he views the archtop guitar as a pianist would view the Steinways his great-grandfather worked on. "I believe that any style of music can be performed on an archtop," Ed explains. "Tradition tells us that most of them are played by jazz players, but being from Texas, I have focused on another group, the Western swing players." His seven-string model has a 14 3/4-inch lower bout and is made entirely of maple. It has a hand-carved flame-maple top and a three-piece flame-maple neck, select European maple back and sides, and a single Kent Armstrong twelve-pole humbucker with volume and tone controls.

LINDSEY BUCKINGHAM'S GUITAR. JASON Z. SCHROEDER. REDDING, CALIFORNIA, 2009. COLLECTION OF LINDSEY BUCKINGHAM.

Jason Schroeder has played guitar since he was a kid, and now gigs several times at month with the band Clear Cut, which provides him with both a musical outlet and a testing ground for the instruments he builds. He says he wants to inspire people to play by making visually striking instruments that feel and sound great. He adds, "A lot of pretty guitars just don't have that 'thump' to my ears. I like a thick, meaty tone that can fill a room and cut through a mix. I also build guitars so that a guy can play a four-hour set with them. I concentrate heavily on the neck shape being just right, and the ergonomics of the guitar are conducive to playing comfortably for long periods."

This unique guitar was built for Lindsey Buckingham of Fleetwood Mac, whom Jason first met in 2008. Later that year, the band invited Jason to spend three days at their rehearsals for the Unleashed tour. He brought about seven guitars with him, two of which the band ended up using on the tour. "On the second day I was there," Jason recalls, "Neale Heywood [a guitarist who toured with the band] asked me to build something special for Lindsey. The guidelines were fairly straightforward—make it feel like his old Turners, but bring the Schroeder aesthetic to the guitar. I was able to take measurements from his original Turner and plug it in to his rig to get a sense of what it was like.

"I wanted something familiar but more akin to an archtop aesthetic. One of the most important aspects was to get the neck carve right. It so happened that his neck was essentially a big '59 LP type of neck, which I know quite well. I also had to hit the sweet spot of the angled pickup that Lindsey uses on his Turners. So I measured that angle and position so I could set it on this guitar. It presented all kinds of design challenges and opportunities, because you end up with this really funny space between the neck and the pickup. So I worked with it and came up with the angled pick guard orientation. Another big thing about the Turners is that they employ a preamp boost, so they are loud as hell when plugged in. This is a secret to Lindsey's sound. His guitar is so loud that it drives his preamp tubes for his signature breakup. On the Turner, there is a plastic 'tailpiece' that I wanted to improve upon. I made a steel stop bar like the one on the Turner to hold the ball ends of the strings. On my guitar, an ebony tailpiece wraps over it to conceal it—the tailpiece also conceals the battery compartment and a custom Demeter boost system that is adjustable via a knob under the tailpiece. I made the boost modular so that if Lindsey ever wanted to change out or customize the frequencies he wanted boosted, we could pull the boost out and plug in a new one.

"The body is flame black limba with a quilt-maple top, and both the top and back are carved. The neck is solid Indian rosewood with an ebony fingerboard, and I used ebony for the tailpiece, knobs, backplate, pick guard, pickup ring, truss-rod cover, and headstock inlays. All the body and neck bindings are wood [three-ply ebony, maple, and rosewood], and the vine inlay on the body is rosewood. I used a Jim Wagner Shredder humbucker, and, as is customary on my guitars, I installed jumbo stainless steel frets and Waverly tuners."

The guitar started life as a non-cutaway, but when Jason brought the finished guitar to a show in San Jose, he says the Fleetwood camp loved the guitar "but there was some heartburn about it not having a cutaway. So I took it back home with me and did a major surgery, creating the cutaway as it is now.

"The timing of the modification was perfect to deliver the guitar to Lindsey for his sixtieth birthday. The date on the back of the headstock is 10-3-09, which was Lindsey's birthday. The LX on the truss-rod cover signifies sixty, and carries a bit of double meaning for the L *in Lindsey."*

FANNED EIGHT-STRING. MICHAEL SHERMAN. BARKHAMSTED, CONNECTICUT, 2010.

"We are not your average guitar company here," Mike Sherman states flatly. "One-offs are our specialty, and we have been building multiscale and multistringed instruments for several years." Sherman recently expanded his offerings to include two eight-string guitar models, and says he has a "very special" ten-string guitar currently under construction for a client. A bass player himself, he also builds extended-range multiscale basses with up to a dozen strings.

Sherman has an engineering background and more than thirty years of experience building custom instruments. Before opening his own shop, he worked in R & D at Hohner, ran the final assembly department at Ovation, and ran Washburn's custom shop. Among the many artists he has worked with over the years are Cheap Trick, Def Leppard, Derek Trucks, Joe Perry, No Doubt, Living Colour, Judas Priest, Albert Collins, Todd Rundgren, the Cars, and Sammy Hagar. When he is not building guitars, he plays bass with two bands, Flipper Dave and Shortness, and pursues his other passion—Grand Prix motorcycle racing and restoring historic Grand Prix motorcycles—which means he can often be found at the racetracks in Loudon, New Hampshire, and Lime Rock, Connecticut, where Paul Newman spent his spare time.

This 25½-inch-scale, eight-string fanned-fret guitar is tuned BEADGBEG, and gives the player an extra string and increased range on both the bass and treble sides. It has an African mahogany body and neck, a curly-maple top, and a bocote fret board with multicolored fiber-optic fret markers. Like all Sherman guitars, it is finished with a polyurethane-lacquer mixture that Sherman concocts in-house and applies in a labor-intensive twelve-coat process—a mixture that he also feels adds depth and clarity to the sound.

SWAN. JAMES SOLOWAY. PORTLAND, OREGON, 2005.

Jim Soloway's long-neck, semihollow-body Swan guitars all feature an unusual extended 27-inch scale length, which Soloway says "produces a level of clarity, presence, and articulation that most guitarists have never experienced. Notes just seem to jump off the guitar."

The extended scale length also enhances bass response, giving the guitar a big, full bottom end. ("Long necks and big bottoms" is the tagline for the Swan.) Soloway also is known for his seven-string guitars—his quest for the perfect seven-string first led him to the 27-inch scale length—and so he also offers the Swan as a seven-string, with an added low B string. Although the Swan is intended to be tuned normally, some players find that dropping the pitch to D takes the best advantage of the instrument's strengths.

PARADIS 6N. ROLF SPULER. GEBENSTORF, SWITZERLAND, 2009.

Al Di Meola, Béla Fleck, and Andreas Vollenweider are among the many world-class musicians who have taken advantage of Rolf Spuler's breakthrough designs. As an inspiration for his work, Spuler cites Albert Einstein, who said, "If at first the idea is not absurd, then there is no hope for it." Spuler also points out that before Leo Fender created the first widely available solid-body electric guitars, what musicians were really looking for was a regular acoustic guitar that could be played extremely loud. "This was the starting point of my vision," Spuler explains. "With the Paradis, I wanted to make available what in 1950 had remained a dream: a stage-friendly guitar, staying true to its natural sound at any volume level, for nylon and steel strings alike." The 6N shown here is the nylon-string version of the Spuler guitar; the 6S carries steel strings.

The Paradis combines Spuler's proprietary piezo pickup system with state-of-the-art electronics and an integrated polybass device that supplements the guitar's round, acoustic sound with fat suboctave bass notes. The sound of the strings is picked up at the same spot where it is transmitted to the body in acoustic instruments—in the bridge, straight below the string, where the fullest range of wavelengths is accessible. A separate sensor for each string transforms this vibration into electrical signals. The Paradis also has a FireWire module, which allows it to be linked directly to a computer and used as a digital guitar.

Spuler crafts the bodies from single pieces or book-matched pairs of choice wood, with a tuned cavity that enhances the acoustic properties. The unique head cover, which hides the tuning machines, is made from the same wood as the body. The headstock caps are fixed in place with magnets and can be simply lifted off to change strings. Spuler carves every neck from solid rosewood, and keeps a supply of fifty-year-old jacaranda on hand for discriminating customers.

NEAR RIGHT **ZT-3 CUSTOM.** NED STEINBERGER. NASHVILLE, TENNESSEE, 2008.

Ned Steinberger has been an important innovator in guitar design since 1980, when he introduced a radical minimalist headless bass guitar made of high-tech, space-age materials. Continuing his tradition of innovation, the ZT-3 Custom guitar is equipped with a revolutionary new version of Steinberger's TransTrem transposing tremolo system, which allows players to change keys "on the fly" by simply moving the tremolo arm. When the tremolo arm is locked, the player can dial any one of five keys, from D to F♯, and then quickly lock in the new key. The unlocked arm allows extreme pitch bending, both down and up, with perfect intonations, because, unlike any other tremolo system, the TT3 (the third-generation TransTrem) bends each string in perfect relative pitch to all the others. This also allows players to use the tremolo arm to raise or lower entire chords in perfect pitch and produce a variety of pedal-steel and slide-guitar effects.

Although the guitar is headless and made from both natural and synthetic materials, its body is fairly conventional in shape and is topped with traditional flame maple. The headless design means the ZT-3 is only thirty-five inches long, and will fit into overhead bins for air travel.

FAR RIGHT **T3/B.** TAYLOR GUITARS. EL CAJON, CALIFORNIA, 2010.

Taylor Guitars, which was cofounded by Bob Taylor and Kurt Listug in 1974, has built its reputation on high-quality acoustic guitars and currently employs more than three hundred people. The company's recent entry into the world of electric guitars was fueled by innovative new pickups created by senior product developer David Hosler.

The T3 is Taylor's souped-up semihollow-body model, which combines the company's high-definition Style 2 HD humbuckers with a coil-splitting application. A three-way switch covers the three standard pickup configurations—full neck, neck-bridge, and full bridge. Pulling up on the volume knob activates the coil splitter, which in effect turns the humbuckers into single-coils.

The T3's body is hollow except for a solid block of wood that runs down the length of the center. The quilt-maple top is laid directly on top of the internal block. The T3/B combines its added Bigsby with a roller bridge, thereby eliminating the problems with tuning stability that occur when a Bigsby is attached to a traditional fixed bridge.

Bigsby
LICENSED

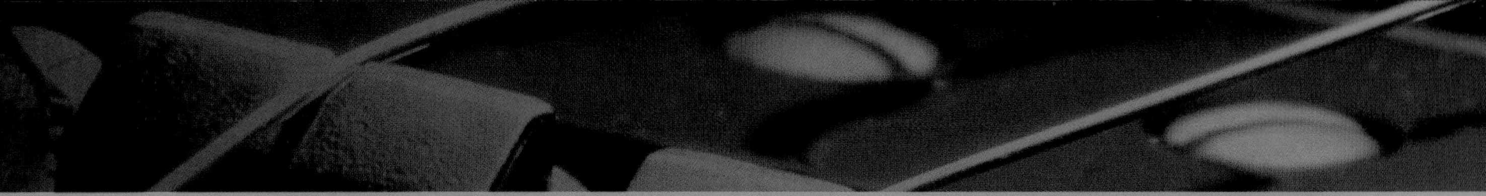

FAR LEFT **ARTISAN MASTER.** RON THORN. GLENDALE, CALIFORNIA, 2008.

Ron Thorn builds a dozen of his Artisan Master guitars each year, each unique example featuring hand-selected tonewoods, what he describes as "extreme" inlays, and a variety of custom appointments. He uses a large Haas Automation CNC machine for the woodwork, and two smaller CNCs for his intricate pearl inlays. As a believer in the use of computer-assisted machinery, Thorn is quick to point out it takes him an average of five hours and twenty minutes to make a single guitar when he works with a CNC machine, whereas it takes sixty-nine hours and thirty minutes to make the same guitar by hand, not counting the time that might be spent on a custom inlay that he or his father would do with a jeweler's saw and a minirouter.

"However short those five hours and twenty minutes might seem," says Thorn, "they are very important to the outcome of the guitar. The machine's accuracy and consistency are unmatched. There are features, such as my double-offset purfling, that just can't physically be done by hand. Fret slots can be made accurate to within a half-thousandth of an inch—heck, the wood will expand or contract more than that by the time I turn the lights off in the shop at the end of the day—but it's good to know that the slots are as accurate as they can be. Can I build a guitar without a CNC? Sure. Would I? I doubt it, because I would always feel that the guitar isn't as good as it could have been if I had used one."

0130 PROFESSIONAL. CHUCK THORNTON, CP THORNTON GUITARS. SUMNER, MAINE, 2009.

Chuck Thornton is a born Mainer who, among other things, has earned five martial-arts belts, studied guitar at the Berklee College of Music, built his own house, and worked with master acoustic luthier Dana Bourgeois. He founded Cp Thornton Guitars in 2004, and offers five hollow-body and two solid-body electric models. Thornton says the semihollow-body Professional is the most versatile guitar he makes. "I have heard this instrument play so many different styles, and it seems to do them all extremely well," he explains. "The combination of mahogany and maple has a woodiness and sustain to die for." This custom example has a 5A-grade flame-maple top, a solid mahogany back and neck, a rosewood fret board with deluxe inlay, and gold hardware.

CARVE TOP DELUXE. MICHAEL TUTTLE. SAUGUS, CALIFORNIA, 2010.

Michael Tuttle was a professional musician long before he began building guitars, and he worked with both Valley Arts Guitars and Don Grosh of Grosh Guitars before launching his own business in 2003. While working at Grosh, he gained a reputation for his fret work, and his Best Frets repair service continues to offer his expertise in that area to players. As a musician himself, Tuttle's motto is, "It's all about the feel," and he says he makes the necks of his guitars "feel like they've been part of your hand from the minute you pick them up."

Tuttle's new Carve Top Deluxe model has a mahogany body with an Eastern red leaf maple top, plus a two-piece mahogany neck and a Madagascar rosewood fingerboard. The finish is a super-thin nitrocellulose lacquer, which adds to the liveliness of the instrument.

MODEL 1. RICK TURNER, RICK TURNER GUITAR COMPANY. SANTA CRUZ, CALIFORNIA, 2007.

Rick Turner, who has been building guitars for more than forty years, is one of the acknowledged masters of electric-guitar design. His Model 1, which combines old-world aesthetics with a modern, full-bodied tonal range, is probably his best known design, primarily through its use by Lindsey Buckingham of Fleetwood Mac.

Although the Model 1 looks like an acoustic guitar, it is actually a unique single-pickup electric. As a student of guitar history, Turner based the instrument's body shape on a nineteenth-century Viennese acoustic guitar that was possibly made by Johann Stauffer, C. F. Martin's mentor. Both the top and back of the Model 1 are arched, and what appears at first glance to be a sound hole is actually a custom Turner rotating humbucking pickup mounted in a black high-impact Plexiglas plate. The plate can be rotated to change the angle of the pickup and emphasize different tonal characteristics.

With considerable evidence from Buckingham's playing to back him up, Turner claims that the Model 1 sounds incredibly acoustic and detailed when it is played clean, "but when the volume kicks up, it screams louder and longer than any guitar you've played . . . without unwanted feedback or breakup."

STUDIO ELITE BURNING WATER 2K. JAMES TYLER, JAMES TYLER GUITARS. VAN NUYS, CALIFORNIA, 2008.

Jim Tyler is a masterful builder and clever marketer who is perhaps best known for his array of highly original finishes, which—in addition to a wide variety of solid, transparent, sunburst, and candy colors—includes Malibu Beach Schmear, Ice Water, and two versions of Burning Water. And, if a Hazmat Schmear or Psychedelic Vomit finish is not enough for you—or if, as Tyler puts it, you "hate 'pretty' guitars, and you don't give a flyin' _____"—he also offers a "Joe-Rat" guitar that "your mom won't buy for you" and that looks like it has been "run over, broken, patched up, left for dead, and patched some more. It exudes attitude."

Putting humor aside, Tyler has been making serious guitars for more than twenty years, and his clients have included the likes of Walter Becker, Jackson Browne, Rick Derringer, Robben Ford, Faith Hill, John Fogerty, Madonna, Joni Mitchell, and Prince. The Studio Elite, which was introduced in 1987, was one of the first Super Strats offered by a custom builder, and has a deeper cutaway on the treble side than a Fender Strat for easier access to the upper frets. Ever the perfectionist, Tyler has designed his own pickups for this and his other guitars, and continues to tinker with old and new designs alike.

BLACKGUARD T. CHAD UNDERWOOD. LEXINGTON, KENTUCKY, 2010. COLLECTION OF CHARLES DAUGHTRY.

Although his name is not well known, more than a few prominent guitarists think Chad Underwood builds some of the best Teles and Strats ever made. Among those who play Underwoods are Anson Funderburgh, Buddy Guy, David Grissom, Matte Henderson, and Jimmy Vaughan. Paul Reed Smith, who knows a thing or two about high-quality guitars and craftsmanship, owns four of Underwood's instruments.

Underwood, who plays lead guitar in the Lexington blues band Big Boss Man, has a deep knowledge of and passion for classic-era Fullerton masterpieces. His attention to detail is second to none, and his patented nitrocellulose lacquer–based finishing process lovingly and faithfully re-creates the burnished look and feel of a well played, fifty-or-more-year-old guitar.

Underwood makes both ash- and pine-bodied Ts, which by all accounts sound completely different from each other. Collector Charlie Daughtry, who commissioned this pine-bodied T, describes it as sounding "like a killer old [Les Paul] Junior with the tone rolled off slightly. The lows and mids on it are incredible, and the relicing on this thing is unbelievable, too. The guitar looks so real, and so old. It feels old, too . . . and, more important, it sounds old, thanks in good part to the killer Ron Ellis pickups on it."

SWIFT ELECTRIC GRYPHON HIGH 12. JOE VEILLETTE. WOODSTOCK, NEW YORK, 2010.

Joe Veillette is a singer, guitarist, and luthier who is best known for his hybrid acoustic-electric instruments and experiments with unusual scale lengths. His eclectic client list includes Jeff "Skunk" Baxter, Ani DiFranco, Lauryn Hill, Henry Kaiser, Jorma Kaukonen, David Lindley, Dave Matthews, David Torn, James Taylor, and Eddie Van Halen.

Veillette studied and practiced architecture before he started building acoustic guitars as an apprentice to Michael Gurian in 1971. He then worked in partnership with Harvey Citron for a number of years and spent eight years as a full-time musician before returning to lutherie. He founded Veillette Guitars in 1995, and continues to build innovative instruments while still finding time to perform with several different groups of singers and musicians.

The Swift Electric Gryphon High 12 is a small-bodied, high-strung twelve-string with an 18 ½-inch scale length and both a piezo and a magnetic pickup. It is strung with six pairs of mandolin-like unison strings and is tuned to D, almost one octave higher than a regular guitar. Joe explains that the doubled strings "provide incredible punch and cut, with complex high overtones that bring to mind instruments like the tres, cuatro, and bouzouki." This example has a claro-walnut top on a poplar body and a maple neck.

EXCALIBUR SURFRETER SPECIAL HSH. PATRICE VIGIER, VIGIER INSTRUMENTS. GRIGNY, FRANCE, 2009.

Founded by master luthier and fretless guitar visionary Patrice Vigier in 1980, Vigier Instruments has pioneered the use of carbon-fiber necks, metal fingerboards, and other technical advances that push the envelope of the guitar's capabilities.

Vigier's fretless Surfreter models, which were introduced in 1997, are like Stratocasters with the wheels off. The lack of frets opens the door to new sounds and ideas, including slide guitar without the need for a slide, vibrato effects without a vibrato unit, pitch bends without bending, the ability to produce Indian raga modes and quarter-tone scales, and beyond. The metal fretless fingerboard provides a hard surface that Vigier claims will stay even for years. According to him, "No wooden fingerboard can offer this kind of sound and lengthy sustain. Its sound is so rich in harmonics that you'll even hear them evolve throughout the length of your note."

The solid body is made of two center-joined pieces of alder, and the neck is maple, made using Vigier's 10/90 neck system, which replaces the traditional metal truss rod with a dense carbon strip—resulting in a solidly reinforced neck that is 10 percent carbon, 90 percent wood. Vigier explains, "We never believed it was logical to drill a hole through a neck and then insert a rod of metal inside. Because wooden necks vibrate, they can absorb the energy of the string and shorten sustain. The 10/90 neck allows notes to ring longer, and creates a sound that is precise and powerful."

S-STYLE SUNSCAPE. FRANK VERRILLI, FV CUSTOM GUITARS. ATLANTA, GEORGIA, 2009.

Frank Verrilli is an accomplished studio artist who, in addition to making hand-carved guitars, has had a successful career creating paintings, furniture, and sculpture in wood, metal, and stone. Then, he explains, "I really starting slowing down with the fine art and was giving much more attention to building guitars, playing guitars, and collecting vintage amps. I was getting burned out on the art scene and, more important, I was feeling that I had said most of what I wanted to say as a sculptor. Making guitars also gave me a chance to go back to the process of my earlier art, I wanted to be strictly hand-carving on wood, with no electric tools, safety glasses, earplugs, or dust masks."

This lightweight S-style (i.e., Stratocaster-type) guitar has a one-piece alder body and a black walnut pick guard. The body has what Verrilli describes as a "very earthy" custom antique oil finish, and the one-piece maple neck has a warm amber nitrocellulose finish. In addition to three Lindy Fralin pickups, the guitar also has an EMG Afterburner booster that activates with a push/pull knob and gives the player up to twenty decibels of preset variable gain to help produce clean overdrive and distortion. Verrilli found room for the Afterburner's battery by carving out a little wood from under the jack plate.

LEFT **ARTIFACT SC 56 WG.** VINCE CUNETTO, VINETTO MUSICAL INSTRUMENTS, LLC. SAINT LOUIS, MISSOURI, 2007. COLLECTION OF JUSTIN MOODIE.

Vince Cunetto pioneered guitar aging when he worked in the Fender Custom Shop, and many consider his Artifact the gold standard in modern Tele-style instruments. Cunetto told The ToneQuest Report *that the whole idea came when he and Jay Black of the Fender Custom Shop "were just shooting the breeze one day. People were buying blue jeans that were already beat up, they would spend a lot of extra money on a worn leather jacket, and the vintage market was going nuts with people paying ten thousand dollars for an old Strat. Why not guitars?" Black brought one of the guitars that Cunetto had subsequently made and artificially aged to John Page, who was running the custom shop. According to Cunetto, "John looked at it and said, 'Cool, another old Strat.' And Jay said, 'No, John, this is a new Strat.' "*

This Artifact has a swamp-ash body in a blond finish, a quartersawn, one-piece maple neck, a Glendale bridge and brass compensated saddles, Jason Lollar pickups, Gotoh tuning machines, and a Callaham control plate that places the volume knob a half-inch closer to the tone knob than it is on a Fender. The London-based businessman, publisher, and guitarist Justin Moodie, who owns this instrument, had Damian Probett of Probett Guitars in Farnham, England, add belly and forearm cuts, and purposefully left them unfinished in what he calls "that classic Jeff Beck Esquire style." He adds, "It's not to everyone's taste, but I like the honesty of it."

RIGHT **PHOENIX.** SCOTT WALKER, STEVE KIMOCK, JOHN CUTLER, AND JASON LOLLAR, S. WALKER ELECTRIC GUITARS. SANTA CRUZ, CALIFORNIA, 2009.

Before opening his own business, Scott Walker worked at the Santa Cruz Guitar Company, one of America's top builders of high-quality acoustic flattops, where he carved guitar necks for the likes of Norman Blake and Tony Rice and eventually became shop foreman. This guitar, offered by S. Walker Electric Guitars, is the result of a collaboration that began with Walker and guitarist and designer Steve Kimock, and expanded to include electronics wizard John Cutler, who brought his expertise in onboard guitar preamps to the project, and pickup designer Jason Lollar, who worked with Cutler on the electronics.

Walker calls the Phoenix "a crazy guitar—stereo/mono, active/passive, and capable of selecting which pickup goes to which amp." The Phoenix can be played in stereo, with a stereo Y cable, or played in mono with a standard cable. When played in stereo, the legs of the Y cable become two channels: channel 1 connects to the neck pickup and channel 2 connects to the bridge pickup. This allows the player to send each pickup to a different amp and ultimately have two chains of effects in each channel. There also are three minitoggle switches on the guitar. The pickup reverse switch allows the player to switch which pickup goes to which amp in a live setting, and the stereo/mono switch allows the guitar to be played in either stereo or mono. In addition, if the player is using the stereo Y cable, it allows both pickups to be sent to either channel 1 or channel 2.

The third minitoggle is the active/passive switch, which changes the signal from high to low impedance. The active, or low impedance, setting produces a clear, transparent tone and avoids the loaded-down signal from cables and effects pedals, whereas the passive, or high impedance, setting offers a more traditional sound. There are volume and tone controls as well as phase selectors for each pickup to assure that it is in phase with the amplifier. Jason Lollar explains that his pickups for the Phoenix are wound "similar to vintage Jazzmaster pickups—the neck pickup has a similar turn count, DC resistance, and coil shape, but the bridge is wound quite a bit hotter than a stock Jazzmaster. The iron blades on the pickups add to the inductance, which gives you a fuller sound with a little more output than is standard, and the sustain on these blade pickups is noticeably longer than on standard Fender pickups."

The Phoenix's body and neck are carved from choice curly mahogany, and its fingerboard is old-growth Brazilian rosewood salvaged from fallen trees. The electronics are shielded by a copper pick guard that Scott patinated and engraved.

LEFT **ARLEN ROTH SIGNATURE.** DON WARREN. GREENWICH, NEW YORK, 2009.

Arlen Roth is a Telecaster wizard best known for his soulful and technically astonishing instrumental renditions of such classic '60s tunes as "When a Man Loves a Woman" and "Ballad of a Thin Man." Don Warren says that when he first met Roth, "he told me of the many attempts other companies had made to re-create the tone and feel of his prized 1953 classic [Telecaster]. Arlen knows he doesn't have to settle and didn't allow me to, either. My challenge was to meet those expectations as well as provide the vast array of tones heard on my [Strat-style, three-pickup] Classic II model," which Vintage Guitar *described as having "some of the most usable-yet-innovative passive electronics we've seen, offering a virtual arsenal of guitar tones at your fingertips."*

This signature model was built to Roth's exacting specifications: it includes a vintage bridge with a solid-brass compensated saddle for true intonation, vintage string spacing, and a bridge pickup that is slightly hotter than usual. Warren describes it as a guitar that "embodies the tones of the golden age, with the addition of beautifully balanced acoustic tone, gut-wrenching grind, and singing sustain along with all the quack and twang you can imagine."

RIGHT **ROXY.** MARC LUPIEN, XXL GUITARS. MONTREAL, QUEBEC, 2010.

In 2003, luthier Marc Lupien of XXL Guitars asked himself a question: how would a Danelectro guitar sound if it weren't made of cheap materials? What would happen if he were to copy the original guitar structure developed by Nathan Daniels in the '50s—i.e., a body made of a softwood core sandwiched between two thin plates of denser material—but instead of sandwiching cheap pine between Masonite plates he were to use cedar or British Columbian fir capped with mahogany?

To find out, Lupien disassembled his beloved 1963 Silvertone U1 to take measurements and make templates, and then began to create what would become the XXL Guitars prototype. The results surprised even him. "The instrument was very light and had good sustain," he recalls, "but, above all, it had soul!"

After getting an enthusiastic response from a friend, the extraordinary Canadian guitarist Steve Hill, Lupien decided to put the guitar into production and began turning out small runs of luthier-quality instruments. He explains that each XXL guitar is unique. "Even though the instruments are made in small batches of about ten each, they do not all have exactly the same dimensions. We let the wood decide. Some pieces of wood are denser and must be thinned more radically, while some are less dense and may be left thicker."

The Roxy is a much bigger instrument than Lupien usually makes. The core is cedar with a top and back of book-matched mahogany. The core is sculpted in a way that maintains structural integrity yet leaves the top and back as free to vibrate as possible, and the braces used to stiffen the top are sculpted directly into the core. The neck is a multilaminate of maple, mahogany, and figured maple, and the fret board is book-matched Honduran rosewood. The guitar also has a Bigsby tremolo tailpiece and is equipped with a pair of Jason Lollar P-90 pickups.

ABOVE **CURLY KOA OVER MAHOGANY AND BRAZILIAN ROSEWOOD OVER MAHOGANY.** JOSEPH YANUZIELLO, YANUZIELLO ELECTRIC GUITARS. TORONTO, ONTARIO, 2010.

Joe Yanuziello is a versatile luthier who builds elegant acoustic and electric guitars and electric mandolins. These hollow-body electrics have tops made of gorgeous tonewoods and clear ivoroid-bound pick guards that allow the wood to show through. Both have mahogany necks, sides, and backs, and are equipped with humbucking pickups that Lindy Fralin designed especially for Yanuziello's instruments. The curly-koa guitar, on the left, has an ebony fingerboard; Yanuziello extended the theme of the Brazilian rosewood guitar, on the right, to its fingerboard and headstock, matching both to the top wood.

SHANGRILA. MICHAEL BLANK, ZUNI CUSTOM GUITARS. ALTO PASS, ILLINOIS, 2008.

Michael Blank has been harvesting and selling instrument-grade wood for more than twenty-five years. Before founding Zuni Custom Guitars, he supplied instrument wood and veneer to Gibson, Washburn, Ernie Ball, and other major companies. He recently decided to sell wood to smaller custom builders, and his new company specializes in native, highly figured woods such as curly, quilt, bird's-eye, spalted, and fiddleback maple, all of which figure prominently in Zuni guitars. "These are freaks of nature and very rare," he explains. "Some can go for ten thousand dollars a log."

Zuni guitars are entirely handmade from sustainable North American hardwoods that Blank cuts himself. Even the pickup rings and cover plates are made out of sustainable figured maple, and most of the knobs and tuners are made out of elk or deer antlers that he harvests after they are shed. Each Zuni features a unique combination of woods and finish colors. Like all Zunis, Shangrila is a 24¾-inch-scale instrument equipped with a pair of humbuckers. But she is set apart by a black-ash body topped with spectacular quilt maple, a curly-maple neck, a bird's-eye-maple fingerboard with pyramid inlays of abalone and mother-of-pearl, and a natural bone nut. The neck binding and pickup rings are also curly maple, and the body covers are curly hard maple.

FURTHER READING AND RESOURCES

FURTHER READING

Bacon, Tony. *Electric Guitars: The Illustrated Encyclopedia.* London: Balafon Books, 2000.
A comprehensive encyclopedia, with 314 oversized pages of images and detailed information.

Carter, Walter. *Gibson Guitars: 100 Years of an American Icon.* Los Angeles: General Publishing Group, 1994.
A huge coffee-table book produced by Gibson, with hundreds of great photos and anecdotes.

Evans, Tom and Mary Anne. *Guitars: Music, History, Construction, and Players from the Renaissance to Rock.* New York and London: Paddington Press, 1977.
The most ambitious and informative historical overview of the guitar, still unmatched in its breadth and depth.

Gruhn, George, and Walter Carter. *Electric Guitars and Basses: A Photographic History.* Milwaukee, WI: Backbeat Books, 1994.
An excellent survey by two of the most knowledgeable guitar historians in the business.

Kuronen, Darcy. *Dangerous Curves: The Art of the Guitar.* Boston: MFA Publications, 2000.
A catalog of an exhibition at the Boston Museum of Fine Arts, tracing the guitar from its roots to the turn of the millennium.

Lospennato, Leonardo. *Electric Guitar & Bass Design*. Berlin: HL Publishing, 2010.
A clear and thoughtful introduction to the design process and the myriad choices a builder needs to make along the way.

Palmer, Robert. *Rock and Roll: An Unruly History.* New York: Random House, 1996.
The brilliant companion book to a PBS series by arguably the greatest of all rock writers.

Santelli, Robert, Holly George-Warren, and Jim Brown, eds. *American Roots Music.* New York: Harry N. Abrams, 2002.
This companion book to a PBS series is an excellent, heavily illustrated introduction to a variety of American roots music, including country, blues, gospel, Cajun and zydeco, and rhythm and blues—and, ultimately, rock and roll.

Schmidt, Paul. *Art That Sings: The Life and Times of Luthier Steve Klein.* Clifton, NJ: Doctorow Communications, Inc., 2003.

Shaw, Robert. *Great Guitars.* Southport, CT: Hugh Lauter Levin Associates, 1997.
Full-page photos and information on forty-eight acoustic and electric masterpieces, from the Renaissance to the Parker Fly.

———. *Hand Made, Hand Played: The Art & Craft of Contemporary Guitars.* Asheville, NC: Lark Books, 2008.
A comprehensive overview of every type of contemporary guitar, including historic reproductions of early European instruments, classical and flamenco, harp guitars, archtops, acoustic and electric basses, and more.

Trynka, Paul, ed. *The Electric Guitar: An Illustrated History.* London: Virgin Books, 1993.
Produced to accompany an exhibition at the Design Museum in London, this is the best book available on twentieth-century electrics, with contributions from Tony Bacon, Tom Wheeler, and other experts.

———. *The Chinery Collection: 150 Years of American Guitars.* London: Outline Press, Ltd., 1999.
A lavish, limited-edition overview of the late Scott Chinery's extraordinary collection of American masterpieces.

Wheeler, Tom. *American Guitars: An Illustrated History.* New York: Harper & Row, 1992.
Still the most comprehensive and thoroughly researched of all books on the subject.

RESOURCES

guitar shows

Dallas International Guitar Festival
http://www.guitarshow.com
4222 Rosehill Road, Suite 3
Garland, TX 75043
(972) 240-2206

Frankfurt Musikmesse
http://musik.messefrankfurt.com
Messe Frankfurt Exhibition GmbH
Ludwig-Erhard-Anlage 1
60327 Frankfurt, Germany
49-69-75-75-194-12

London Guitar Festival
International Guitar Foundation
http://www.igf.org.uk/International_Guitar_Foundation/London_Guitar_Festival.html

Montreal Guitar Show
http://www.salondeguitaredemontreal.com
400 de Maisonneuve West Boulevard, 9th floor
Montreal, Quebec H3A 1L4
(514) 525-7732

Newport Guitar Festival
http://www.newportguitarfestival.com
(305) 531 9428

lutherie schools

American School of Lutherie
http://www.americanschooloflutherie.com
2745 SW Scenic Drive
Portland, OR 97225
(503) 292-2385

Harry Fleishman's Luthiers School International
http://www.fleishmaninstruments.com
1533 Welter Court
Sebastopol, CA 95472
(707) 823-3537

Roberto-Venn School of Luthiery
http://www.roberto-venn.com
4011 South 16th Street
Phoenix, AZ 85040
(602) 243-1179

guitar dealers

Boutique Guitar Resource
http://boutiqueguitarresource.com

Destroy All Guitars
http://www.destroyallguitars.com
2124 Stone Pasture Road
Fuquay-Varina, NC 27526
919-552-3047

Elderly Instruments
http://www.elderly.com
P.O. Box 14210
Lansing, MI 48901
(888) 473-5810

Gruhn Guitars, Inc.
http://www.gruhn.com
400 Broadway
Nashville, TN 37203
(615) 256-2033

Norman's Rare Guitars
http://www.normansrareguitars.com
18969 Ventura Boulevard
Tarzana, CA 91356
(818) 344-8300

Premier Builders Guild
http://premierbuildersguild.com
201 South Highland Avenue
Pittsburgh, PA 15206
(714) 514-0647

Wildwood Guitars
http://www.wildwoodguitars.com
804 Main Street
Louisville, CO 80027
(303) 665-7733

electric guitars on the web

Gbase
http://www.gbase.com
47 Old Hills Lane
Greenlawn, NY 11740
(877) 968-4642

The Gear Page
http://www.thegearpage.net
Harmony Central
http://www.harmonycentral.com

luthiers

Alembic
http://www.alembic.com
3005 Wiljan Court
Santa Rosa, CA 95407

Jean-Yves Alquier
http://www.alquier-guitar.com
Le Soler, France

Matt Artinger
http://www.artingerguitar.com
4035 Main Road West
Emmaus, PA 18049

Asher Guitars & Lap Steels
http://www.asherguitars.com
2554 Lincoln Boulevard, Box 1037
Venice, CA 90291

AW Custom Guitars
http://www.awguitars.com
Aloha, OR

J. Backlund Designs
http://www.jbacklund.com
100 Cherokee Boulevard, Suite 123
Chattanooga, TN 37405

Gene Baker
http://www.finetunedinstruments.com

Victor Baker
http://www.victorbakerguitars.com
544 Park Avenue, Suite 2B
Brooklyn, NY 11205

Beltona Resonator Instruments
http://www.beltona.net
Old Parua Bay Road
RD 5 Whangarei, New Zealand

Blindworm Guitars
http://blindwormguitars.com
121 Yale Avenue
Colorado Springs, CO 80904

Blueberry Guitars
http://www.blueberryguitars.com
4420 Poirier
Ville St. Laurent, Quebec H4R 2C5

Bolin Guitars
http://www.bolinguitars.com
4021 North 36th Street
Boise, ID 83703

Born to Rock
http://www.borntorock.com
New York, NY

Siggi Braun: Fine Young Guitars
http://www.siggi-braun.com
Adolf-Safft Strasse 13
D-73037 Göppingen, Germany

Breedlove Guitar Company
http://www.breedlovemusic.com
2843 NW Lolo Drive
Bend, OR 97701

Briggs Guitars
http://www.briggsguitars.com
P.O. Box 98043
Raleigh, NC 27624

Bruton String Works
http://www.brutonstringworks.com
63 Kirkgate Drive
Spencerport, NY 14559

Campbell American Guitars
http://www.campbellamerican.com
P.O. Box 460
Westwood, MA 02090

Cardinal Instruments
http://www.cardinalinstruments.com
2317 Lafayette Avenue
Austin, TX 78722

Harvey Citron Enterprises
http://www.citron-guitars.com
282 Chestnut Hill Road
Woodstock, NY 12498

Collings Guitars
http://www.collingsguitars.com
11210 West Highway 290
Austin, TX 78737

Comins Guitars
http://www.cominsguitars.com
P.O. Box 611
Willow Grove, PA 19090

Conklin Guitars and Basses
http://www.conklinguitars.com
P.O. Box 1394
Springfield, MO 65801

Crow Hill Guitars
http://www.crowhillguitars.com
Fairfield, IA

Dagmar Custom Guitars
http://www.dagmarcustomguitars.com
Niagara Parkway
Niagara-on-the-Lake, Ontario L0S 1J0

Destroy All Guitars
http://www.destroyallguitars.com
2124 Stone Pasture Road
Fuquay-Varina, NC 27526

Michael DeTemple
http://www.detempleguitars.com
P.O. Box 56626
Sherman Oaks, CA 91413

Engel Guitars
http://www.engelguitars.com
Stamford, CT

Enke Designs
http://www.enkedesigns.com
La Veta, CO

Eugen Guitars
http://www.eugen.no
P.O. Box 1710, Nordnes
5816 Bergen, Norway

EVH Guitars, Amplifiers, and Musical Products
http://www.evhgear.com
8860 East Chaparral Road, Suite 100
Scottsdale, AZ 85250

Fender Musical Instruments Corporation
http://www.fender.com
8860 East Chaparral Road, Suite 100
Scottsdale, AZ 85250

Fibenare Guitars
http://www.fibenare-guitars.com
Budapest, Hungary

Fleishman Instruments
http://fleishmaninstruments.com
1533 Welter Court
Sebastopol, CA 95472

Charles Fox
http://www.charlesfoxguitars.com
Portland, OR

Scott French
http://www.scottfrench.com
P.O. Box 562
Auburn, CA 95603

Fujigen, Inc.
http://www.fgnguitars.com
3680-1 Tokiwa Omachi
Nagano 398-0004, Japan

Gibson Custom, Art & Historic Division
http://www.gibsoncustom.com
1612 Elm Hill Pike
Nashville, TN 37210

Roger Giffin
http://www.giffinguitars.com
Beaverton, OR

Gigliotti Custom Guitars
http://www.gigliottiguitars.com
Tacoma, WA

Goldbug Products
http://www.goldbugproducts.com
P.O. Box 922
Delavan, WI 53115

Goulding Guitars
http://www.gouldingguitars.com
Essex, England

Gretsch Guitars
http://www.gretschguitars.com
FMI Specialty Sales
8860 East Chaparral Road, Suite 100
Scottsdale, AZ 85250

Grosh Guitars
http://www.groshguitars.com
7223 West 118th Place, Unit I
Broomfield, CO 80020

Johan Gustavsson Guitars
http://www.jgguitars.com
Magasinsgatan 9
21613 Limhamn, Sweden

Hahn Guitars
http://www.hahnguitars.com
Garnerville Arts and Industrial Center
55 Railroad Avenue, Unit 10F
Garnerville, NY 10923

Harden Engineering
http://hardenengineering.com
1045 North Western Avenue
Chicago, Il 60622

Frank Hartung
http://www.hartung-guitars.com
Karl-Marx Strasse 24
D-98704 Langewiesen, Germany

Henman Guitars
http://www.henmanguitars.com
33583 Mulholland Highway
Malibu, CA 90265

Hottie Guitars
http://hottieguitars.com
10699 SE Happy Valley Drive
Portland, OR 97086

Nik Huber Guitars
http://www.nikhuber-guitars.com
Borsigstrasse 13
63110 Rodgau, Germany

Ian A. Guitars
http://www.iaguitars.com
P.O. Box 503482
San Diego, CA 92150

Joseph Jesselli
http://www.jesselli-guitars.com
Huntington, NY

TV Jones, Inc.
http://www.tvjones.com
P.O. Box 2802
Poulsbo, WA 98370

William Jeffrey Jones
http://williamjeffreyjonesguitars.com
Neosho, MO

Ron Kirn Signature Guitars
http://www.ronkirn.com
P.O. Box 600301
Jacksonville, FL 32260

Steve Klein, Timberdance Guitars
http://www.timberdance.com
Orinda, CA

Knowlton Guitars & Basses
http://www.knowltonguitars.com
Portland, OR

Koll Guitar Company
http://www.kollguitars.com
Portland, OR

Lacey Guitars
http://www.laceyguitars.com
P.O. Box 634
Kingston Springs, TN 37082

Langcaster
http://www.langcaster.com
Auckland, New Zealand

Lindsay Wilson Guitars
http://lindsaywilsonguitars.co.uk
Church House, Bratton Fleming
Barnstaple
North Devon EX31 4SA, England

Liquid Metal Guitar Company
http://www.liquidmetalguitars.com
Vancouver, BC

Leonardo Lospennato
http://www.lospennato.com
Berlin, Germany

LsL Instruments
http://www.lslinstruments.com
15111 Keswick Street
Van Nuys, CA 91405

M-tone Guitars
http://m-tone.com
Portland, OR

S. B. MacDonald Custom Instruments
http://www.customguitars.com
Huntington, NY

Malinoski Art Guitars
http://www.petermalinoskiart.com
Hyattsville, MD

Manne Guitars
http://www.manne.com
Via Paraiso 28
36015 Schio, Italy

Master Handmade Guitars
http://www.master-guitars.com
Los Angeles, CA

Brian Monty
http://www.brianmonty.com
Ontario, Canada

Mørch Guitars
http://www.morch-guitars.dk
Voer Færgevej 104
DK-8950 Ørsted, Denmark

MotorAve Guitars
http://www.motorave.com
Durham, NC

Myka Guitars
http://www.mykaguitars.com
Seattle, WA

Novax Guitars
http://www.novaxguitars.com
88708 Gentry Road
Eugene, OR 97402

Occhineri Custom Guitars
http://www.occhineriguitars.com
Bloomfield, CT

John Page Guitars
http://www.pageguitars.com
Wolf Creek, OR

Pagelli Guitars
http://www.pagelli.com
CH-7412 Scharans Graubünden
Switzerland

Parker Guitars
http://www.parkerguitars.com
444 East Courtland Street
Mundelein, IL 60060

Pheo Guitars
http://www.philandjoanworld.com/index.php/pheo_guitars
Portland, OR

Phifer Designs
http://www.phiferdesigns.com
P.O. Box 262
Garnerville, NY 10923

Potvin Guitars
http://www.potvinguitars.com
Ottawa, Ontario

Probett Guitars
http://www.probettguitars.co.uk
Surrey, England

Ribbecke Guitars
http://www.ribbecke.com
P.O. Box 2215
Healdsburg, CA 95448

Ritter Instruments
http://www.ritter-instruments.com
Weinstrasse 19
67146 Deidesheim, Germany

Larry Robinson
http://robinsoninlays.com
P.O. Box 308
Valley Ford, CA 94972

Jaden Rose Guitars
www.jadenroseguitars.com
London, England

Ruokangas Guitars
http://www.ruokangas.com
Kankurinkatu 4–6
Fin-05800 Hyvinkää, Finland

Mike Sabre
http://www.mike-sabre.com
La Tour Sarrazine
51 avenue du 3 septembre
06320 Cap d'Ail, France

Schaefer Guitars
http://www.schaeferguitars.com
2415 East 5th Street, Building C1
Austin, TX 78702

Jason Z. Schroeder Guitars
http://schroederguitars.com
2561 Radio Lane
Redding, CA 96001

Michael Sherman Guitars
http://www.sherman-customs.com
Barkhamsted, CT

Paul Reed Smith Guitars
http://www.prsguitars.com
380 Log Canoe Circle
Stevensville, MD 21666

Soloway Guitars
http://www.solowayguitars.com
Portland, OR

Spalt Instruments
http://www.spaltinstruments.com
Vienna, Austria

Rolf Spuler Guitars
http://www.rolfspuler.com
Im Halt 25
Ch-5412 Gebenstorf
Switzerland

Steinberger
http://www.steinberger.com
Nashville, TN

Michael Stevens
http://www.stevensguitars.com
P.O. Box 1082
Alpine, TX 79831

Taylor Guitars
http://www.taylorguitars.com/guitars/electric
1980 Gillespie Way
El Cajon, CA 92020

Ulrich Teuffel
http://www.teuffel.com
Weissenhorner Strasse 13
89233 Neu-Ulm, Germany

Teye Guitars
http://teye-guitars.com
Austin, TX

Thorn Custom Guitars
http://www.thornguitars.com
815 Western Avenue, Unit 1
Glendale, CA 91201

Cp Thornton Guitars
http://www.cpthorntonguitars.com
51 Butterfield Road
Sumner, ME 04292

James Trussart Custom Guitars
http://www.jamestrussart.com
1307 Allesandro Street
Los Angeles, CA 90026

Michael Tuttle Guitars
http://www.bestfrets.com
Los Angeles, CA

Rick Turner Guitar Company
http://www.renaissanceguitars.com
815 Almar Avenue
Santa Cruz, CA 95060

James Tyler Guitars
http://tylerguitars.com
6166 Sepulveda Boulevard
Van Nuys, CA 91411

Underwood Guitars
http://underwoodguitars.com
Yucca Valley, CA

Veillette Guitars
http://www.veilletteguitars.com/
2628 Route 212
Woodstock, NY 12498
(845) 679-6154

Frank Verrilli
http://fvcustomguitars.com
Atlanta, GA

Vigier Guitars
http://www.vigierguitars.com
10-12 rue de l'abbé Grégoire
Z.A.C. des radars
91350 Grigny, France

Vinetto Guitars
http://www.vinettoguitars.com
2828A Breckenridge Industrial Court
St. Louis, MO 63144

S. Walker Electric Guitars
http://www.scottwalkerguitars.com
Santa Cruz, CA

Warren Guitars
http://www.warrenguitars.com
8 Mill Hollow, Apartment D
Greenwich, NY 12834

XXL Guitars
http://xxlguitars.com
Les ateliers de la corde
5425 de Bordeaux, Suite 003
Montreal, Quebec H2H 2P9

Yanuziello Stringed Instruments
http://www.yanuziello.com
442 Dufferin Street, Studio T
Toronto, Ontario M6K 2A3

Zemaitis Guitars
http://www.zemaitis-guitars.com
Tokyo, Japan

Zuni Custom Guitars
http://www.zuniguitars.com
P.O. Box 4, 10 Main Street
Alto Pass, IL 62905

This book, which had its genesis in the heart of the impassioned fourteen-year-old rocker who still lives inside me, would not have been possible without the help of many new and old friends and colleagues.

First, my profound thanks to all the busy luthiers who so generously shared their work, time, photos, and thoughts with me. This book would not have been possible without their cooperation and involvement, and their enthusiasm for the project helped fuel its fires from start to finish. Thank you, one and all.

Thanks also to George Benson, George Borst, Lindsey Buckingham, Charlie Daughtry, Jeff Doctorow, Jacques-André Dupont, Dr. Frank Guerra, Robert Hansen-Sturm, Alex Härtel, Calvary Kendrick, Matias Kupiainen, Jared Meeker, Richard Mermer, Vincent D. Mills, Bob Miles, Justin Moodie, Bill Nelson, Marnie Stern, Jim Wallace and his Southpaw Sanctum, Bob and Dave Thomas, Konstantine Zakzanis, and all the other guitarists and collectors who shared wonderful guitars from their personal stashes with me.

Special thanks to Billy F. Gibbons and Steve Miller for allowing me to use photos of them with instruments built by Bolin Guitars, and to John and Jake Bolin for all the time and special attention they gave this project. I am also deeply indebted to Matte Henderson, who kept e-mailing me photos of irresistible guitars he owns with headings like "Seen this?" and "If it's not too late" or "While we're at it"; and to Junior Brown, who took time out of his hectic schedule for a photo session in his rural Texas cabin. Special thanks also to Griff Smith, who photographed Junior and his Guit-Steel, called Old Bud, and to Mike Stevens, who put it all together and sent me wonderful stories and photos of his world in west Texas. I also am deeply grateful to David Myka and Rob Taylor, who walked me through the creation of the Flaretone acoustic-electric guitar that they designed and David built.

Thanks to my agent, Jeanne Fredericks, who made this book possible; to my ever-supportive editor at Sterling Publishing, Barbara Berger, who shared my vision for the book and did everything possible to make it a reality; and to project manager Barbara Clark, whose sharp-eyed editing and thoughtful suggestions improved my work in a thousand ways. Thanks also to Scott Meola and Rachel Maloney, who provided the book's stunning design, and Jason Chow, who designed the cover.

Finally, thanks to my wife, Nancy, who has patiently listened to my ravings about music and guitars of all kinds for nearly thirty years now, and to my daughters, Emma and Georgia, who are still telling me to turn it down.

ILLUSTRATION INDEX

INDEX

A

B

C

D

E

O

P

Q

R

U

V

W

X

Y

Z

PHOTO CREDITS

Courtesy of Jean-Yves Alquier: 152[l], 152[r], 153[l], 153[r] (Photos by Pierre Luc Dufour)
Courtesy of Ian Anderson: 188
Courtesy of Matt Artinger: 26, 27, 28, 29, 30, 31 (Photos by Michael Stewart)
Courtesy of Bill Asher: 154
Courtesy of Jerry Auerswald: 154–55
Courtesy of Victor Baker: 158
Courtesy of Andrea Ballarin: 202[l]
Courtesy of Dave Begalka: 201 (Photo by Bayard Black)
Courtesy of Bruce Bennett: 156
Courtesy of Michael Blank: 236, 237 (Photos by Don Frazier)
Courtesy of Blueberry Guitars: 160 (Photo by Mark D. Goldman)
Courtesy of John Bolin: 32, 33, 36, 37[t], 37[b] (Photos by Tim Brown, Balance Productions); 35[t], 35[b] (Photos by Welsh Studios, Inc.)
Courtesy of Born to Rock Guitars: 161 (Photo by Johan Hornestam)
Courtesy of George Borst: 3, 13, 17, 19, 141, 146, 147[l], 214[l], 214[r] (Photos by Ryan Conley)
Courtesy of Siggi Braun: 162 (Photo by Alexander Härtel)
Courtesy of Breedlove Guitars: 163[l]
Courtesy of Jack Briggs: 163[r]
Courtesy of Ben Bruton: 164
Courtesy of Dean Campbell: 165[t]
Courtesy of Harvey Citron: 166
Courtesy of Collings Guitars: 167 (Photo by Alex Rueb)
Courtesy of Bill Comins: 168[t]
Courtesy of Bill Conklin: 168[b]
Courtesy of Michael DeTemple: 38, 39 (Photo by Fred Morledge, PhotoFM.com); 40[l], 40[r], 41[t], 41[b]
Courtesy of Charles Daughtry: 55, 172, 228–29 (Photos by Charles Daughtry)
Courtesy of Jeff Doctorow: 80, 174, 211 (Photos by Jeff Doctorow)
Courtesy of Rob Engel: 173 (Photo by Paul Johnson)
Courtesy of Jean-Claude Escudie: 187[r]
Courtesy of Henry Eugen: 175
Courtesy of Sam Evans: 165[b]
Courtesy of Steve Evans: 159[t]
Courtesy of Fender Musical Instruments Corporation: 5[b], 6, 16, 23[l], 176, 177
Courtesy of Fibenare: 43, 44, 45, 46, 47
Courtesy of Harry Fleishman: 178[l] (Photo by Harry Fleishman)
Courtesy of Charles Fox: 178[r] (Photo by Denise Fox)
Courtesy of Scott French: 21 (Photo by Alicia Ross); 179[l]
Courtesy of Fugijen, Inc.: 110–11, 112–13
Courtesy of Mark Fuqua: 204–5
Courtesy of Gibson Guitar Corp.: 2, 5[t], 8, 10, 11
Courtesy of Roger Giffin: 48, 49, 50, 51, 52, 53
Courtesy of Patrick Gigliotti: 180 (Photo by Sebastien Miron, Crilaphoto.com)
Courtesy of George Gorodnitski: 202[r]
Courtesy of Anthony Goulding: 184
Courtesy of Grosh Guitars: 185[l]
Courtesy of Johan Gustavsson: 54, 59
Courtesy of Chihoe Hahn: 185[r]
Courtesy of Robert Hansen-Sturm: 126–27 (Photos by Robert Hansen-Sturm, Storm Photo, Inc.)
Courtesy of William Harnden: 186
Courtesy of Frank Hartung: 60, 61, 63, 64[t], 64[b], 65
Courtesy of Matte Henderson: v, 42[t], 42[b], 56[t], 56[b], 57, 179[tr], 179[br], 194[t] (Photos by Matte Henderson)
Courtesy of Graham and Paris Henman: 187[l]
Courtesy of Nik Huber: 66, 68–69, 70[l], 70[r], 71[t], 71[b] (Photos © Atelier Jørn Kiel, Germany)
Courtesy of Joseph Jesselli: 189[l], 189[r], 190[l], 190[r] (Photos by Jurgen Lorenzen)
Courtesy of Thomas V. Jones: 191
Courtesy of William Jeffrey Jones: 72, 73, 74, 75, 76, 77
Courtesy of Ron Kirn: 192 (Photo by Ron Kirn)
Courtesy of Mark Knowlton: 193 (Photo by Holland Studios)
Courtesy of Mark Lacey: 195[t]
Courtesy of Joh Lang: 196[t]
Courtesy of Chris Larsen: 181, 182[t]
Courtesy of Lance Lerman: 199[b]
Courtesy of Liquid Metal Guitars: 197
Courtesy of Leonardo Lospennato: 198–99 (Photo by Dieter Stork)
Courtesy of Marc Lupien: 234[r]
Courtesy of Scott MacDonald: 200[l]
Courtesy of Peter Malinoski: 84[t], 84[b], 85, 86, 87
Courtesy of Vincent D. Mills: 14 (Photo by Vincent D. Mills)
Courtesy of Brian Monty: 88, 89, 90, 91, 92, 93 (Photos by George Pagakis)
Courtesy of Justin Moodie: 128, 128–29, 232 (Photos by the Packshot Factory)
Courtesy of Johnny Mørch: 203
Courtesy of Ralph Novak: 208
Courtesy of Peter Occhineri: 209[l], 209[r]
Courtesy of John Page: 94; 96–97, 98[t], 98[b], 99[t], 99[b] (Photos by John Page)
Courtesy of Claudio and Claudia Pagelli: 100 (Photo by René Tanner, festhalter.ch); 102[t], 102[b], 103[l], 103[r] (Photos by Ralph Feiner); 104[l], 104[r], 105 (Photos by Räto Joos)
Courtesy of Mike Potvin: 212–13
Courtesy of Premier Builders Guild: 157, 194–95
Courtesy of Damian Probett: 213
Courtesy of Matt Proctor: 205
Courtesy of Tom Ribbecke: 215[l] (Photo by John Youngblood)
Courtesy of Jens Ritter: 215[r]

Courtesy of Howard Robinson: 196[b] (Photo by Kevin Rowe)
Courtesy of Larry Robinson: 106; 109, 200[r] (Photos by Larry Robinson)
Courtesy of Jaden Rose: 216 (Photo by John Kingsnorth Photography)
Courtesy of Juga Ruokangas: 22; 114[l], 114[r], 115, 116, 117[l], 117[r]
Courtesy of Mike Sabre: 217[b]
Courtesy of Taku Sakashta: 216–17
Courtesy of Ed Schaefer: 218
Courtesy of Paul Schmidt and Mike Welden: 122, 123 (Photos by Nicolas Cope)
Courtesy of Jason Z. Schroeder: 219
Courtesy of Andrew Scott: 159[b]
Courtesy of Michael Sherman: 220[l]
Shutterstock: ii–iii (© Elja Trum); vi–vii (© Yellowj); viii–1 (© Péter Gudella); 150–51 (© mike.irwin); 238–39 (© Steve Mann)
Courtesy of Erik Smith: 169
Courtesy of J. Griffis Smith: 130, 131[l] (Photos by J. Griffis Smith)
Courtesy of James Soloway: 220[r]
Courtesy of the Southpaw Sanctum: 4 (Photo by James Wallace)
Courtesy of Michael Spalt: 118, 119, 121[t], 121[b]
Courtesy of Rolf Spuler: 221[t], 221[b]
Courtesy of Ned Steinberger, Steinberger.com: 222
Courtesy of Alice J. Stevens: 124, 131[r] (Photos by Alice J. Stevens)
Courtesy of Pete Swanson: 170–71
Courtesy of Philip Sylvester: 210[l], 210[r]
Courtesy of Taylor Guitars: 222–23
Courtesy of Rob Taylor: 206[l], 206[r], 207 (Photos by Rob Taylor)
Courtesy of Ulrich Teuffel: 132, 134, 134–35, 135, 136–37, 137
Courtesy of Teye: 138, 140, 142[l], 142[r], 143 (Photos by Alan Barley)
Courtesy of Ron Thorn: 224[l], 224[r] (Photos by Rob Szajkowski)
Courtesy of Chuck Thornton: 225 (Photo by Richard D. Shapiro)
Courtesy of Timberdance Ergonomic Guitars: 78, 81, 82, 83[t], 83[b] (Photos by Carol Moll)
Courtesy of James Trussart: 144, 145, 147[r], 148, 149
Courtesy of Rick Turner: 226[l]
Courtesy of Michael Tuttle: 226[r]
Courtesy of James Tyler: 227
Courtesy of Joe Veillette: 229
Courtesy of Frank Verrilli: 230 (Photo by Stu Haluski)
Courtesy of Patrice Vigier: 231
Courtesy of Scott Walker: 233[l], 233[r]
Courtesy of Don Warren: 23[r], 234[l]
Courtesy of Sam Winters: 182[b], 183
Courtesy of Andrew Wright: 156
Courtesy of Joseph Yanuziello: 24–25, 235